Treasures in the Darkness

by
Alice Wilson-Sharp

Kingdom Publishers

Treasures in the Darkness

Copyright© Alice Wilson-Sharp

All rights reserved. No part of this book may be reproduced in any form by photocopying or any electronic or mechanical means, including information storage or retrieval systems, without permission in writing from both the copyright owner and the publisher of the book. The right of Alice Wilson-Sharp to be identified as the author of this work has been asserted by her in accordance with the Copyright, Designs and Patents Act 1988 and any subsequent amendments thereto. A catalogue record for this book is available from the British Library.

Scriptures and Word Definitions taken from The Spirit-Filled Life Bible, New King James Version. Copyright © 1991. Used by permission of HarperCollins Christian Publishing. www.harpercollinschristian.com. Definitions taken from The New Strong's Exhaustive Concordance of the Bible by James Strong. Copyright © 1990 by James Strong. Used by permission of HarperCollins Christian Publishing. www.harpercollinschristian.com. Extracts taken from Sitting at the Feet of Rabbi Jesus by Ann Spangler and Lois Tverberg Copyright © 2018 by Ann Spangler and Lois Tverberg. Used by permission of HarperCollins Christian Publishing. www.harpercollinschristian.com. Extracts taken from Captivating by John and Stasi Eldredge Copyright © 2005 by John and Stasi Eldredge. Used by permission of HarperCollins Christian Publishing. www.harpercollinschristian.com. Extracts from The Complete Dictionary of Bible Names by Dr. Judson Cornwall and Dr. Stelman Smith Copyright © 1998. Used by permission of Bridge Logos, Inc. ISBN 978-1-61036-111-8. The Voyage of the Dawn Treader by CS Lewis © copyright 1952 CS Lewis Pte Ltd. Extracts used with permission.

ISBN: 978-1-911697-69-5

1st Edition by Kingdom Publishers, London, UK.

You can purchase copies of this book from any leading bookstore or email contact@kingdompublishers.co.uk

For my family.
All for one...

Contents

Foreword 7

Introduction 9

God's Desires 15

Light 51

Truth 85

Life with God 111

Faith 144

Hope 171

Peace 199

Joy 231

Rest 260

Conclusion 294

Bibliography 298

FOREWORD

When I was at school, we visited the Tower of London. I hadn't grown into my love of history by that point so I found most of the day pretty dull, but I do remember being utterly fascinated by the Crown Jewels. To my great delight, we even got to hold replicas! One bright spark in my class was busy examining a particularly impressive-looking sword when he was heard to mutter something about how it wasn't very sharp, to which our tour guide replied: 'That's because it's a ceremonial sword, not a battle sword.'

This book is all about a sword. This is a book about the Bible, that living, active, double-edged sword which God gives to everyone who wants to learn how to really live. The trouble is, it's all too easy to carry the Bible around in your life like a ceremonial sword: dusting it off every so often, admiring its beauty and maybe even using it to impress others. But what if we got to grips with the truth that this is a battle weapon. That's what Alice has set out to do in 'Treasures in the Darkness.' With her characteristic wit and wisdom, she helps us discover that this sword is very sharp indeed.

But this isn't just a book about the Bible. This is a book full of the Bible. Alice has spent years roaming through its landscapes and getting to know its people, and she introduces them to us like old friends. Her love of history means she notices all those little details which bring the stories to life, and her analytical mind means she delights in finding fresh insights in the most familiar passages. If you're the kind of reader who likes a 'wow I've never seen it that way before' moment, this is a book for you. Alice has read many books about the Bible, but there's no rehashing of old tropes here. This is the work of someone who has taken time to get the sword out of the scabbard, examine it closely and learn its workings. Having said that, this is no dry instruction manual either. Alice's love of God's Word shines through on every page and the treasures she mines for us are gems of wisdom, understanding, comfort, challenge and fun.

Most importantly perhaps, this is a book about what it's like truly to live the Bible. In her introduction, Alice says she wants to, 'help us discover the dynamic power available to us through the Word of God and to know how to apply it in the darkness.' After all, what use a sword which cannot help us in the toughest of battles? What use a sword which doesn't cut through the things that bind us? And what use a sword which, when the dark hours come, we find we don't know how to use? I can commend this book to you because I know that its author knows what it is to try and find hope in dark times. When she speaks of anxiety and depression, she speaks from bleak experience. Yet here is a woman who has chosen to take the Bible to task, to try it and test it, to see if it really does cut through to hope, and she has found that it does.

As well as being insightful and inspiring, this is a practical book. Alice intersperses her teaching with suggestions of things we can do to help us practise using the sword. There are creative and multi-sensory activities, questions to ponder and things to research further. It's not a book to rush through in one sitting. This is a book that leads us through a life-changing journey of reading, thinking, feeling, praying and doing. And since every sword-bearer worth her salt will tell you that swords need oiling, Alice regularly invites us to stop and make space for the Holy Spirit to work.

In Alice's own words: 'Salvation through Jesus Christ is our reason for hope, and it is through Scripture that we find knowledge and encouragement about the wonders of that salvation. It is in the Bible that we find the tools and skills that we need to stand strong despite disappointment, depression and doubt.'

As you read 'Treasures in the Darkness', I pray You will discover the joy of learning to wield your very own battle sword.

Lyndall Bywater
Christian speaker, author and broadcaster

INTRODUCTION

"O you afflicted one, tossed with tempest, and not comforted.
Behold, I will lay your stones with colourful gems,
and lay your foundations with sapphires.
I will make your pinnacles of rubies, your gates of crystal,
and all your walls of precious stones…
In righteousness you shall be established."

Isaiah 54:11-12 and 14

The Bible is a book written about the dark times, for us in our dark times. It is full of stories of people and the darkness they experienced: injustice, war, plagues, journeys, oppression, infertility, famine, imprisonment, betrayal and exile to name a few themes. Yet the glittering thread of redemption, light and life is woven brightly throughout Scripture, because God did not abandon us to the darkness. We see that God gave His people promises and revelations in the darkness, because that was when they were most needed. These words in Isaiah 54 were God's promise to Israel when they were in exile. His people were afflicted, shaken by storms and distressed; but God gave them the hope of a future time when they would be gloriously rebuilt and restored. I believe that these are words for us now, whatever the darkness we face. It is God's desire that we know both salvation and restoration in our lives.

We know that one day we will be amongst those who live on the new earth, in the perfect presence of our Father; but in the meantime, we navigate a world of challenge and difficulties as best we can. As we look around, the darkness is all too evident in life. There is the darkness of the world in which we live – a chaotic place of war, natural disasters and everyone behaving as they see fit. There is the darkness that comes from our personal circumstances, as bereavements, health problems, financial difficulties, job insecurities and so on, can so easily rock the foundations of our lives. Darkness also arises as a result of sin, either our own or the repercussions caused by the sins of others.

It is natural to wonder where God is in the darkness, to doubt His goodness and provision for us. After all, we were designed to live in Eden with a perfect work-life balance, secure in our worth, identity and purpose, walking with our Creator each day. But with the sin of Adam and Eve, humanity was sent into exile and life is not how it was meant to be. Our strength and efforts go into holding everything together each day; balancing our commitments and wishing that there were more hours in the day simply to get the basic tasks done, let alone achieve something mighty for the Lord. Sin changed the narrative from perfect work and rest to fallenness and brokenness, and that is where we stay until we accept both the salvation and the restoration that Jesus Christ offers us.

Simply choosing to trust and obey in dark times is a battle, because our natural instincts tell us to withdraw and protect ourselves when we are getting hurt. In faith, we know that God could resolve this situation in a heartbeat, yet He does not. We do our part by holding onto God's promises but sometimes this does not seem to make a difference. Choosing to trust in such times is a costly act of will; but standing in faith when it is hard takes us so much closer to our Father. We have a God who promises to bring good and benefit out of our trials and tribulations as we look to Him. By opening our hurting hearts to Him, the darkness can be a place where God restores and rebuilds us: from our foundations in salvation, in His truth, in relationship with Him and in faith; to the walls and gates of wisdom, peace, joy and rest; to the pinnacles of hope. With God in our lives, the darkness can become a place of hidden treasures.

During one of the storms of life, I realised that I could keep crying out to God about the storm, getting frustrated and upset; or I could ask God to take me deeper and deeper into His heart. I had a picture where

I saw myself travelling down a steep, narrow shaft into a dark, empty chamber. It was like documentary footage I had seen of the interior of an Ancient Egyptian pyramid. In my picture, here and there, half-submerged in the dirt of the walls of the chamber, I could see gemstones. I could see that there were treasures to be explored in this place of hiddenness and it was not a process that could be rushed. The gifts of God are too valuable to gather quickly and move on. Each treasure would need time and commitment to be fully revealed; and this process would happen in the place of darkness, of hiddenness and of challenge.

God works most in us during the tough times because that is when we need Him most. In the picture God gave me, His treasures were represented as gemstones to be carefully mined. In reality, His treasures are so much more than jewels or precious metals. They are not objects at all, but qualities and gifts that our loving Father plants within us by His Spirit. It is when we are most out of our depth and at the end of our own resources that we need to lean most strongly on our Father, and this is when He causes His treasures to grow and become established in us. God wants us to personally experience that He is exactly who He says He is. How else can we learn that He is sufficient in any trial that we face? He wants us to discover that when our resources are at an end, He can work in us and through us in a way that is far beyond our natural scope and ability. God's treasure enriches us because it is active and dynamic: it sustains, nurtures, strengthens and feeds our souls. It is treasure that enables us to endure; which protects and arms us in those dark times. As we allow the Holy Spirit to work deeply within us during the dark times, we become more like Him.

Dark times are unavoidable and will always be challenging to go through. There will always be times and seasons when we most desperately need to know what is true, to know God's presence, to possess strong hope, faith, peace, joy and rest. But in dark times, the things that we need most to keep going are the things that are hardest to find. Why? Because they are contested: Satan will always use dark times to try to separate us from God and cause us to withdraw from Him. He will use any opportunity to tempt us to doubt God's sovereignty, His goodness, and His willingness to provide for us and protect us.

Satan will whisper doubt and lies to us; playing on our heightened emotions to tell us that we are hopeless, powerless and abandoned. Satan will always work to steal, damage and destroy the things that will help us through. So how do we keep hold of the things of God in the dark times? How can we play our part in unearthing and taking hold of the treasures that God has for us as we go through those challenges?

The Bible is a book written for us for a very real and necessary purpose: it is a manual that teaches us how to find the way, the truth and the life in a broken and dysfunctional world. It shows us the bigger picture of what it is to live in Christ with the hope and inheritance of the Kingdom of God. The Bible contains the tools and strategies we need in a fallen world, but also shows us the way to access the dynamic power of the Holy Spirit that we need to run the race of faith. It is essential to restore our understanding of Scripture so that we recognise the powerful, life-bringing tools it gives us and learn how to use those in the dark times.

We could change the analogy and look at the night sky. We can look up on a clear night with a sense of wonder, enjoying the evening star and numerous constellations – all tiny dots of light across the darkness. We know from Genesis that God made the stars and God Himself tells us that He made the Bear, Orion and the Pleiades, amongst other constellations (Job 9:9). All those little dots of light in the sky are God's gift to us. We look up and are grateful for the beautiful sight and comfort of tiny, twinkling lights in the darkness. We can know that in Christ there is joy, hope, peace and rest. Yet, when we desperately need those things, they can be like stars that we wish upon: attractive but distant and out of our reach, things that make little practical difference in our lives. Scriptures can just be words unless we allow the Holy Spirit to reveal the whole truth and power of them to us.

We are many light years away from the stars. What if we travelled closer to them and learned more about them – what would we find then? A star is 'any massive self-luminous celestial body of gas that shines by radiation derived from its internal energy sources.'[1] Each star is phenomenal in its size and energy. They give out so much light

---

[1] Accessed from: https://www.britannica.com/science/star-astronomy 16 April 2020

energy that we see them here on planet Earth, many light years away. I only recognise one constellation: Orion, the hunter, with its distinctive belt of three stars. So, what does it mean when God tells us that He made Orion?

In its very simplest form, the constellation consists of nine particularly bright stars, including the super-giant stars Rigel and Betelgeuse, one of the brightest in the sky. Our sun is *tiny* in comparison with Betelgeuse. As I researched this, I read that if Betelgeuse replaced our sun it would extend beyond Jupiter. That is just one star of this constellation. If that were not impressive enough, part of the sword is the Orion nebula, which consists of hundreds of young stars, grouped with four huge stars called the Trapezium.

God did not create tiny dots of light. He spoke into being immense, complex spheres of gas in a variety of sizes and clusters that emit light through radiation. One star alone is a stunning creation. The full description of one constellation alone is far more complicated than I can understand. The science is beyond me, but the sense of wonder is not.

As we look up from our patch of Earth, we only see a small part of what is truly there. If we base our understanding of stars on this, we miss something crucial about what they are and what is happening out in space where we cannot witness events. We need a change of perspective.

Where we view Scriptures as tiny dots of light that sound and look nice, we need to see what God truly created for us: extraordinary gifts that are full of energy, light, life and dynamic power. The Scriptures are not just words. Through the revealing work of the Holy Spirit, we find our eyes are opened to discover that they are active and living, releasing the treasures of the Kingdom of God within us.

This book is intended to help us discover the dynamic power available to us through the Word of God and to know how to apply it in the darkness. We will look at the treasures that:

- prepare, equip and arm us
- enable us to stand and withstand in faith
- rebuild, restore and strengthen our foundations, walls, gates and pinnacles so that we can be all that God created us to be.

This is not intended to be a book that you read through in one go and move on. Use it as a workbook – something to annotate, work through, spend time considering. Use it to try out different ways to pray and to invite God to be present in your life in a new way. Use it to put Scriptures into practice in the tough times. Above all, use it as a way to open your heart once more to the Living God and invite Him to partner with you in all that you go through each day, allowing Him to rebuild and restore you in the depths of your soul. In each chapter, there will be opportunities to pause and reflect on the teaching: actively, creatively, intellectually and reflectively. You may want to use one idea, several or none of them – it is simply a way to enable us to engage more deeply with Scripture.

If you want to use this book with a group, I suggest that the response ideas be used. With an existing group, participants could read and respond individually and then bring their thoughts or projects to the group to share. That way, each person can respond in the way that best suits them and there is the benefit of learning how different people engage with Scripture. Alternatively, you could set up a group based on people who all like to respond in the same way. Participants can read the chapter individually and then gather to do a response task altogether. If you have a group of people who love to be active, do a 'head outside' task together and talk as you go. If you love to be artistic, use your group time to create and talk.

However you choose to use this book, I pray that it will be a practical tool that equips and enables you in your walk with Christ.

Let's go treasure-hunting!

GOD'S DESIRES

zeloo (Greek)

'To be zealous for,
to burn with desire,
to pursue ardently...'[2]

Out of all the treasures in the darkness, we begin with the treasure of discovering the desires of God's heart. We may be comfortable with talking about finding out God's will so that we can pray in line with that, and we may be familiar with talking about our own dreams and desires. But do we ever think about God having desires? Does that seem important to how we live life? Is it what we turn our minds to when we face challenges? Probably not, except to wonder how it could be God's desire for us to go through such suffering and hardship. But we start here because it is part of the vital context of the world in which we live and because it introduces us to God's character in a new way.

Before the creation of the world, there was God (Father, Son and Holy Spirit) in perfect love, harmony and relationship. He lacked nothing. Yet He had a desire to create and He acted upon that. As we look at the act of creation and the words of God throughout the Bible, His heart and desires shine out to us. What better place is there to begin than with the desires of God's heart? To hear His voice and better understand what He wants for us, His children.

What is God zealous for? What does He pursue ardently, with eagerness and passion? Let us begin at the beginning.

---

[2] Definition taken from the supplementary notes of *The Spirit-Filled Life Bible, New King James Version*, (Thomas Nelson, 1991) p. 1740

God's Desires at Creation

In Genesis, we have two chapters of wonder as God sets in motion the creation of all that we know. Two chapters of witnessing the Master Craftsman at work, where all is made *perfectly* for the benefit of mankind. As a human characteristic, we view perfectionism as a mixed blessing: we appreciate the attention to detail in getting something absolutely right, but it can involve someone being extremely driven to finish something to his or her own impossibly high standard. God's standards are the highest of all, yet He achieved multi-layered perfection without any struggle at all. What do we learn about God from this?

The process of creation was ordered.

God had the desire and vision to create, but also the pattern and the plans for the process of creation. There was an order and timing to His work. In His infinite power, He could have done everything instantly, without any negative consequences to Himself or the world, but He deliberately chose not to and we need to learn from that. He was establishing a principle for us about work and about ministry.

When we have a desire for something and a vision of it, our enthusiasm can drive us to rush in because we are excited about what could be. How much greater was God's excitement and enthusiasm for His creation! Yet, He still spread His work out over six days. There was a task for each of those days; He did that work and then stopped. He did not rush onto the next thing or work all hours to fulfil the vision. There is a need for us to match our steps to His in what we do, how we go about the task and when we do it. We are called to live at God's pace, not rushing on ahead of Him in our impatience or our enthusiasm.

It also teaches us that whatever we do for God, it will start with the *desire* to do something, the vision for it; then the plans, patterns, process and pace for that. All these things are required in His kingdom. A clear example of this is the instructions given to Noah about building the Ark. God said, "Make yourself an ark ... And this is how you shall make it..." (Gen. 6:14-15). This was done to God's specifications and with the materials He had chosen. We see this also with Moses. In time set apart with God, Moses was given the call to create and build; but God also gave him the pattern for how this should be done, as we read in Hebrews:

> 'They serve at a sanctuary that is a copy and shadow of what is in heaven. This is why Moses was warned when he was about to build the tabernacle: "See to it that you make everything according to the pattern shown you on the mountain."' Heb. 8:5 (NIV)

In this case, it was an earthly version of something that already existed in heaven – there was a need to do things God's way.

Right from the beginning of creation, God models the creative process for us and demonstrates His ability throughout. We see clearly that:

- He is full of vision and desire to create – these two elements provide the motivation and drive to see something come to fulfilment.
- He has the practicality and logic required for carrying out construction – to know what needs to happen, in what order and how that should happen in order to be successful.
- He has the creative imagination to make something stunningly beautiful as well as functional.

Vision and desire alone are insufficient – we need the skill and determination to see a project through to completion, and for us that often involves working in a team so that we can benefit from the strengths and skills given to others.

We know that God is perfect and did not have the same obstacles in His work that we do in ours. He did not find that He had made an error in His measurements for the world. He did not have creative differences with His team or experience doubt over whether He had made the right decisions. He never lost interest, got overtired and overwhelmed or felt stressed about budgets and deadlines. He did not have the temptation to give up and walk away. We are probably all too familiar with these things. God demonstrated to us that we need to work at His pace, rest at His pace, and to persevere so that we see things through to completion. As part of this, we can recognise that God has a desire for His works to come to completion and fruitfulness; then to have that satisfying moment of looking over that work with the recognition that this is good, very good. He desires us to know that satisfaction of work well done.

God desires to create, nurture and sustain life.

God took time over His work of creation. Methodically, He set about creating layer upon layer of the universe, of planets, of atmospheres, of habitats, of living things (plants and animals), of time and place. At the beginning,

> 'The earth was without form, and void; and darkness was on the face of the deep. And the Spirit of God was hovering over the face of the waters.' Gen. 1:2

The satellite images of our planet are so familiar to us now, it is difficult to imagine how it was in this initial phase of development. A planet in darkness, without form and entirely devoid of life, is an unsettling image. Why else is there such fascination with the possibility of there being life on other planets? There is something deep within us that searches for life.

In God's sight, it was certainly not a suitable dwelling-place for His children. So, as His Spirit hovered in darkness, He considered all that we were going to need and all that would delight His children. Our Father gave the order for there to be light, and He created day and night. He went on to create separation with the waters; to create land and vegetation. God spoke the sun, moon and stars into existence, giving them orders to rule over day and night. Previously, all light had just existed at God's word, but now He created visible, physical light sources. Next, sea-creatures, birds and land creatures were called into being, and blessed by their Creator.

Several phrases are repeated within the creation story. It reminds me of children's stories where there is rhyme and repetition to help the young learn to recognise words as they learn to read, and a way of fixing something in our memories. For adults, this repetition can be frustrating and we may skip over those bits rather than keep reading the same thing. We like to get straight to the main points! In this instance, it is a sign that we need to pay attention rather than thinking, I have already read this once and do not need to read it again. One of the aspects that we see repeated is the creation of divisions and boundaries in all that God created:

- God divided the light from the darkness. Lights were created to divide day and night, and to mark out the days, years and seasons. Lights were created that were given rule over day and another to rule the night. (See Gen. 1:4, 14, 16-17)
- A firmament was created to divide the waters above from the waters below. The waters on earth were gathered in one place to allow land to appear. (See Gen. 1:6-7 and 9)
- Out of the whole earth, God created a garden that was set apart to be the dwelling place of man. (Gen. 2:8)

We tend not to think about the need for there to be separation between land and water until that boundary is breached, when rivers flood causing great distress to those affected. However, this principle of 'this far and no further' in creation also applies to our lives. Boundaries are a vital part of God's plan to give us conditions in which we would be emotionally, physically and spiritually healthy. Without these boundaries, we all too easily become overwhelmed and flooded with anxieties, commitments and burdens which diminish and damage us. Godly boundaries support and sustain us.

God desires to show us His glory.

It is an intriguing thought that God could have simply created the Earth, its moon and the sun and nothing else. It would have been enough for us to live and live well. The moon would have regulated ocean tides and given us light for some nights during the month. The sun would have given the light and warmth we needed. We did not actually need anything more.

But God chose not to do this. He chose to create Earth as part of a solar system with stars and other planets, each planet with a different appearance and construction. He chose to create this solar system as part of a vast universe. Have you ever wondered why? We do not need other galaxies or even other planets in order to have life. It tells us that He does not want to give us 'just enough' - He delights in abundance and variety.

Spend a moment looking at pictures of the planets in our solar system – each one so distinctive and with its own characteristics. Jupiter's immense size is beyond my comprehension, but who can forget that distinctive red spot? Neptune appears blue in colour; Saturn has those beautiful rings around it. Just imagine the delight God took in creating each of these! Yes, creation was an ordered process, but it is impossible to ignore the idea that God was brimming over with enthusiasm and joy in His work. Therefore, how can we avoid drawing the conclusion that the rest of creation is there for us simply to explore and enjoy with God; something to provoke a sense of wonder and delight? We know that God is relational and that is partly expressed through great generosity. Out of His delight in creating, He gave us a vast universe so that we can enjoy and share in these beautiful wonders of His heart with Him. He did not want to give 'just enough' to His children, but desires to share the greatness of His love and heart with us.

We can take this one step further. God was clearly not creating something that was simply functional in order to fulfil a need – in this case, the basic things required to sustain life. If that were the case, He would simply have created Earth and the bare necessities, without variety or character. He created something that was also stunningly beautiful. Why? Because creation was intended to declare the glory of God.

Just pause for a moment in awe of the sheer magnitude of such a project. The work of creation necessarily had to point to the glory of God: His magnificence, His power, His goodness, His love, His imaginative flair, His technical ability to design cells and systems that work together with perfect accuracy, His provision for all living things. Creation testifies to His limitlessness. What is time or space to Him? Why create one planet or sun when several galaxies can be brought into being without any difficulty, each with its own character and design? Yet, He also creates the microscopic. Creation, in all its different components, points to the glory of God. He desires us to recognise that so that we will then rejoice in it and in Him. Our God desires to bless us abundantly, freely, open-handedly with all the good things of His heart and kingdom. This is part of His glory.

When we compare God's leadership with that of rulers who have come and gone through history, we find out how remarkable this is. Powerful rulers on Earth tend to exhibit a degree of ruthlessness. Dictators have absolute power and control, but this is achieved through the removal of personal freedoms and the exercising of an oppressive regime. They do not freely give to all, because neither their power or resources are perfectly secure, eternal or limitless. They tend to give generously to those whose support they need in order to stay in power. In these situations, the human heart craves control and retaining that power over others at any cost, rather than freely giving and allowing others the choice to stay or go.

God's power and majesty are unchanging and eternal. He gives abundantly because His power and resources have no limit but also because His heart is perfectly generous and loving. It is an astonishing truth that the only one who is truly in absolute power and authority is God, but He is no dictator. His rule is eternal and perfectly secure, so He does not need to bribe or coerce anyone to do anything. His rule will never be usurped or corrupted. This absolute ruler is the only one who is worthy of all our praise and devotion:

- because He gave us life
- because He gave us the whole of creation to enjoy and revel in
- because He gave His only Son to die in our place so that we might have eternal life with Him.
- because, having given us everything - *everything!* - He also gives us the freedom, the right and responsibility to choose whether we stay with Him or go.

God desired mankind to be in His image.

When God created man, it was with the words:

> "'Let Us make man in Our image, according to Our likeness; let them have dominion over the fish of the sea, over the birds of the air, and over the cattle, over all the earth and

over every creeping thing that creeps on the earth." So God created man in His own image; in the image of God He created him; male and female He created them. Then God blessed them, and God said to them, "Be fruitful and multiply; fill the earth and subdue it; have dominion over the fish of the sea, over the birds of the air, and over every living thing that moves on the earth."' Gen. 1:26-28

In contrast to other living things that were called into being 'according to its kind,' man was created according to the likeness of God. What was God's intention in this? In what way was man to be His likeness?

God is relational and there is complete union of heart, mind and purpose within the Trinity. There was and is no disagreement between the Father, Son and Holy Spirit, nor will there ever be. They are one in all that is desired, planned and worked out. We are intended to live and work in unity with God and with our fellow believers.

God is love, joy, peace, hope, goodness, kindness, gentleness, faithfulness, life, satisfaction - we are created for these things. Remember, there is no record of Adam or Eve being dissatisfied or complaining of any lack or want in their lives until the serpent came. They had lived for a length of time with the tree of good and evil in the garden with them, and there is no indication that they had given it any thought until that moment when Eve entered into conversation with the serpent.

God is just and true, glorious, eternal. God is creative and life-bringing; one who desires to see us built up, fruitful and satisfied. God's creation was a witness to His glory. We are made in His likeness – made to bear and reflect His glory. That seems hard to believe, but we consider this after the Fall. It is difficult to understand that, originally, mankind was as glorious as a sunset or a summer's day. As part of this reflecting of God's glory, mankind was called to fulfil this great commission:

- to be fruitful and multiply.
- to fill the earth and subdue it.
- to have dominion over all other creatures.

All living creatures were to be fruitful and multiply, but God conferred authority and responsibility on mankind alone; no other living thing was to reflect the governance of God.

Again, we read this after the Fall so it is difficult to imagine these original intentions and perhaps to see the relevance. We can read and know that God's desire was for man to have dominion over creation, but what does that mean for us now? We may rephrase this to mean that we are called to be stewards over the earth God created and that is a helpful way to consider this; however, we see the words *dominion* and *subdue* here. These are not words that we are comfortable with. After centuries of living in a fallen world, we are more aware than ever that mankind has caused all manner of damage to the earth and to each other, so we associate dominion with the abuse of power and the taking away of someone else's rights. What does godly dominion over the created world mean and involve? What was the role of mankind to be? Apart from the naming of things, we do not find out too much about this in Genesis, but we do learn that God's ultimate intention is to create a new heaven and a new earth where these things will be re-established. We will have godly dominion over the new earth, as God had originally planned. (See Revelation 21:1 and 22:5)

God's desires at the beginning of the world will be fulfilled and brought to completion one day. In the meantime, whenever our hearts cry out that something is not as it should be it is a witness to the fact that we are created in God's likeness, created for His kingdom. God has placed 'eternity in our hearts' so that we search for life and for all that God intended us to have. (Eccl. 3:11)

When we are impacted by sin, disease and death, our hearts cry out that this was not what was meant to be. Of course not. When we are impacted by injustice, poverty and crime, we know that this is not how things should be; of course not. This was not what God created us for. We were created to have hearts for justice, eternity, glory and unity because we are created in the likeness of God. We were created to live in love, joy, peace, faithfulness, goodness, gentleness, kindness and so on, because we are created in the likeness of God. We are continuously on a search for life in all its fullness because God *is* life in all its fullness. We are created for union with Him.

We have these eternal things placed in our hearts: the desire for soul-satisfying work and rest, and, most importantly, a face-to-face relationship with our Father and Creator. Life in the garden that God planted for man, to the east in Eden, is the pattern for what life should have been for humanity. A place where life was breathed into us, where our needs were perfectly met, where there was no doubt that God exists because of His manifest presence and involvement in our lives. God never intended to be distant from us – He intended to walk with us, talk with us, share life with us, face to face. There was no need for salvation at that point because all was as it should be.

God's creation was intended to sustain and nurture life for His children in all its fullness. Not just meeting our basic needs so that we could function and exist but creating a world that would fascinate and engage us. It was the place for us to grow joyfully to be like our heavenly Father, securely in relationship with Him and exercising our ability to rule and create within clear boundaries in a stimulating and awe-inspiring environment. This is what we need to be healthy and whole. After all, God created all things whilst being in a perfect union of Father, Son and Holy Spirit. Satisfying love, unity and agreement in relationship was there before anything else.

Reflect and Respond Ideas

Head outside: Allow the created world to testify to the creative imagination, workmanship and glory of God: go star-gazing, head to the coast or the moors – whatever is manageable.

Research something: Find out more about something God has created and marvel at how intricate that work is. For example, you could find out about how a leaf is formed or about the cells that form blood or about how an animal is suited for its habitat.

Ponder further: Have you ever considered God as having desires before? How does that change how you think about Him?

Get creative: Is there something in particular that helps you experience awe and wonder at what God has made for us? Draw it, paint it, make a model of it or do some creative writing as if you were there watching it being made.

The Separation

God never made anything that failed to match with His original vision. At the beginning, everything was made exactly to fulfil His vision and desire. However, as we know, His work was marred by mankind. As mankind was made in God's image, we can recognise that having desires is a way in which we are made in His likeness. However, whereas His desires are divinely holy and perfect, ours are held in the frailty of humanity.

Before Eve was created, God had made it clear to Adam that there was one tree, just one tree in the whole of the garden, which was not to be used for food. This was the tree of the knowledge of good and evil – eating the fruit of this tree would lead to death (Gen. 2:16-17). But the day came when Eve encountered a serpent.

The first thing that the Bible tells us about the serpent was that it was 'more cunning than any beast of the field.' (Gen. 3:1) Therefore, when we look at this exchange between it and Eve, we should expect to see cunning at work. In the light of this, we notice that the serpent never directly incited Eve to eat the fruit, nor said anything particularly persuasive. If we think about the nature that persuasion takes when someone is tempting us with cake or dessert, for example, we could expect the serpent to point out how delicious the fruit looks and will taste, to persuade us that it is only polite to try a little, that there are not that many calories in it and we all deserve a treat on occasion. But the serpent neither coaxed her into eating the fruit nor told her to eat it. In fact, we only find it saying two things.

It begins with a question to ascertain Eve's understanding and interpretation of God's instruction: 'Has God indeed said, "You shall not eat of every tree of the garden?"' (Gen. 3:1) We could note that Eve added in an extra rule when she responded, as she said that they were not allowed to eat from it *or touch it* which was not true. Although there was an addition or an exaggeration of God's words here, she was correct in saying that God had told them not to eat of one tree because the consequence was death. This is the critical point: Eve knew that God had told them not to eat the fruit of this one tree and she knew that death would result (See Gen. 2:17). The point was clear and unequivocal. It was this that the serpent addressed when it spoke for the second time:

"You will not surely die. For God knows that in the day you eat of it your eyes will be opened and you will be like God, knowing good and evil." Gen. 3:4-5

The serpent implied that God was lying to protect His own position; that God wanted Adam and Eve to be ignorant of good and evil, because otherwise they would be like Him.

As a result of the serpent's words, this tree that had not previously been of much interest to her was suddenly so fascinating that Eve could not take her eyes away from it. The serpent did not need to say another word: Eve did the rest herself.

She did not engage with either statement that the serpent made. Instead, she took the words that the serpent had said and allowed them to open up a new pathway for her – the pathway of disobeying God. She added in her own words and ideas to justify taking that pathway: the tree was so pleasant to look at, good for food, and desirable to make one wise. (Gen. 3:3-6) Eve went from being perfectly satisfied to feeling that there was something missing – something she suddenly felt that she needed to have and could not live without. A desire was awakened and, now that she had considered disobeying God, the means to meet that desire was readily available.

God did not step in to remind Eve or Adam of His instructions, but they had the ability to remind themselves of His character (which had been revealed through their time spent with Him) and that He had only ever denied them two things. He directly told them not to eat the fruit of this tree and, in so doing, He also denied them the knowledge of evil. It is interesting to note that God did not go into detail about what the knowledge of evil involved. He simply told Adam and Eve not to eat the fruit.

It is also important to note that Satan approached in the guise of a serpent. God had given Adam and Eve dominion over 'every creeping thing,' which would include serpents. As God did not intervene, we can see this as Him allowing man to have this moment of choice where they could exert freewill. They could choose to trust God or turn away. They could exert their God-given authority over the serpent and subdue it, or they could allow the serpent to influence them. Eve considered and gave weight to the serpent's words, choosing to eat the fruit. She let herself be guided by something she should have exercised dominion over. Both Eve and Adam convinced themselves that acting independently of God was the correct choice. The consequences of Eve and Adam's sin became quickly apparent.

Firstly, Adam and Eve discovered what it was to be vulnerable and to desire protection. For the first time, but certainly not the last, God's children hid from Him in shame, guilt, fear and insecurity when they heard His voice. For the first time, they had that sick feeling that they were in trouble; that what they had done was wrong and that there would be consequences. We are familiar with this from an early age, but Adam and Eve had never known that before.

Secondly, they were exposed to the knowledge of evil, when previously all that they had known was the goodness of God. We have never been in a situation where all we know and experience was pure and holy, as Adam and Eve did; but we will have had moments of horrified shock during our lives when we are suddenly confronted with a new knowledge of evil. Surely that was what Adam and Eve experienced.

Thirdly, God spoke over each of those involved in this situation, in the order of when they rebelled: the serpent, the woman, the man.

He cursed the serpent and put enmity between it and the woman; then prophesied as to the coming of the Messiah who would bruise the serpent's head. (Gen. 3:14-15)

For Eve (whose name means *life, life-giving*[3]) the consequence was to know sorrow and pain in conception and bringing forth life. Secondly, her desire would be for her husband and he would rule over her. (Gen. 3:16)

For Adam (whose name means *earthy, of the ground*[4]) the consequence was to know futility and struggle in working the ground and in providing food. Indeed, the ground itself would be cursed so, regardless of how well and hard he worked, Adam would see thorns and thistles grow alongside the grain in the land he worked. Even creating a basic food item like bread would involve hard work and sweat. (Gen. 3:17-19)

---

[3] Dr. Judson Cornwall and Dr. Stelman Smith, *The Complete Dictionary of Bible Names,* (Bridge-Logos, 1998) p.54

[4] Cornwall and Smith, *Bible Names*, p.5

In other words, Eve and Adam were given restrictions around the commission they had been given. They would experience struggle and heartache in being fruitful and multiplying, in filling and subduing the earth, and in having dominion over the earth. This does not apply just to childbirth, marriage or agricultural work but indicates that there will be a measure of struggle and suffering in whatever way we work to bring forth life.

God also spoke change into their relationship. Although He spoke to Eve about this, it directly impacted Adam as well. It is an uncomfortable part of Scripture that a husband should rule over his wife, but this should be read in the light of God's understanding of what that should be like. We could look into the Song of Songs, which fully explores the language of love and covenant relationship; or the book of Hosea, where God describes Himself as a husband desiring His unfaithful wife to return. It is also made abundantly clear in the New Testament that a husband should love his wife as Christ loves the church (See Eph. 5:25-29). God twice uses the word 'cursed' - toward the serpent and the ground, but not towards the man or the woman, so this change is not to be read in that light. (Gen. 3:14 and 17) We are to see these things as the consequence of sin but also as something that is to act constructively to bring redemption. So, what was the purpose of this?

As a result of her sin, Eve's desire was to be for her husband. There was a consequence in the area of desire because this was at the root of her decision to disobey God. That was one sin. However, she then led Adam into sin as well. Now, Eve had been formed to be both companion and a help to Adam; one out of all creation who was 'comparable to him' (Gen. 2:18). By help, this means a partner in work and in providing vital aid. The Hebrew word *ezer* is only used in one other context and that is to describe the LORD coming to our aid when we are in desperate circumstances.[5] In offering Adam the fruit, she had gone against this role as his help; she encouraged him to be disobedient rather than leading him away from trouble. Therefore, directing Eve's desire back to her husband would open the way for her to fulfil her role as *ezer* with vigilance and heartfelt willingness. With her de-

---

[5] John and Stasi Eldredge, *Captivating*, (Thomas Nelson, 2005) p.31-32

sire connected to her husband, Eve's heart and soul would be invested in her husband's well-being with greater faithfulness.

Adam was also to rule over Eve which, based on the little we see of their relationship, I suspect would not have come naturally to either of them. God gave Adam authority over Eve because he needed to be called to take an active role in Eve's life. Although Adam recognised that she was, "bone of my bones and flesh of my flesh," and that she was one with him, he had not taken that to the full extent of God's intention: that he should love her as himself, and as God loved them. (Gen. 2:23) Instead, Adam's natural response had been to hold back and stay silent as Eve sinned. Therefore, he was called to overcome this reluctance or unwillingness to stand up for Eve and to stand against the enemy on her behalf. What he had not naturally done was now given to him as a divine responsibility.

He also sinned because he simply did what Eve said and ate what she gave him, even though he knew it was against God's command. I do not believe that it was wrong for Adam to follow Eve's lead *per se*. The problem was that in this instance, Eve was clearly leading Adam into disobedience and death rather than into obedience, life and rescue as she was called to do, and Adam knew that. He knew that taking and eating that fruit was unquestionably wrong, but he did not act to bring life and rescue to Eve or to himself. Now, Adam was being given authority over Eve and was expected to use it – not to oppress her, but to keep them both walking rightly before God. In this way, they each had a protective and supportive role to play for the other: Adam, in his new role as ruler – one who was to rise above his natural inclination to opt out and to act with authority for his wife's well-being; and Eve as his *ezer* – one who was to come to the rescue when her husband was desperately in need.

For this to work well, both Adam and Eve needed to depend on God to supply them with the grace to live this way. Adam's call to rule over his wife was a sacred responsibility. The only ruler that Adam and Eve had experience of was God Himself, so that should give us an insight into what God intended in this role. God's rule over us is one of self-sacrificial love, wisdom and the desire for His children to know life and goodness. Adam was called to rule in such a way that would enable Eve to know life and goodness, leading out of wisdom and love. We easily fall short of what God intended – we can tell ourselves we are acting with right and godly authority, when actually we are being domineering or manipulative so that we can get our own way. We need to stay close to God, in the flow of the Holy Spirit, to live as near to His call as we can.

Eve was called to accept that rule, even though her natural response was to act independently of Adam and God, so this would have also required grace. It costs us to ask for help or to receive correction; it costs us to submit to someone else, even in a godly relationship of love, trust and empathy. We do not naturally respond well when someone offers advice or tells us we need to change what we are doing. We tend to react defensively or angrily. Equally, if we try to discuss something and feel that we are not listened to, communication and unity breaks down. These are things that cause us to create and allow separation between us. It is all too easy for us to step outside of our God-appointed roles and to allow separations to take hold, so we need to stay close to God in how we interact with each other.

God's desires are completely good and pure; but we are made of flesh and bone, fallen and human, so our desires do not naturally line up with God's. We need the Holy Spirit to work within our desires to bring them in line with God's and also to develop within us the resolution to seek the fulfilment of those desires from God alone. It is also the Holy Spirit who helps us to submit to the leadership of God when our natural inclinations urge us to go our own way. It costs us something to submit our will to God's, or to someone that God has placed in a position of covering over us, but it is part of living with spiritual discipline. It is one of the glorious mercies of God that as we submit our will to His, we find Him fulfilling our desires in a new way. God wanted and still wants His children to be satisfied, fruitful and wise; but we need to learn to seek those things from Him and with Him.

Finally, they were sent away from Eden. Interestingly, the reason for this is given in God's own words:

> '"Behold, the man has become like one of Us, to know good and evil. And now, lest he put out his hand and take also

of the tree of life, and eat, and live forever" – therefore the LORD God sent him out of the garden of Eden to till the ground from which he was taken. So He drove out the man; and He placed cherubim at the east of the garden of Eden, and a flaming sword which turned every way, to guard the way to the tree of life.' Gen. 3:22-24

We are made in God's likeness: in the image of one who is and always will be glorious, pure, holy, just, true, faithful, good, and so on. Knowing God's goodness brought complete fullness of life to Adam and Eve. It was not His intention that we should know evil as He did, because that would corrupt, damage and destroy us. This was the one area where we were not to be like Him. Knowing evil would not and does not bring life and health to us.

Although God did not directly address the subject of death, it was upon this matter alone that Satan had directly contradicted Him. As a result of their sin, Adam and Eve still lived physically, but they would no longer have eternal life in an earthly paradise, where God walked with them each evening. They would have a temporary physical life, in which they would know evil as well as good. Because it was not good that man should live forever in a sin-filled, fallen world it was essential that man could no longer access the tree of life. Therefore, man was cast out of Eden and the way back was guarded. We read in Genesis 6 that God restricted human life span still further from many hundreds of years to one hundred and twenty, because of the sin of man.

From eternal life to limited life-span, from physical perfection to bodies that succumb to aches, pains, illnesses and the aging process. This is far from what we were designed for but, through Christ, we can receive the gift of eternal life once more and will live in His presence, timelessly, just as God always intended. Just as Adam and Eve once had access to the tree of life, we will have access to the tree of life when the new heaven and the new earth are formed and sin is no more. (Rev. 22:2) The glorious life we were meant to have will be restored once and for all.

Reflect and Respond Ideas

Head outside: Go for a run or a walk. On the way out, pay attention to things that show the consequences of sin entering the world. On the way back, reverse those things and give thanks for all that will one day be restored in glory.

Research something: Head into the Bible and look at some of the passages where God describes Himself as a husband. Why did He choose that particular metaphor?

Ponder further: What are your experiences of being under leadership (in the home, at school growing up, at work or church, in marriage)? What has been positive or negative about them? How has that impacted you and how you see figures of authority?

Get creative: So many stories revolve around the need for a rescuer. What stories have most caught your imagination? What was it about them that impacted you? Who did you want to be like? Draw, paint or journal about the rescuer character that most impacted you.

God's Desire for Righteousness and Restoration

From the very opening of the Bible, we discover that our God is relational. After all, God is Father, Son and Holy Spirit, in completeness, wholeness and perfection. He created mankind for relationship, for unity with the Trinity. If we look at an overview of the Old Testament, we see that the story of mankind is one of either turning to God or away from Him. Turning to God involved faithful commitment to Him, with all due obedience and submission. Deliberately and repeatedly turning away from Him involved rebellion. Rebellion led to judgement and exile from God's place of blessing and provision. Repentance led to return, restoration and rebuilding.

Sacrifice is not a comfortable subject for us, but we see it as part of the atonement process throughout the Old Testament. The shedding of blood was a necessary part of this, but it was never enough to bridge the gap between God and man once and for all. The priests acted as intermediary between man and God, and the blood of the animals covered the sin committed. Lambs without blemish were offered as sacrifices, and a goat would be sent ceremoniously outside the camp to atone for sin (the scapegoat), but this had to keep happening to keep

Israel right before God. It is into this context, that the coming of a Deliverer was prophesied.

Location One   Eden

God created man and, out of the whole earth, designed a garden for us to live in, where we could be in relationship with Him. There was perfect goodness, hope, life, peace, joy, work and rest. This was His desire fulfilled. But Eve and Adam turned away from God's provision, eating fruit from the one source forbidden to them. They sinned and the judgement was exile from the face to face contact we were supposed to have with God. Mankind was moved from a fruitful garden to the wilderness. Even at this point, God promised a future reckoning between the Serpent (Satan) and the offspring of woman – the Messiah. (See Gen. 3:15)

Location Two   Exile to the East of Eden

Outside Eden, Adam and Eve discovered what it was to struggle in work and relationship; they discovered what it was to be insecure, fearful and fractious. Their son, Cain, attained notoriety for being the first murderer. Cain's brother, Abel, was righteous before God and had given a sacrificial first-fruits offering that was pleasing to Him. In contrast, Cain's offering was not sacrificial which displeased God. Instead of repenting of any wrong heart attitude or disobedience in the offering, Cain turned away in anger and killed Abel.

Over time, the people attained such a state of wickedness that God brought a flood to cover the Earth, destroying everything but the family of Noah who, alone, was righteous before Him. God began again with Noah, with restoration and covenant. God's instruction to Noah was to "be fruitful and multiply," just as it had been to Adam and Eve, and man's authority over other living creatures was reaffirmed. (Gen. 9:1-2)

Location Three   The Flood-Washed Earth

God's desire was still to have a dwelling-place for His people. After the Flood, God had a Promised Land in mind for His people – a land flowing with milk and honey – where He would lead His people in perfect love and perfect justice.

God called Abraham to follow Him, wherever He led. Because of Abraham's righteousness, God promised him that he would be the father of nations, the father of God's chosen people. Abraham was shown the land that would belong to his descendants, who would be numerous and blessed in God. (Gen. 12 – 13, 15, 21:1-7)

From one favoured man came one promised child of God, from whom the nation of Israel grew, being fruitful and multiplying, increasingly filling and subduing the earth. Many generations later, Israel found itself enslaved in Egypt; and it was out of that place of captivity that God intended to lead them into His land and dwelling-place with them. God brought a further covenant with His people through Moses, to help them live rightly before Him.

The tribe of Levi was called to be set apart as a priestly order before God, which was a serious and solemn duty. The fact that God called one tribe of the twelve to be set apart specifically to focus on guarding and maintaining the sanctification and holiness of the people indicates just how important this was to God and how much the people needed to be kept focused. In Exodus chapter 28, Moses received instructions for the priests, as led by Aaron and his sons. God had the vision, the plans and the patterns for what was to be; and He filled gifted artisans with the spirit of wisdom in order that they might make garments of glory and beauty for the priests. They were not just functional garments, but symbolic and artistic.

Aaron, head of the priestly Levite tribe, was to wear a fine linen tunic, sash and trousers. In addition, he was to wear:

- *a breastplate of judgement,* with precious stones to signify the sons of Israel, as a memorial before the LORD. The Urim and the Thummin would be over Aaron's heart, which were a means of discerning God's will.
- *an ephod* with stones engraved with the names of the sons of Israel.
- *a blue robe* with pomegranates of blue, purple and red thread around the hem, and golden bells in between. God's instruction was that,

"...it shall be upon Aaron when he ministers, and its sound will be heard when he goes into the holy place before the LORD and when he comes out, that he may not die." Ex. 28:35

- *a turban made of the best linen*, that should have the following:

"... a plate of pure gold and [engraved] on it, like the engraving of a signet: HOLINESS TO THE LORD... it shall be on the front of the turban. So it shall be on Aaron's forehead..." Ex. 28:36-38

This is a far cry from the relationship that Adam and Eve had known with God in Eden. Here, God was using clothing to remind His people of the need to take their relationship with God seriously, both for the priests wearing these garments and those around them who would see them. There was a need for His people to come to Him with hearts like Abel, offering the best of their produce, lives and hearts to their God; not carelessly giving with hearts that did not desire to honour Him, like Cain.

God's design was specific and detailed: He had chosen the colours of the threads, and the style and symbolism He desired, which would act as a reminder of the significance of the role they had been given. It was a high calling, a vocation and one that carried immense responsibility. As they put on these ceremonial garments, they would be reminded of the need to prepare their hearts and minds ready to carry out their priestly duties. After all, deliberately approaching God with an attitude of carelessness or disrespect for His holiness could lead to death. Imagine what it would be like to go to work or drive a car with the words 'holiness to the LORD' across our foreheads! How would that change our attitudes and our behaviour? Or when we go to church or approach God? How would it change the way we speak to people who slow us down, annoy us, belittle us?

God also had strict rules for what was an acceptable sacrifice in the Old Testament. There were rules for grain offerings, drink offerings, freewill offerings, peace offerings, sin offerings. (See Leviticus 22:17-33.) This was not to be undertaken lightly, as a careless, superficial act that meant nothing to the person bringing the offering; but with a right sense of fearing the LORD: knowing that He was and is holy and that heart attitude was essential in presenting an acceptable offering to Him. The people needed to esteem their God. He was not an inanimate idol, crafted and created by man, that could be taken out or put away in a bag as required. Their God was not created by man but was the Creator of man. Israel constantly needed these reminders of this difference between their God and idols.

In addition to this, there was a specific day set aside at the end of the agricultural year for Israel to atone for their sins before God. Israel was instructed to offer burned sacrifices and no work was allowed at all,

> "For any person who is not afflicted *in soul* on that same day shall be cut off from his people. And any person who does any work on that same day, that person I will destroy from among his people. You shall do no manner of work ... It shall be to you a Sabbath of solemn rest, and you shall afflict your souls..." Lev. 23:29-32 (my emphasis)

God allowed no room for misunderstanding in this. The people were to take this seriously, at the risk of death. This was not something for the priests to do on behalf of the people, but for each person to do on his or her own behalf. They were to recognise and acknowledge from the depths of their souls that they had fallen short and to turn back to God in repentance.

Location Four   The Promised Land

Over time, the tribes of Israel took the land promised to them; they settled and established themselves. God had made the situation abundantly clear to Israel – blessing and favour were dependent on righteous behaviour and hearts before Him.

This should have been the place of relationship with God and righteousness before God, yet even here there was ongoing tension between the knowledge of God Most High and the pull to idolatry. This tug of war continued for centuries. If we read through the book of Judges, we see that the nation alternated between leaders who remembered and honoured the LORD, and those who acted wickedly in His sight. The book ends with the phrase, 'everyone did what was right in his own eyes,' not God's. (Judges 21:25) The more Israel followed pagan ways and took credit for the blessings that God had given, claiming that they had earned what they had, the more Israel came under God's judgement. Covenant was a two-way agreement and God had kept His part; but, yet again, mankind turned away from their part because they wanted to be like everyone else. Breaking the covenant had clear consequences:

> "Because you did not serve the LORD your God with joy and gladness of heart, for the abundance of everything, therefore you shall serve your enemies ...The LORD will bring a nation against you ... a nation whose language you will not understand, a nation of fierce countenance ... and they shall eat the increase of your livestock and the produce of your land until you are destroyed ... They shall besiege you at all your gates until your high and fortified walls, in which you trust, come down throughout all your land ..."
> Deut. 28:47-52

God did not speak this out lightly. We approach this from the knowledge of God's grace extended to us abundantly through Christ, so this strikes us as being brutal; but this was long before He died for us all. We are very quick to respond if we feel that God has broken a promise to us, but Israel repeatedly broke its promise to trust and obey God. God had rescued His people from slavery and given them a new land, but they had defiled it and themselves with their sin and rebellion. Through the prophets, He sent call after call to His beloved children to come back to Him and live in His goodness and perfect provision. Time and time again, His children refused to listen. Mankind had gained the knowledge of evil and there were seasons where God's people found it desirable.

From the sheer number of books containing warnings of the consequences of sin and promises of restoration to God's people, we can see just how much God's heart was calling His people to choose wisely. During the time of Israel and Judah's wickedness and exile, the prophets Joel, Amos, Hosea, Isaiah, Micah, Zephaniah, Jeremiah, Nahum and Habakkuk were all raised up to speak out the words of the LORD to His people.

If we ever wanted to hear the true cry of God's heart, it is in these books of His voice calling out to His rebellious, sinful people who no longer cared about the things He had lovingly prepared for them. Instead, they chose to worship idols, they behaved in immoral ways that caused disease and broken relationships, they cheated in business. Their hearts were far from God, their behaviour was evil, but repeatedly God called to them through the prophets who listened and who carried that burden of the people's sin. In Hosea, we read God's cry:

> "When Israel was a child, I loved him, and out of Egypt I called My son ... they sacrificed to the Baals, and burned incense to carved images. I taught Ephraim to walk, taking them by their arms; but they did not know that I healed them. I drew them with gentle cords, with bands of love ... I stooped and fed them.
>
> How can I give you up, Ephraim? How can I hand you over, Israel? How can I make you like Admah? How can I set you like Zeboiim? My heart churns within Me..." From Hosea 11:1-4,8

How could His people prefer the wickedness of the world when they had known the eternal goodness of God and His heart to bless them? In His majesty and mercy, God stooped to feed His children. He lovingly raised them, helped them walk, healed them, set them free from slavery. But they turned to other gods, took the credit for all that went well and treated others unjustly. God was waiting for them to repent and turn back to Him, but they refused and continued in rebellion. He had promised Noah that He would not send a flood to cover the earth again, which He had done before because of wickedness; but there was still the option to destroy Israel, as He had the wicked places of Sodom and Gomorrah, Admah and Zeboiim.

God's love is so powerfully evident in this passage as He put into words His Father-heart longing for His children. He did not want to destroy them. No wonder His heart churned within Him. His desire was for the restoration of His people to righteousness and relationship with Him. He warned and He rebuked, but He would not wait forever for them to repent because that way more and more people would be lost to Him. Through the prophet Zephaniah, God spoke, saying:

> "And it shall come to pass at that time that I will search Jerusalem with lamps, and punish the men who are settled in complacency, who say in their heart, 'The LORD will not do good, nor will He do evil.'" Zeph. 1:12

> "This is the rejoicing city that dwelt securely, that said in her heart, 'I am it, and there is none besides me.' How has she become a desolation ... Woe to her who is rebellious and polluted, to the oppressing city! She has not obeyed His voice, she has not received correction; she has not trusted in the LORD, she has not drawn near to her God."
> Zeph. 2:15 and 3:1-2

What our hearts say is so revealing – both as individuals and as communities. The hearts of God's people spoke of self-sufficiency and a rejection of God *(...there is none besides me)* but also of God being indifferent to their behaviour. *(The LORD will not do good, nor will He do evil.)* Jerusalem rejoiced in its state of sin, idolatry and immorality; but God saw its desolation.

Remember that Satan's deceitful statement to Eve was, "you will not surely die." This is the essential lie behind our justification of sin: we will not surely die if we eat the fruit forbidden to us. We will not surely die if we go into church with a heart full of anger, bitterness and unforgiveness. We will not surely die if we covet, or lie, or disobey God's instructions about righteous living. We will not surely die if we reject God and take the glory for ourselves. God will not respond with good or evil, so our behaviour does not matter. As Adam and Eve found out, they did not instantly die physically, but the repercussions of sin led to desolation – to spiritual and physical decay and eventual death.

The fact that God spoke of searching Jerusalem *with lamps*, indicates that He was intending to search a place that was in darkness; that He would be looking at things that did not belong in His kingdom of light. What did He find? In these two passages alone, we read of:

- complacency - not believing that God will respond to our behaviour either way.
- rebellion and disobedience.
- refusing to listen to correction.
- not trusting God.
- not drawing close to God.
- allowing themselves to be 'polluted' by rebellion and idolatry.

We can also infer the existence of pride and arrogance, which left no room for God and accepted no need of Him.

When we start talking about punishment or judgement, we tend to start wondering if the consequence is proportionate to the crime; something which becomes debatable and subjective. God's words in Ezekiel 16 help with this. Out of His love for them, He had adorned them,

> "'...with gold and silver, and your clothing was of fine linen, silk and embroidered cloth. You ate pastry of fine flour, honey and oil. You were exceedingly beautiful, and succeeded to royalty. Your fame went out among the nations because of your beauty, for it was perfect through My splendour which I had bestowed upon you," says the Lord GOD.' Ezek. 16:13-14

He had given His best for their benefit and blessing, even bestowing His splendour and royalty upon them. But they had turned to false gods who could not compare to Him; acted with such wickedness in their worship of those idols, that God could not continue to wait for them to come to repentance. Where they had been under the impression that God would neither do good or evil, He told them through the prophet Ezekiel:

> "I will deal with you as you deserve ..." Ezek. 16:59, NIV

All discussion and debate end at that point. The people would get what they deserved: exile from all the good He had given them and all the protection He had provided.

Whilst exile was a severe consequence, His people were not destroyed. God allowed them to live because of His covenant love for them, and so that they still had the way to repentance and restoration before them. His mercy was at work alongside judgement, regardless of whether the people recognised that. But because of their repeated rebellion the Promised Land would be attacked; the holy city of Jerusalem, which had not been rightly valued by God's people, would be destroyed. God's people would be forced to serve their enemies (such as Babylon and Assyria), they would lose their natural resources (the produce of the land and their livestock) and their physical defences would be destroyed (the walls and gates). God's people would be exiled from the land given to them, just as Adam and Eve had been exiled from Eden.

When we turn the Zephaniah passage around to see the behaviour that would have pleased God, what we see is God's desire for His people to draw close to Him. It is such a touching and simple desire that speaks volumes about God's heart for relationship. He wanted to be chosen and sought out; to be seen, spoken to, consulted, delighted in and honoured. Out of that, God's desire was for Israel to respond to correction and choose to live rightly before Him in obedience and trust, acknowledging God's existence, sovereignty and engagement in their lives. In other words, to recognise that He was God: all-powerful, all-glorious and relational. Because sin separates us from God, it was only on these terms that He could pour out His goodness and blessing as He wanted.

The messages of the prophets vary in detail, but the essential message is the same: there are warnings about the consequences of rebellion against God and the promise of restoration if they repent. The way open was always there, through repentance. We hear God's pain over the wickedness of His beloved children, who had chosen worthless things over all the riches of His heart and Kingdom; and we hear His desire for restoration and rebuilding ringing loud and clear. He spoke through Amos to promise:

"I will raise up the tabernacle of David, which has fallen

> down, and repair its damages; I will raise up its ruins,
> and rebuild it as in the days of old ... I will bring back the
> captives of My people Israel; they shall build the waste cities
> and inhabit them; they shall plant vineyards and drink wine
> from them; they shall also make gardens and eat fruit from
> them." Amos 9:11 and 14

God's desires here are all constructive – rebuilding cities for habitation, planting vineyards to produce wine, making gardens to produce fruit. The physical restoration and building up was to be matched by a spiritual restoration with Israel once more planted in healthy ground and fruitful. He promised that heartfelt repentance would meet with blessing:

> "'Turn to Me with all your heart, with fasting, with weeping,
> and with mourning." So rend your heart, and not your
> garments; return to the LORD your God, for He is gracious
> and merciful... "Behold, I will send you grain and new wine
> and oil, and you will be satisfied by them; I will no longer make
> you a reproach among the nations.'" From Joel 2:12-13 and 19

Even in the midst of judgement, God had already planned for the restoration of Israel and Judah: firstly, in the Promised Land, secondly in the sending of the Messiah, thirdly in the pouring out of the Holy Spirit, then finally in the new earth. God's heart was for His people to be established in *righteousness*. That was Israel's part of the covenant, and that was where Israel repeatedly fell. What Israel could not, or would not, achieve through keeping the Law, Jesus would fulfil for them; and then the Holy Spirit would be poured out on those who received Jesus as the promised Messiah and Saviour. God's gifts and promises were firm, substantial and beyond price; for God planned and promised to come in increasing measure and intimacy to His people. God Himself would meet the needs of His people with His own body and Spirit.

In the final book of the Old Testament, it says that God noted all those who were faithful to Him, saying,

> "'They shall be Mine," says the LORD of hosts, "on the day

that I make them My jewels. And I will spare them as a man spares his own son who serves him.'" Mal. 3:17

We fall short so easily, it is hard to imagine that the LORD of hosts – the Commander of the armies of angels in heaven, angels so powerful that one angel alone can defeat an army – would consider us as His treasure, His jewels, His sons; but this is how He views those who are faithful to Him. He sees those who are righteous and faithful to Him, and He values them.

The prophetic ministry of warning, rebuking and promising restoration continued. We read of the glory departing from the temple in the book of Ezekiel; we have the words of Obadiah, written around the time that Jerusalem fell to Babylon; and we read the story of some of the exiles in Babylon in the book of Daniel.

Reflect and Respond Ideas

Head outside: Exile is a common theme in the Old Testament. Next time you head out, consider what it would have been like to leave home and know you would not be returning. On the way back, give thanks for God's grace and forgiveness that always allows us to return home to Him.

Research something: Find out more about the temple and the different areas it included. What were they for? Who was allowed into each section? What objects or furnishings were in each area?

Ponder further: What would you like God to do in your life? How would you like Him to restore you from areas where you have been 'tossed with tempest, and not comforted' to being established in beauty and righteousness?

Get creative: These passages of Scripture are so descriptive and evocative. Which one fires your imagination? Draw, paint, craft, make a model to go with one of these passages. Or you could create an illustrated version of one of the passages.

Rebuilding and Restoration in the Promised Land

When the people had turned to repentance and God began the process of restoring them to the land, there was the need to rebuild the temple, walls and gates of the city. These were the physical structures in which the people had wrongly trusted and placed their pride. We read of this in the book of Ezra, at the end of the Babylonian captivity; the rebuilding of the temple in the time of Haggai, then Zechariah; the challenge to the people in Malachi and the rebuilding of Jerusalem's walls and gates in Nehemiah.

In the book of Haggai, we find that people were focusing on establishing their own homes when the temple lay in ruins. The physical ruin of the temple was a symbol of hearts that had not been restored completely to God; of priorities that were not aligned to His. Those outer, visible structures represented an invisible spiritual truth.

In Nehemiah, the walls and gates of the city remained unrestored, which brought shame and reproach upon Israel. This was a vital part of the physical protection for the city; those barriers kept dangers out and enabled the people to exercise judgement and control over who entered. It represented a deeper truth that the spiritual walls and gates of the people had already been destroyed by their idolatry. They had opened the gates to other gods and pagan worship; wilfully ignoring the commands of God. Therefore, when the rebuilding took place, it was not just a physical process of building, but a spiritual one. As the physical structure rose, so the shame was being removed and the spiritual places were being rebuilt inside the people. They relearned what was pleasing to God, recognising His power and holiness, and His presence with them in the challenges they faced. There was a restoration of righteousness, which also brought an emotional and mental healing. We are designed to find wholeness in God, and to stand in His strength and wisdom whilst He works in us.

Restoration through Messiah

There is another link between the messages of the Old Testament prophets, from Isaiah to Malachi: the prophecies of the one who was to come, the Servant, the Messiah. His coming was prophesied centuries before His birth and they were words of hope in the dark times of waiting. What was Israel to expect from the Messiah? To look at just a few of the prophecies of Isaiah, they knew that the Messiah would be:

- One who would break the yoke that burdened the people (Is. 9:4)

- One who would govern upon the throne of David with a rule of peace, judgement and justice, that had no end (Is. 9:6-7)
- One who would be a son born of a virgin, called Immanuel, Wonderful, Counsellor, Mighty God, Everlasting Father, Prince of Peace. (Is. 7:14 and 9:6)
- One upon whom the Spirit of the LORD shall rest, bringing wisdom and understanding, counsel and might, knowledge and the fear of the LORD. (Is. 11:2)
- One who would not lean on His own understanding (Is. 11:3)
- One who would be faithful and righteous (Is. 11:5)
- One who would be a banner to the people, a rallying point for Jews and Gentiles. (Is. 11:10)

We see promises to bring freedom and righteous government to us, through one who would be perfectly and uniquely able to provide all that we need.

We can also turn to Isaiah 61, where we find a prophecy and a promise to God's people which was fulfilled in Jesus Christ. Indeed, it was this passage that Jesus preached on in the temple, to announce His ministry. (See Luke 4:16-22) God promised to:

- heal us and set us free; exchanging all shame and grief for beauty and joy (Is. 61:1-3)
- make us trees of righteousness; deeply rooted in Him and upright before Him (Is. 61:3)
- enable us to rebuild, repair and raise up the ruins and desolated places (Is. 61:4).

This was and is His promise of what He would do for us, flowing out of His desire for us. His intention was to heal and restore us, to bring us strength through Him, so that we could then minister to others.

Whatever Israel may have expected and desired, what they needed was a sinless sacrifice without blemish to atone for their sins. Israel sought freedom from the oppression of temporal nations, dealing with the immediate and visible situation that they faced; but God saw the spiritual oppression and planned to defeat the evil one for all people both at that time and in centuries to come. Only the sacrifice of a sinless man could bridge the separation between God and His children once and for all; only the willing sacrifice of the son of God would defeat sin and death. And so, God Most High once more acted to lead His people out of slavery; He once more stooped low for His children.

God Himself became man. God Himself became the spotless lamb without blemish, who would be offered as a blood sacrifice for all the people of the time and those to come. God Himself was taken outside the city as the scapegoat upon whom all the sins of humanity were placed.

Jesus' blood paid for our sins. It is only through this perfect sacrifice of God's son that we are now able to approach His throne and receive the promises of restoration. These go hand in hand: restored relationship with God, then our restoration into wholeness and into oaks of righteousness; the joining with God in His work of rebuilding and replanting.

Reflect and Respond Ideas

Head outside: Go to a wood or forest, where you can appreciate the height and sturdiness of the trees – how does that speak to you of how God sees people of faith? Or do some gardening as a way to consider how God restores the barren places and the wastelands. If you do not have a garden (or cannot help someone else in theirs) you could plant up some herbs for the kitchen.

Research something: Head into the Bible to find the Scriptures that show the fulfilment of those prophecies in Isaiah. Or do some research into oak trees – how long they can live, how the root system works, what part they play in the eco-system of woodlands.

Ponder further: What would it be like for us to be involved in rebuilding the ruined cities and part of Jesus's Isaiah 61 ministry? What might that look like for you?

Get creative: Do some creative writing about a destroyed city being restored. Create a banner that is a rallying point for people to come to Jesus.

God's Desires for Us

We live in the days after Pentecost, so instead of focusing on a sacred building being the place where God dwells, we recognise that the Holy Spirit dwells within us. We, as believers in Christ and part of the covenant of His blood, are the dwelling-place of God on Earth and God desires to restore us. We are called to live in faith and in righteousness before God and man. Now, more than ever, we need to have strong spiritual foundations in righteousness and truth.

We enter into salvation when we accept Jesus Christ as our Lord and Saviour. We recognise that we have 'sinned and fallen short' and that we need His blood to cover our sin. (Rom. 3:23) This acceptance of His deliverance causes us to become new creations – people within whom the Spirit of God dwells. We become part of His Isaiah 61 ministry of healing and restoration, being established as oaks of righteousness, then released to rebuild and restore the ruins. That is *His* work in us; His desire for our healing and wholeness being put into action within us according to His plans, purposes and patterns.

However, we also need salvation as an ongoing process. We need salvation when we get it wrong, when we have experienced trauma, when we are in circumstances that are overwhelming or feel that they are crushing us. Satan does not care what method works to turn us away from our relationship with God; he is only interested in the end result of a collapsed faith, a relationship with God destroyed. He wants to block our restoration in Christ. Therefore, we need God's perspective to see this bigger picture of what is going on around us; to recognise the true cause of what we are coming up against.

In medieval warfare, there were three approaches to attacking a castle: tunnelling to undermine the foundations, bombarding the walls with missiles to weaken them and create a breach, or laying siege to the castle to starve the people to a point of surrender. Satan uses exactly the same strategies with us. He attempts to undermine our foundations by destabilising our understanding of the truth with deception, twisted theology, misapplied Scripture and so on, until our trust and faith in God collapses. He tries to weaken our faith with disappointments, griefs and grievances against God so that we withdraw from Him and cut off communications with Him. He unleashes missiles at us with the aim of causing our defences to become worn down and eventually collapse. He will bring about the feeling of being under siege – the sense that we are surrounded, abandoned and being starved of all that we need to survive. When our reserves of spiritual food and water are low, it is difficult to endure the challenges of life. Into this, Satan brings the undermining lies of abandonment and rejection: *there is no help coming, no relief and no hope to come... God does not care; you were not hearing His voice... This siege is all there is; imprisonment is all there is... You are helpless – give up, surrender.*

With our building analogy, the foundations are the hidden part of the structure that give stability, strength and soundness; we know that they are there but they are not seen. The proof of the strength of those foundations is how they stand in challenge. Our spiritual foundations need to be securely grounded in God's kingdom of light, consisting of truth, faith and our relationship with God. We need to be built up in wisdom, hope, joy and peace; established in righteousness and filled with the good things of the Kingdom. This strong structure, a life built in this way, can stand and withstand in the day of trouble; something which will also point others to Christ.

For Israel, the temple was a place of enormous significance as the focus of worship. It was the physical dwelling place of God, where worship and sacrifice was offered. Now, we are the holy place of God, His dwelling-place. It is one of the mysteries of God's creation that we are flesh and blood, but also spirit. We are called to offer ourselves as living sacrifices to God and to offer sacrifices of praise. That place of worship needs to have priority in us.

We have things in which we place our trust and confidence: our high and fortified walls. Wherever our trust is in something other than God, we can expect those walls to fall at some point because only God is unchanging and perfect. God's heart is to be all the protection and defence we need; He wants to be the only source of our trust and confidence. He wants to be the wall around us and the glory within us. (See Zech. 2:5) What a breath-taking desire for our God to have! If God is the glory in our midst, then we do not need to chase success in the eyes of the world.

The Promises to Come

The ultimate restoration is still to come, when God will complete what He has begun in us for life everlasting in His presence. How we live matters not just for the here and now, but also for what is to come. He has in mind a new heaven and a new earth, with the ultimate restoration of all things. As God promised through Isaiah,

> "'Violence shall no longer be heard in your land, neither wasting nor destruction within your borders; but you shall call your walls Salvation and your gates Praise.'" Is. 60:18

Do we ever see salvation and praise as solid structures for defence and protection? That is what will be fulfilled perfectly one day, even though now we still live in a world of violence, wasting away and destruction. God desires us to be armed and protected in all the troubles, opposition, trials and temptations that we face, and so we need to play our part in keeping our walls and gates strong and complete.

Nowhere in Scripture does God promise us an easy life. Far from it. Regardless of religious belief or lack thereof, we will all know troubles and tribulations. The choice is whether we want to go through trials with God or without Him? We all face physical death. The question is, do we want to know everlasting life in the new heaven and earth that God will create for us, where sin and death will be no more; where we find out what it was supposed to be like for mankind, in the dwelling-place our Lord has created for us? Trials, tribulations and death are common to all mankind, but we find hope and joy in knowing that there is something glorious beyond description waiting for us.

It is difficult to read the Bible without recognising that there is a need to be faithful, to endure and to overcome. We are told clearly that:

> "'... you will be hated by all for My name's sake. But he who endures to the end will be saved.'" Matt. 10:22

> 'Blessed is the man who endures temptation; for when he has been approved, he will receive the crown of life which the Lord has promised to those who love Him.' James 1:12

God does not want the trials and tribulations to come as a horrible shock, but as something that we can expect and something that He will see us through. He wants us to be increasingly whole and restored, as then we react better and recover more quickly. He wants us to be able to endure in righteousness and faith, which is why so much of the New Testament is information about how to stay strong in faith whatever our circumstances are. We need help with that because it is hard. But the rewards of enduring are fruitfulness and life: access to the river of life, the tree of life and the crown of life in the New Jerusalem where all hell has passed away and God's desires are finally and completely fulfilled.

Reflect and Respond Ideas

Head outside: If you are able to, visit a castle and notice all the different defensive aspects to it. Where was it built and why? Look for a well and consider how essential that would be in a siege. Relate that to how God wants us to feel in His kingdom.

Research something: Find out about an area in the world where Christians face persecution simply because they believe that Jesus Christ is Lord. Pray for them to endure and proclaim that they will receive the crown of life.

Ponder further: Finding out that our faith in Jesus means that some will hate us is tough. Spend some time to process that – perhaps you have already experienced people responding in hatred because of your faith. Balance that out with what God promises us as we endure with our eyes fixed on Jesus.

Get creative: Read Revelation 21 and 22 and respond in art, music, creative writing ...

LIGHT

phos (Greek)

'From *phao* (to shine, or make manifest, especially by rays);
Luminousness (in the widest application: natural or artificial,
abstract or concrete, literary or figurative)
Fire, light.'[6]

Is it possible to define the importance and value of light to mankind? Sunlight is a necessary factor in life, growth and well-being. Even when we take it for granted, natural light is essential to our lives physically, emotionally and mentally. We can study the science of light, but this does not explain why light is something that impacts our mood and engages our sense of wonder. In difficult times, we use the metaphor of darkness and the need to find light at the end of the tunnel. Light is associated with hope, health and well-being, not just existence.

Sunlight is transformative. An overcast day can easily make us feel low and unmotivated, but when the clouds clear to let the sunlight through, we find our mood lifting and we become more positive. The bare trees of winter become beautiful rather than barren when lit by the sun. This morning, our attic windows were covered in stunning frost patterns like fern leaves, which sparkled in the sunlight. It became a moment to pause in wonder and thanksgiving.

Spectacular sunrises or sunsets can stay in our memories for many years. They are moments to savour; time taken out of the ordinary in order to enjoy the colours. Who else but God would make a functional

---

[6] James *Strong, The New Strong's Exhaustive Concordance of the Bible*, (Thomas Nelson Publishers, 1990) Greek, number 5457. This is the most common word used for light in the New Testament.

process, like the transition of night into day and day into night, so glorious? No two sunsets are identical; each one is unique.

Light can help us transcend the ordinary for a few moments; giving some respite. It seems to be universal that firelight captures our attention, causing us simply to stop and watch the flames for a while. It is restful - like time has stopped for a while. How often does that normally happen in life, that we feel compelled to stop and watch something? A candle flame can have the same mesmerising quality that draws us to be still and focus on that light and its movement. Light impacts us and speaks to us in a profound way, whether it is the flickering of starlight or firelight, or the shifting shades of colour illuminating the sky as the sun sets.

Would you ever choose to sit in complete darkness, simply to consider the quality of that darkness and to marvel at it? We do not go out at night to stand in awe at the darkness, but at the lights we see in it – the stars, moon, comets, perhaps even the space station passing by which reflects the light of the sun. People travel to the Arctic Circle not because they want to see the complete darkness of the sky, but in the hope of seeing the aurora borealis with its ethereal light show dancing across the night sky.

Light also shows us things that need dealing with and can spur us on to action. Surely the tradition of spring cleaning has something to do with the stronger sunlight showing up the dust and cobwebs more clearly!

Light speaks to us so profoundly because it touches upon an eternal truth that God has placed within His children. We were made to live in His kingdom of light: of truth, salvation, goodness, grace and wholeness. It is only in Him that we find these things in complete perfection, without fault or failing. We looked at how things went wrong with Adam and Eve, but there was a rebellion before that which shaped the world we live in.

The First Rebellion

Whilst it is completely true that we have a loving Father who desires to bring us life in all its fullness, it is also true that we have an enemy whose aim is to separate us from God. His name is Satan. It is impossible to look into the story of this clash of kingdoms without considering the theme of light.

What do we know of Satan? He began as an angel in heaven called Lucifer. Very few angels in the Bible are known to us by name, but Lucifer was one of them. His name meant *light-bearer, the shining one, shining*.[7] We are told that the seraphim before the throne of the Living God cover their eyes in worship because His holiness is so overwhelming; but Lucifer did not want to be a worshipper of his Creator – he wanted to be the one worshipped and so he rebelled. (Is. 6:1-3) We read of this moment in Isaiah:

> "'How you are fallen from heaven, O Lucifer, son of the morning! How you are cut down to the ground, you who weakened the nations! For you have said in your heart: I will ascend into heaven, I will exalt my throne above the stars of God; I will also sit on the mount of the congregation on the farthest sides of the north; I will ascend above the heights of the clouds, I will be like the Most High.'" Isaiah 14:12-14

The attitudes and desires of Lucifer's heart led to the action of rebellion; not just on his own part but in causing others to rebel against God and choosing to serve him instead. Isaiah recorded five 'I will...' statements of Satan's heart:

1. I will ascend into heaven (God's dwelling-place)

2. I will exalt my throne above the stars of God (above God's creation)

3. I will ascend above the heights of the clouds

4. I will sit on the mount of the congregation (indicating Jerusalem)

5. I will be like the Most High

Lucifer was not content to serve or worship another, even if that was God Most High. He wanted glory for himself. Lucifer desired his own

---

[7] Cornwall and Smith, *Bible Names*, p.122

throne, high over the created world. He desired to be like God.

This desire to be '*like* the Most High' is interesting because at no point does Satan imply or state that he is able to replace or supplant God. He knows that God is the one and only Most High and that nothing will change that. The best he could aim for was to be 'like' the Most High in being high, exalted, enthroned, worshipped. He did not, however, want to be like God in His creativity and life-bringing work, or like God in His desire to establish things with perfect order and beauty. Satan did not want to be like God in loving others and sacrificially pouring himself out for the good of mankind. No, the only area in which Satan wanted to be *like* God was in His glory.

Ironically, it is in this that he is most *unlike* God. God has no need to harbour ambitions to elevate and exalt Himself, because by His nature He was and is and always will be all-glorious, omnipotent, incomparable, above all things – nothing can change that truth or alter His nature. He cannot increase or decrease in power, splendour or might. This awesome, all-powerful God who reigns gloriously in the splendour and majesty coveted by Satan, is also the servant-hearted God who loved humanity so profoundly that He took human form and experienced mortal life from birth to death. There is nothing selfish about the Most High. Even before creation, there was perfect love within the Trinity – relationship, intimacy. Now, our God reaches down to those He created and offers us salvation and life eternal with Him, raising us up with a loving hand each time we fall and fail. This is the indescribably awesome glory of God: that He is perfect power, majesty and justice; but also, perfect goodness, mercy, generosity, love, compassion and humility.

Everything about God that draws us to love and pursue Him, was rejected and despised by Lucifer. Having rebelled against God Most High in his heart and in his actions, Lucifer was cast out of heaven. Jesus described this event as seeing Satan, '"...fall like lightning from heaven."' (Luke 10:18) Lightning is the result of a violent clash of particles, which releases an enormous amount of heat and light energy into the sky. We do not see the particles react as such, but we do see the lightning bolt and hear the sound of thunder moments later. The casting out of this angel is compared to this sudden, explosive release of energy. Lucifer, the bearer of light, became Satan, the adversary of God and all who follow Him.[8] This angel, 'cut down to the ground,' is doing all he can to gain high position now, whilst he still can.

After only two chapters of perfection, Satan made his move to damage and destroy what God had created. Man's sin allowed that process to happen. Instead of being able to walk in the cool of the garden with our loving Father, mankind was exiled from Eden and the blessings of direct contact with God. In the Isaiah passage, we see that Satan 'weakened the nations' by separating us from God and establishing his kingdom of spiritual darkness upon the Earth. Satan wants mankind to rebel and sin, just as he did, rejecting everything to do with God.

In the natural world, light and dark work together; day merges peacefully into night and back again as the Earth rotates around the sun. Spiritually, this cannot happen because the darkness reacts violently to the light. Whereas Satan's kingdom is one of darkness and destruction; Jesus's kingdom is light and life. There is no goodness, joy, truth, peace or love in Satan's kingdom; there is no evil or injustice in God's kingdom. We live in this state of entirely opposite, incompatible forces, which clash violently when they meet.

God placed limitations on mankind so that in our need and struggle we would turn to Him for strength and enabling; but also so that our time in a fallen world would not last forever. God knew that enduring in a fallen world would be a struggle because of our own sin but also because Satan continuously works to block God's desires for us. We need to know this as the background to all that we experience in life.

God is light – there is no darkness in Him. Therefore, there is no darkness in His kingdom. He is the source of light, and all that brings light to our souls: goodness, hope, joy, truth, peace, wholeness, and so on. He is the source of all that we need to live and live well before Him. His kingdom is the place where we can abide and dwell in His presence, both now but also in the new Earth when all is made new.

---

[8] Cornwall and Smith, *Bible Names*, p.162

Reflect and Respond Ideas

Head outside: Spend some time outside on a dull day and be alert to how it affects your mood and your attitude to the things that are on your mind. Then spend some time outside on a sunny day and do the same exercise. Consider how living in God's light can impact our mood and attitudes.

Research something: Find out some more about the different names of God. What does this tell us about Him, about His heart for us and His kingdom? In contrast, what does this tell us about Satan and his kingdom?

Ponder further: Find a space to contemplate the importance of light, whether in a dark room with a candle, or looking up at the stars. Reflect on the contrast between dark and light, and about how the light impacts you.

Get creative: The fall of Lucifer was described as being like lightning. Explore that with art, sound, dance, creative writing. If you had been there, what words would you have used to describe it? Record those words in a way that reflects their meaning.

The Choice We Have

Jesus did not present His disciples with a choice of light or darkness. He taught His followers that they had a choice of routes in life, using the metaphor of gates and paths. Many choose the wide gate and the broad path; few find the narrow gate and follow the difficult path. (Matt. 7:13-14). Two verses, two sentences, two gates, two paths. This is clearly contrary to the popular view that there are many paths to God – there is only the narrow way through Jesus Christ. We choose one or the other. Even if we ignore this, we are still making a choice.

The unspoken similarity is that both paths involve tribulations - no one escapes or avoids tribulation or the costs of life in a fallen and broken world. If we were in any doubt about that, John 16:33 records Jesus explicitly telling His disciples that they will have tribulation in life, facing difficulties and distress. Neither option promises an easy life, but the ultimate outcome is completely different depending on which path we choose. The narrow gate and the difficult way lead to life. The wide gate and the broad path lead to destruction.

What can we expect from the narrow path? When we follow Jesus, we take up our cross and follow Him – not just once, but many times.

Submitting to His will not only is a narrow path but it enrages Satan. Satan does not want us to be obedient and faithful to God; or wide awake spiritually, praying as the Holy Spirit leads us and praying for the kingdom of God to be established here on Earth; he does not want us to be fulfilling the mandate to make disciples and baptise them in the name of Jesus. We will experience those powerful lightning clashes as Satan opposes our pursuit of Jesus.

Jesus told the disciples that, "'the thief does not come except to steal, and to kill, and to destroy.'" (John 10:10) Satan wants to sow distrust, dishonesty and misunderstanding in our relationships so that they break down. Satan wants to cause rifts in churches, where Christians feel so hurt and betrayed that they will not look to the narrow path of reconciliation and forgiveness but simply leave. Satan wants to steal and destroy our confidence and identity in Christ. Satan twists, distorts and questions truth, introducing doubt and confusion (did God *really* say that?).

Darkness exists and the spiritual battle exists whether we want it to or not. However, the darkness is not the end of the story.

When we follow Jesus, we gain access to all the resources of the Kingdom of Light. He does not leave us unprepared or unprotected: we have the Bible and the Holy Spirit to guide us through, plus all that we gain through Christ.

When we follow Him, it is not just on the sacrificial path to Calvary, but on the triumphant path to everlasting life, joy, wholeness and goodness. This path that can hurt like hell is also the path of the eternal and glorious victory of Christ over sin, death and all darkness.

The tribulation we inevitably face, the darkness we go through, is only ever half of the story. If we read the whole of John 16:33, Jesus says,

> 'In this world you will have tribulation; but be of good cheer, I have overcome the world.'

If we read the whole of Jesus' statement in John 10:10, we find that,

> "'The thief does not come except to steal, and to kill, and to destroy [but] I have come that they may have life, and that

they may have it more abundantly."'

Jesus has overcome the enemy, the darkness, sin and death. Jesus is the way to eternal life and relationship with God, who alone is the source of all goodness and truth, life and wholeness. When we recognise and acknowledge Jesus Christ as Lord and Saviour, we need to know that He promises to be all we need in the darkness. Our response should always be to reach out to Jesus as the way, the truth and the life in every circumstance; for this is not just true of the moment of salvation, but true of every moment when we need to know the saving presence and guidance of Jesus in our lives. Fundamentally, the darkness is designed to draw us away from relationship with God. So, we need to do the opposite by drawing ever closer to God, letting Him work in us and through us especially in our darkest moments.

We may not be entirely comfortable with the military metaphors we find in the Bible – we use terms such as spiritual warfare, spiritual battle and putting on the armour and it can seem a little ... strange. However, if we found ourselves in a war zone that we could see, hear and experience around us, we would definitely want every available resource to keep ourselves safe and protected.

Paul was in no doubt about there being an unseen spiritual war raging around him and his fellow believers. He suffered greatly for proclaiming the Gospel, so it is wise to look at his ever-practical advice on dealing with the darkness we face. He wrote these words to the church in Ephesus:

> '... be strong in the Lord and in the power of His might. Put on the whole armour of God, that you may be able to stand against the wiles of the devil. For we do not wrestle against flesh and blood, but against principalities, against powers, against the rulers of the darkness of this age, against spiritual hosts of wickedness in the heavenly places.' Eph. 6:10-12

Paul wanted the Ephesian believers to look beyond the flesh and blood situations that they faced so that they could see the spiritual problem going on behind the scenes. He listed various spiritual foes: the wiles of the devil, principalities, powers, rulers of the darkness of this age and spiritual hosts of wickedness. This was not to cause fear amongst the church of Ephesus but to explain what was really going on. Ephesus was a bustling city of pagan worship, where it was acceptable to worship any manner and number of gods. However, claiming that there was only one true God and only one path of salvation was disruptive and strongly rejected by many.

It is important to remember that Paul was a teacher and a mentor: his focus was always to build other believers up in faith and to show them how to deal with the obstacles they faced. Paul did not want the believers to focus on the arguments and troubles they had with the people around them, but to recognise that there was a spiritual realm where that opposition and persecution was being generated. He knew that if the believers of Ephesus focused on wrestling flesh and blood, they would simply become exhausted and potentially give up. They needed to know how to identify the real enemy and know how to be spiritually armed and how to pray.

Notice that there is no conditional clause of, '*if* you come against the wiles of the devil *then* you might like to consider this option'; or '*if* a fiery dart should happen to come your way, *then* you could try this'. There was no doubt in Paul's mind that believers of Christ would come against the evil one, so he commanded them to be strong in the Lord by arming themselves spiritually. It was only through this spiritual protection through Jesus Christ that they could withstand whatever came against them. This is just as true for believers now. The armour of God is available to us through Christ, but we need to choose to put it on through prayer.

Paul continued:

'Therefore, take up the whole armour of God, that you may be able to withstand in the evil day, and having done all, to stand. Stand therefore, having girded your waist with truth, having put on the breastplate of righteousness, and having shod your feet with the preparation of the gospel of peace; above all, taking the shield of faith with which you will be able to quench all the fiery darts of the wicked one. And take the helmet of salvation, and the sword of the Spirit, which is the word of

God; praying always with all prayer and supplication in the Spirit, being watchful to this end with all perseverance and supplication for all the saints...' Eph. 6:13-18

It is because of all the spiritual opposition that we take up the whole armour of God: this is how we protect and arm ourselves spiritually. It is our choice to do this – it is a deliberate process of choosing to recognise that there is a need for arming and that it is not just a metaphor but a tool that has real impact in the spiritual places.

'Take up the whole armour of God...'

I take up the whole armour in a way I can easily remember, and that is to start at the helmet and work down to the shoes.

I put on the helmet of salvation and give thanks that Jesus died for me at Calvary so that I can draw close to the Living God who created me. I pray for God's protection over every part of my mind and give the Holy Spirit freedom to do whatever He needs. I welcome His work of salvation (of rescue, deliverance and help) in all I face.

I put on the breastplate of righteousness, again giving thanks that this is not my righteousness but His. I ask God to protect every area of my heart and invite the Spirit to move where He needs to. I put on the belt of truth and give thanks that God's word is unchanging, eternal and definitive. The shoes of the Gospel of peace go on next, as I give thanks for all that is possible through Jesus Christ who died and rose again. I take up the shield of faith and the sword of the Spirit, asking God to give me alertness to any fiery arrows and the ability to handle them with faith and truth, in His might.

With any of these areas, I pray more specifically as the Holy Spirit leads me. For instance, I may bring areas of mental processing to be covered by Jesus' salvation (such as my judgement, if I have a decision to make; my imagination, memory, sub-conscious, will, attitudes, memories). I might bring areas of my heart to be covered by Jesus' righteousness (my emotions, calling, desires, femininity, identity). It is good to give thanks for specific words of truth that I can stand on, as they come to mind, and to meditate on all that Jesus accomplished for us with thanksgiving and praise.

I also find it helpful to proclaim that Jesus is Lord over each part of my life and over situations I have to deal with, so that I can speak out that He has authority and sovereignty over everything. It puts Him in position before and over all things.

'...that you may be able to stand ...'

The purpose of the armour of God is to enable us to stand and withstand in whatever the spiritual battle is. When we are clothed in the salvation and righteousness of Christ, we can stand. When we have the truth of the word of God wrapped around us and in our hand, ready to use, we can stand. When we have faith before us, we can stand. When we have our feet enclosed in the glorious good news of the victory of Christ over the evil one, we can stand.

When Moses led the Israelites out of Egypt, there came a point when they were blocked in front by the Red Sea and became aware that the Egyptian army was bearing down on them from behind. From the Scriptures, we know that this was God's plan, but the Israelites only saw that certain death awaited them. Their sight knowledge of the situation left them without options. However, God showed them how to position themselves before Him and He opened a way for them that they could never have created themselves.

In the NIV version of Exodus 13:18, it says, 'The Israelites went up out of Egypt armed for battle,' and were described as boldly marching out. (Ex. 14:8). They were not yet trained in battle, but they left Egypt as soldiers, armed and marching out with courage and strength of heart. As the Egyptians bore down on them and their courage fled, Moses instructed them with God's command:

> "'Do not be afraid. Stand still, and see the salvation of the LORD, which He will accomplish for you today. For the Egyptians whom you see today, you shall see again no more forever. The LORD will fight for you, and you shall hold your peace.'" Ex. 14:13-14

Our positioning of heart, mind and spirit so often needs to be this: to be spiritually armed with the things of God and to stand firm in faith and obedience. Repeatedly in the Ephesians passage, Paul tells us that being armed spiritually enables us to:

- stand against the wiles of the devil (temptations, deceit, fiery arrows...)
- withstand in the evil day (the darkness around us)
- and having done all, to stand
- stand therefore.

We see this in action again, many years after the Exodus, when the kingdom of Judah was facing attack. God's instruction was given to one of the Levites:

> "'Position yourselves, stand still and see the salvation of the LORD, who is with you, O Judah and Jerusalem! Do not fear or be dismayed ...'" 2 Chron. 20:17

If we change our view of God in these situations to seeing Him as our commanding officer, we begin to see Him as the one who is leading us, the one who has the strategy. We submit to God, our commanding officer, so that Satan will flee from us. We can know that our God will win the victory and lead us through, but our part is to position ourselves, in the whole armour of God, so that we can stand and see the salvation of the LORD who is with us.

'...praying always...'

We are intended to engage in an ongoing conversation with the Father, bringing everything before Him and interacting with Him in all that goes on in our day. Conversation involves both talking and listening, showing an interest in someone else's perspective on what is going on. With this, there is no room for adopting a special prayer voice or manner of speaking: it is just talking to God out of the reality of life, whether that is doing the washing, preparing for a meeting, heading to the airport for a flight...

No matter how close we are to other people, the only one who can truly and deeply engage with us in all that we do and are, is the Almighty God of the universe. He will not lose interest in what you are doing, what you are thinking, what your hopes and dreams are. You do not need to take care of Him or worry that you are taking up too much of His time. You are His beloved child, and He is there for you every second of the day and night. Chat with Him. Invite His involvement in whatever is going on and listen to what He has to say. A Scripture may come to mind that helps, or a way forward that had not occurred to you before.

'...with all prayer and supplication...'

We come before God out of whatever is in our hearts and out of what the Holy Spirit prompts us to pray. This could be prayers of repentance, prayers of thanksgiving and praise, prayers of supplication and request, prayers of trust and worship, prayers of lament, prayers for yourself or others.

In Jewish tradition, there are phrases of blessing or praise that are spoken throughout the day, which are designed to refocus our minds from our own instinct to rely on ourselves and do everything on our own, back onto the sovereignty, presence and provision of God. It is described as a way of 'kneeling down' before God during the day.[9] This does not need to have a set formula, but an attitude that chooses to bless God and kneel before Him. As you wake up, 'blessed are you, O Lord, for creating a new day,' or 'I praise you, Lord God, for the work you have given me.' It could simply be, 'I thank and praise you, Lord, for giving me life.'

If you know that you work with someone you do not get on with, bring that to God. Acknowledge the ways in which you struggle to work with them. Then pause and recognise that there are probably ways in which you are difficult to work with too! Invite God to work in your attitude to that person and ask the Holy Spirit to be at work in all your interactions with that person. Do not expect them to change, but you can expect you and your attitude to change. Bless God that He is with you wherever you go. Bless God for the job He has given you. Bless God for the Holy Spirit, who will guide you through the frustrations.

---

[9] Ann Spangler and Lois Tverberg, *Sitting at the Feet of Rabbi Jesus*, (Zondervan, 2018), pp.98-101

'...in the Spirit...'

One of the most beautiful things of the Christian faith is that our Heavenly Father knows that we are going to find it difficult to follow Him and so gave us the Holy Spirit to guide us, help us, prompt us, enable us. He has not set us an impossible task and then sat back to watch us fail. He is in this with us. When we do not know what to pray, when we cannot put words to what we feel, the Holy Spirit helps us (see Romans 8:26).

Invite the Holy Spirit to teach you to pray, to guide you and prompt you. This might be with a Scripture or song that comes to mind; a person that comes to mind and a nudge to pray for them and to send them a message. The Holy Spirit knows the full picture that we cannot see. It requires humility to put aside our own understanding of circumstances and situations, but as we learn to do this and to ask the Holy Spirit to reveal the truth to us, it opens the way for God to work in us and through us.

'...being watchful...'

It is so important to develop this skill of spiritual alertness, which comes through becoming increasingly sensitive to the leading of the Holy Spirit. Paul gives this instruction in the midst of teaching about arming ourselves spiritually and in praying for other believers. We are to be aware of our own need for spiritual protection and also to be alert on behalf of our brothers and sisters in Christ. It is the Holy Spirit who reveals to us what is happening in the spiritual places so we can look past the part of the problem in front of us and deal with the spiritual opposition. Being watchful is so important wherever Christians work together because unity is so deeply opposed by Satan. We need to be quick to spot spiritual obstacles and opposition to the Kingdom work of Christ on Earth.

Reflect and Respond Ideas

Head outside: If you like action, you might want to find an assault course to take on. As you go through, compare it to our spiritual lives – the way is not easy, there are challenges, but getting to the end is amazing!

Research something: Find out more about ancient Ephesus – where is it, what gods were worshipped there, who traded there, what languages would have been heard there, what is still left that shows us what the city was like?

Ponder further: Are you aware of moments in your life where a decision involved choosing between the narrow path or a wide path? What were the clues that showed you that one path was aligned with God's will and the other was not?

Get creative: Try creating a maze on paper or as a model, that shows different pathways – some leading to life, others leading to destruction. Or choose one piece of the spiritual armour and explore what its design might be.

Living in the Light

As we learn through reading God's plans for mankind in Genesis and again in the new Earth to come, we were designed to live in God's light. Rather than this being an automatic thing now, it becomes something that we need to choose and remember.

John's Gospel begins with a few verses that are packed full of truth and the mysteries of God's kingdom:

> 'In the beginning was the Word, and the Word was with God, and the Word was God…. In Him was life, and the life was the light of men. And the light shines in the darkness, and the darkness did not comprehend it.' John 1:1, 4-5

We have Jesus as the Word who was with God and who was God from before creation. Light and life are interwoven in Christ; they are part of His being. This light of Christ was not understood by the kingdom of darkness, nor could it be extinguished or diminished by it. Satan tried to destroy Jesus several times, but Jesus only gave up His life at the time appointed by the Father, and in a way that fulfilled the prophecies of old.

Jesus also described Himself as light:

> "'I am the light of the world. He who follows Me shall not walk in darkness, but have the light of life.'" John 8:12

These are such familiar words to us, but we do not necessarily live in the full truth of what this means for us. We know that this is not about Him being a literal light source - He did not come and glow wherever He went. This is also not just a nice idea or image; something poetic and sentimental. Jesus came as the spiritual light to those in the kingdom of darkness. This is about rescue, salvation, deliverance from evil; it is about bringing hope and a way out for those in the imprisonment of spiritual darkness. God knew that we needed spiritual light and Jesus was to be that light, to all who call upon His name. He brought the light of hope through salvation, but also the essential teaching that we still use today to equip us to choose wisely in life.

This dual role is so important for us to understand. Jesus came to bring us eternal salvation but also the *equipping* that we need to endure and resist the darkness for the entirety of our lives on Earth. Jesus never offered platitudes of false comfort or attempted to downplay what we would experience in life. Instead, He promised that when we follow Him, we shall not walk in darkness – even in the fallen world we live in. We shall not walk in darkness, because in Christ we have the light of life.

Focus on this promise for a moment: no matter what it feels like, when you follow Christ you shall not walk in darkness because you have the 'light of life' that comes from Christ in you and with you. This is God's desire for you and His promise to you. Bear this in mind as we read these words of Paul, written to the church in Ephesus:

> '...you were once darkness, but now you are light in the Lord. Walk as children of light (for the fruit of the Spirit is in all goodness, righteousness, and truth), finding out what is acceptable to the Lord. And have no fellowship with the unfruitful works of darkness...' Eph. 5:8-11

This is such a key part of our testimony of God's redemptive work in us. We were darkness – not that we were simply in darkness, but that our very being was darkness. Now, we are light in the Lord – not just that we have the gift of light through Christ, but that He restores our *identity* to being light. This is a profound shift which occurs as we accept Jesus Christ as our Lord and Saviour. We are taken out of darkness, and darkness is taken out of us; we are brought into the light of Christ, and His light is placed within us. Our identity and dwelling place change from one kingdom to another.

This is part of our being in Christ and Him in us, but we also have a part to play in this. We were designed to bear God's likeness in being light, but this is no longer a natural or automatic way for us to live and be. Paul knew this so, in writing to believers in Ephesus, he first reminded them of the truth that they were now light. He followed up this statement of identity with practical steps for living this out. His advice was never a theoretical, 'do as I say, but not as I do,' but the bold approach of 'see how I live – this is what I live out and I have found that this works.' So, what does Paul tell us to do?

'Walk as children of light…'

Satan was an angel, a light-bearer, but he rebelled against God and chose to go his own way. He is now eternally in darkness, doing whatever he can to take other children of light with him – to take *us* with him. How else can he hurt God?

Having this example in mind, we need to ensure that we walk as children of light, in obedience and fellowship with God. Through the work of the Holy Spirit within us, we should be walking in goodness, righteousness and truth. This shows our heritage and identity as children of light, not just as a testimony and witness to others but for our own well-being.

'…find out what is acceptable to the Lord.'

Like any child, we have to learn how to do things God's way – even if we have been Christians for many years. We need to keep going back to the Word of God and immersing ourselves in it, and we need to stay close to His heart in all things. The more we know the Bible, the more the Holy Spirit can bring those verses to mind when we most need them.

Neither of these instructions involves being passive: we are to *walk* in light and to *find out* what pleases God. We have a choice and resolution to make in how we are going to live and what we will pursue.

'Have no fellowship with the unfruitful works of darkness.'

The use of the word *fellowship* is interesting here - we are not to be in harmony or at peace with the works of darkness; we are not to stand in a position of friendship with them; we are not to engage with them or participate in them; we are not to compromise or find understanding with them. In another letter, Paul takes this point further:

> 'For what fellowship has righteousness with lawlessness? And what communion has light with darkness? And what accord has Christ with Belial? Or what part has a believer with an unbeliever? And what agreement has the temple of God with idols? For you are the temple of the living God.
>
> As God has said: "I will dwell in them and walk among them. I will be their God, and they shall be My people." Therefore, "Come out from among them and be separate," says the Lord. 'Do not touch what is unclean, and I will receive you.' 2 Cor. 6:14-17

We need to be so wise in this. Our walk with Christ puts us on a path that is entirely incompatible with the things of darkness. We cannot have a foot on each path as they lead in opposing directions. If we keep a foot on the broad path, we cannot progress along the path of light. It was idolatry that kept pulling Israel away from God's path of righteousness – they continued to find the ways of darkness attractive and adopted the practices of the surrounding pagan nations. Israel could not walk in two opposing directions at the same time; nor could they look in two directions at the same time, any more than we can. We have to choose one or the other; not just once, when we first come to Christ, but throughout our lives.

When we choose Christ, we give Him lordship of our lives. However, we still have to make that choice regularly. Will we submit to God's leadership in how we treat someone we find difficult? Will we submit to Him each time we make a choice in what we watch, how we use our time and finances? Rather than asking ourselves whether we are turning to an idol, it is more straight-forward to consider which path we are walking on in those decisions. Is it one that will bring us closer to God, or further away? If God has prompted us to do something and we say no, then we are turning away from Him and blocking our ability to hear Him next time. We always have free will in our choices, so we always have the choice to choose God's kingdom and leadership or to turn away from it.

Paul did not mean that we remove ourselves from the world and refuse to interact with non-believers. Far from it. Remember that Paul did not live in a secluded hermitage, avoiding contact with other people. He preached the Gospel to unbelievers in cities that hosted a wide range of religious beliefs and practices, with sorcerers and the demonic present. But Paul remained set apart for Christ in his heart and did not compromise in his walk of faith, no matter what that cost him. He did not have fellowship with those things of darkness. In his heart, mind and soul, Paul was entirely committed to God's kingdom of light, life and love. This was his foundation, his bottom line. If it did not honour God, he wanted none of it.

Paul was whole-hearted in his love for Christ, but he was also whole-hearted in his love and commitment to people who needed salvation or discipleship. He loved his fellow believers and wanted them to know that this was at the root of his response to them, as we see in 2 Corinthians:

> 'For out of much affliction and anguish of heart I wrote to you, with many tears, not that you should be grieved, but that you might know the love which I have so abundantly for you.' 2 Cor. 2:4

Paul chafed at imprisonment because it kept him out of the world; confined and unable to visit those he loved and those who needed discipleship and encouragement. It kept him away from those who needed to hear the Gospel. He continued to mentor, teach and encourage via letter but he longed to be with them in person. He was a people person, passionately engaged with their choices and lives.

Why was Paul so committed to pursuing God? Because he had personally encountered Jesus Christ and was profoundly changed by the grace that lifted him out of darkness and sin when he deserved judgement. In the light of this, he knew that nothing else was worth pursuing, nor did he want anyone to be left out of such joy. Towards the end of Revelation, we find out that one day all the light we need, will be provided by Jesus once more. In the description of the New Jerusalem, John saw that,

> 'The city had no need of the sun or of the moon to shine in it, for the glory of God illuminated it. The Lamb is its light.'
> Rev. 21:23

There was a prize to come that was worth dying for: the life that God always intended us to have, in the glory and light of His presence. From the beginning to eternity, God is the light and life to all men; and this light will not be extinguished by the darkness. On the contrary, the light of Christ will continue to shine and there is no power of hell that can stop that.

Reflect and Respond Ideas

Head outside: Take a walk (or go for a run or bike ride) in your neighbourhood as a child of light. Proclaim as you go that Jesus Christ is Lord; that He has the victory over all darkness.

Research something: Research someone who lived as a child of light – how did they make such a difference through their lives that their names have been remembered? Examples could be: Corrie Ten Boom, Watchman Nee, Amy Carmichael, Bilquis Sheikh.

Ponder further: How would life be different if we were able to live with complete conviction that God can and will defeat the darkness? If we walked in confidence that we were bringing the light of Christ with us wherever we went and that this makes a difference?

Get creative: Speak, sing, shout, draw, paint about the sovereignty and victory of God over darkness. You might want to do this generally, speaking out over things going on in the world today, or specifically, speaking out over situations that you face.

Praying for Light in the Darkness

Knowing this, we then need to consider the light of God as something that we desperately need to go through life. We find references to God being our light in the context of encounters with darkness, danger and difficulty. It is part of God's provision for us in the darkness –a valuable and necessary part of our defences and our enabling. Turning to the light needs to become an instinctive response mechanism in whatever darkness we deal with, so how do we go about that?

We have already seen from Scripture that:

- God is light and there is no darkness in Him.
- Jesus came as the light to the world to both Jews and Gentiles, for all time.
- We *have* the light of life – it is something that we now possess because we follow Christ.
- We *are* light in the Lord – this is our identity in Christ.
- We are children *of* light – made in the likeness of God and now adopted into God's family; living in His kingdom, under His sovereignty and Fatherhood.

Turning to these truths and proclaiming them reminds us of our heritage and identity in Christ; it restores a foundation of necessary fact and restores an important perspective

We also read in the Psalms that the Word of God is a lamp unto our feet. A lamp is needed in order to travel in the darkness, so we can see where it is safe to put our feet. The Word of God is the light that shows us where we take our stand and withstand the work of the evil one. It is our first resource in finding the way, the truth and the life in a situation that otherwise seems hopeless. It is possible to read pages of Scripture and not be any the wiser or more protected. That is because we find the light of God through the Bible *and* through the revelation and help of the Holy Spirit. The Word of God (the Bible), the Word (Jesus Christ) and the Holy Spirit together open the way for us to discover the spiritual perspective we need on our circumstances.

David began Psalm 27 with the following declaration:

'The LORD is my light and my salvation; whom shall I fear? The LORD is the strength of my life; of whom shall I be afraid?' Ps. 27:1

In the New King James Bible, this chapter is described as 'an exuberant declaration of faith.' David was confident that God was faithful, mighty to save and would be with him in his present situation. David used rhetorical questions for which his unspoken response was 'no one.' But for us, this rhetorical question may not be helpful. We can know that the answer is 'no one,' but it may not impact our heart attitude. We can read this verse and hope for a change in our emotions, yet still experience fear. We might even read it and then feel condemnation that we do not have that same faith and confidence in our circumstances. How can we turn this from theory into a tool?

I re-read this recently, not as a confident proclamation of faith where there was no doubt, but as a deliberate stirring up of faith in a time of fear. Instead of reading it as a rhetorical question, we can take it as a question requiring an answer. Once we read it as something to consider and weigh up, it gives us a different perspective; something that we apply to our own heart responses and allow to become a powerful tool.

David began with what he knew to be true about God: that He Himself was the light that David needed, and that He Himself was David's salvation. Based on that knowledge: was there anyone that David should fear? Based on that knowledge: is there anyone that you should fear?

Ponder this in your heart for a while. What is it that you face? What fear does that cause? There will be a trigger for fear (such as an illness) and the emotion of fear that it causes. The emotional response is powerful and can limit our ability to find perspective on the 'trigger' situation. For those who have ongoing trouble with anxiety, this will be a familiar state of affairs. We still have a choice to stand on truth, but it will feel like a battle to do this.

Proclaim over that situation:

'The LORD is my light...'

God Himself is the source of light. Because it is part of His being, it is a living, powerful and transformative light at work in our hearts and in our circumstances. It is not something distant, but present with us and in us.

Bring to mind the most glorious sunrise or sunset you have seen – God's light and glory are even greater and more breath-taking than that.

When we talk about the LORD being our light, we mean that He is the one who brings us revelation, salvation, the way through, life, supernatural vision and hope. This is all available to you through Christ.

Make it personal to you – right now, the Almighty God, who created the vastness of the universe, is *your* light in what *you* are dealing with.

'The LORD is my salvation ...'

He is the one who has redeemed you from all darkness and changed your identity to being His child, His beloved. He has brought you eternal life with Him; but He is also your salvation in the circumstances you face now. Salvation brings us a supernatural way through something; a way which otherwise would not exist. We could not be in the relationship with God that we have without it; His salvation supernaturally opened the way for us. His salvation also opens a way through our circumstances as we look to Him.

Because of Jesus, you have the light of life. He has overcome the darkness and has complete victory over the evil one.

'The LORD is the strength of my life...'

God is the source of all the strength you need; therefore, you do not need to find the strength yourself. He wants His strength to flow through you, especially when you feel out of your depth. Lean into His strength and let Him take the weight of your burdens. Lean into His understanding rather than your own and let Him lead you through.

Proclaim that the LORD is the strength of your life in that situation and that all you need is available through Christ.

Fear may not immediately leave, but as we stand and withstand in these truths we become stronger in our spirits and begin to build faith. The fact that David selects these three aspects of God's character indicate that these are the ones that enabled him to reject fear, to disempower fear and to remove the hold that fear had on him. God is light, salvation and strength. He is the one who enables us to see clearly and know where to step; He is the one who supernaturally brings us a way through; He is the one who gives us the strength we need to keep going. Therefore, '...whom shall I fear?' Through this change in perspective, caused by considering and proclaiming the greatness of God, David was able to recognise that fear had no right to be there. God was and would continue to be all that he needed to deal with his situation.

He is your light, salvation and strength – do you still need to fear those things you face? Again, if anxiety is an ongoing struggle, your emotions will be telling you that fearing is exactly the right thing to do. Standing on truth and trust in God will be hard, but it is good to find a word of truth and then take a stand on that. For instance, 'I will not fear because God is my light, my salvation, my strength.' This is making a choice to stand, no matter what.

As a result of this process of considering his circumstances in the perspective of God's character, David's faith was stirred up and enabled him to boldly proclaim his confidence in God's provision. He mentioned two fears and then stated his refusal to be weakened by them:

> 'Though an army may encamp against me, my heart shall not fear; though war may rise against me, in this I will be confident.' Ps. 27:3

David resolved that he would maintain a confident and courageous heart even if an army was raised against him and war came. Why? Because even in these worst-case scenarios, the LORD would be present with him in all His mighty dynamic and transformative power.

Bring your worst-case scenario to God and spend some time to bring that into the context of these truths. Your heart will not automatically feel confident and may resist this. We are flesh as well as spirit. Like David, we need to resolve, proclaim and stir our hearts up to faith-filled trust in God as our light in the darkness we face. But as we deliberately stand on these truths in our spirit, then the heart will follow.

Respond

Let the truth of the light, salvation and strength of God fill you each day so that you are equipped and protected in all that you face daily. Use the Scriptures above in situations you face, even small ones, so that the Scriptures and the truth become fixed in your heart and memory.

Write your own 'exuberant declaration of faith' to encourage yourself:

Though………………… may happen, my heart shall not fear;

though …………………… may come against me, in this I will be confident:

that the LORD is *my* light and *my* salvation; the LORD is the strength of my life.

God at Work in the Dark Times

Even if we know that God is with us, it can be incredibly difficult to get any sense of what God is working out in the dark times – it tends to feel as though God is absent. It is often only once we look back that we can see how God has changed us, or what He has been doing behind the scenes. Reading the Bible gives us testimony after testimony of how God came through for His people when they cried out to Him. We see the beginning, middle and end of those stories. But we do not have the benefit of that complete vision with our own stories. We can believe that God worked any number of miracles that we read about in the Bible, but we are not so sure that He will work miraculously in our own lives. And maybe He will not do things the same way. We do not ever know how He will resolve things.

Perhaps we all too easily forget that we are participants in a much bigger story than our own lives; or perhaps we yearn for a bigger role in the kingdom and are unprepared for what we come up against. Our circumstances must not be a measure of God's love for us or of the quality of our faith. Those who desire to serve God can expect to be shaped and moulded, refined and purified. We go through a narrow gate and walk along a difficult path.

Sometimes, we will face tough times as a result of sin. The Bible is clear that we have all sinned and fallen short of the glory of God (Romans 3:23). Our sinful actions have consequences for ourselves, especially in our relationship with God, but they can also have repercussions for those around us. The Holy Spirit will always be ready to alert us to sin in our own lives and a willing heart will choose repentance. Often, this will come as an awareness that we need to correct an attitude to someone we struggle to work with, or a nudge that our words to someone were harsh and critical. When the Holy Spirit shines a light on something so that we can no longer ignore it, we have the choice to come to Jesus in repentance and ask the Spirit to help us put the matter right and to become more like Christ in that area.

It is not now necessary to offer blood sacrifices, because Jesus gave Himself once and for all to atone for our sins. But our God is still holy and righteous, and our sin is still an obstacle to our relationship with God until we turn back to God, with a humble and repentant heart. Our sacrifice now is to offer ourselves in service and worship to the only one who is worthy of our praise; to the one who first gave Himself for us. We are still called to be pure and righteous, as God is. We need to be quick to respond in repentance when we sin and look to the grace of God to restore us, but also to show us where we need to put things right with those we have sinned against.

When we are affected by the sin of others, the difficulty is to forgive so that grace can be released; and to keep our own heart attitudes pure before God, confessing any bitterness, resentment, anger, and so on. A remarkable example of this comes in the life and death of Stephen, told in Acts 6:8-15 and Acts 7:1-60.

Stephen was a godly man, 'full of faith and power,' who spoke with wisdom through the Holy Spirit (Acts 6:8 –10). This angered the religious authorities, who sought to silence him by inciting men to make false accusations of blasphemy. When brought before the high priest to answer the charges, Stephen's Holy Spirit-filled response caused those listening to be 'cut to the heart,' but with murderous anger, not with repentance. Even as he was being stoned to death, he cried out,

"'Lord, do not charge them with this sin.'" (Acts 7:60) Stephen was not sinless, by any means, but he was a man of God who found himself on trial quite unjustly. He was innocent of the charges against him but subject to those who wanted to silence the Gospel. Yet, he spoke with grace towards those who had sinned against him, so grievously.

There is such a stark contrast between Stephen and those accusing him. It must have been infuriating for those present who saw him as a blasphemer, one who dared to call them 'betrayers and murderers, "who have received the law by the direction of angels and have not kept it,"' by one who was so clearly unaffected by their anger and willingness to kill him. (Acts 7:52-53) Surely, Stephen's physical sight informed him accurately of the anger of the people listening and the danger he was in. Yet, we do not find Stephen acting in fear, because his spiritual vision had so overwhelmed him with wonder.

> 'Stephen, being full of the Holy Spirit, gazed into heaven and saw the glory of God, and Jesus standing at the right hand of God, and said, "Look! I see the heavens opened and the Son of Man standing at the right hand of God!"' Acts 7:55-56

Through the power and presence of the Holy Spirit, Stephen's mind and heart were full of God's glory rather than the fear of man. At this moment of darkness, his gaze was heavenwards. He saw God's perfect splendour and the crucified Christ standing at God's right hand in power and majesty. Based on this account, I wonder whether he would have counted it a gain to stay on earth when he had seen such a joyous and awe-inspiring vision of heaven? It was certainly the grace of God that filled Stephen with such joy at such a moment. But it remains a hard truth that Stephen did not experience a reprieve or a miraculous rescue. He followed God faithfully, preached the Gospel, lived in the guiding of the Holy Spirit, and was brutally murdered. But even in that, He lived with an open heart before God and released grace to those who destroyed him.

It is in this passage that we are introduced to Saul – we are told that he was present at Stephen's execution and had agreed to it; we are also told that Saul was vehemently against the church, actively persecuting all those who followed Jesus, 'breathing threats and murder against the disciples of the Lord,' (Acts 7:58, 8:1-3, 9:1). Was it a result of Stephen's prayer in his final moments that Saul, the persecutor of Christians who was present at the stoning, encountered Jesus on the Damascus road?

Stephen prayed that God would not hold the sin of his murder against those present. This did not mean that God forgot, or that it did not matter that those who loved Him had been murdered because they followed Christ. It mattered deeply to God. How do we know this? Because of Jesus's words to Saul:

"'Saul, Saul, why are you persecuting *Me*?'" Acts 9:4
(my emphasis.)

Every time one of His followers was persecuted, Jesus saw that as an action against Him. Whatever we suffer as a result of choosing Christ matters to Him; it is personal to Him. However, He transformed Saul's life by the forgiveness of his sins and the outpouring of grace upon his life. It was grace that enabled him to serve God willingly through all that he suffered for the sake of living and preaching Jesus Christ. Stephen died with his eyes full of the glory of God and with words of grace on his lips. As a result, Saul's life became one lived for Jesus Christ; and through him countless lives were saved and discipled.

It is rare that our circumstances in life are perfect, even if it is unlikely that we will find ourselves in the same situation as Stephen. We will experience tribulation of some kind and we will have to make the choice of whether we continue to look to God or turn away.

We could look at the story of Daniel, in the Old Testament, who lived a life devoted to God's service whilst in exile. He knew that his primary call in life was to serve God. Even though he was sentenced to death for worshipping God and disobeying the order to worship the King of Babylon, Daniel refused to compromise on the things of God. This was lived out daily, over many years. This was not just a *season* of life - it *was* Daniel's life.

Or we could look at John in the New Testament, exiled to Patmos. Like Daniel, his circumstances were not what he would have chosen and his physical life was in the hands of others; but he knew his priority was to serve God wherever he was. Both men were subject to the worldly powers who could dictate to them and who could have them killed; they both knew hardship, loneliness, confusion, heartache. But both served God diligently throughout their lives, refusing to stop what God had told them to do. They knew tribulation, but they lived rightly before God in their hearts. Because of this, God used them powerfully. They were deeply involved in the work of God's kingdom and had astonishing experiences as a result, seeing visions of spiritual revelation that were mind-blowing in their significance, to the point that God sent an angel to help Daniel understand. It was in exile that John received the revelations of the end times that we read in the book of Revelation. The visions were for a purpose and part of a high calling before God.

Following Christ as spiritual forces clash around us is hard. Did John ever wonder why he had been exiled when so many of his fellow believers were being killed? Did he ever wonder about God's choice in that? Perhaps. But I believe that he, along with the other disciples, had so committed their lives to God that they accepted the life-span He had allotted to them, seeking to glorify God in all things. They had seen their friend and Lord crucified and resurrected. They knew that they would die on Earth at some point, in some way, but would also be raised again to eternal life. As will we.

As we look at the lives of those who have gone before we can look at their example in dealing with tribulation:

- being full of the Holy Spirit
- turning our eyes towards the glory of God and the victory of Christ, enthroned eternally
- prioritising the things of God's kingdom
- positioning our hearts to love, serve and honour God above all else in every circumstance.
- releasing those who have hurt us to God; refusing to allow the offence to have a hold in us so that we can be free and allow God to move in that.

These things matter – they are internal and spiritual foundations for responding to tribulation so that we are able to stand despite what is happening.

However, we have another response which is powerful and important. In the Lord's prayer we are taught to pray, 'Your kingdom come. Your will be done on Earth as it is in Heaven.' (Luke 11:2) Perhaps because it is something that we generally recite corporately in church, we can lose the impact of just what we are doing here. But if we look at this in military terms, it takes on a different significance. Satan has established his kingdom of darkness on Earth. When we pray, 'Your kingdom come,' we are asking God to break through the enemy lines established on Earth, to drive out the enemy and replace that foothold of darkness with His kingdom of light and resurrection power.

When we face tribulation and pray for God's will to be done and for His kingdom to be established in that situation, we are powerfully partnering with God in the spiritual battle. It is a way to come before God, acknowledging the situation but refusing to let Satan have his own way. We respond knowing that God is greater than any demonic power, and that He can make a way where there seems to be no way out.

It was during the darkness of night that the waters of the Red Sea were rolled back so that Israel could walk away from the Egyptian army. (Ex. 14:21)

At Calvary, the Light of the World allowed Himself to be slain so that we could be redeemed by the perfect blood sacrifice of the son of God. However, all the disciples could see and understand was that their beloved friend and Lord was dead. No miraculous rescue had taken place. Jesus had been crucified and darkness covered the land as He gave up His perfect life for us. His body was placed in a borrowed tomb and a stone rolled in front to block it. The Sabbath came and went, with nothing changed. Night-time came again.

> 'Mary Magdalene went to the tomb early *while it was still dark* and saw that the stone had been taken away from the tomb ...' John 20:1 (my emphasis)

The most dramatic moment in human history took place in the most understated manner: during the night, without fanfare or human witnesses, Jesus Christ was raised to life again. At His birth there was the star that alerted the wise men to the prophesied birth, there were angelic visitations and a host of heaven filling the sky with praise. It was visible, for those who were invited to witness the moment. But at the resurrection, there is no mention of an angelic choir, no carefully orchestrated public statement of victory, no press conferences or stirring speeches. I wonder what it would have been to witness what happened *behind* the scenes on those days when it seemed that it was all over, that all was lost. At some point, during the night, Jesus was raised to life in glorious victory: He had defeated sin and death, taken the keys of hell away from Satan, and no man suspected, saw or heard a thing.

Darkness does not stop God from working His purposes out. Our role is to keep praying and declaring that God's will be done in the situations we face; to pray for the Kingdom of God to be established in that situation.

Reflect and Respond Ideas

Head outside: During the night hours, God parted the Red Sea and raised Jesus from the dead. Spend some time on a dark night to ask God what is happening in the darkness that we cannot see.

Research something: Return to the story of Stephen in the Bible in Acts 6 and 7. Imagine that you were one of the people listening to him speak. How would you have responded?

Ponder further: Stephen spoke with wisdom through the Holy Spirit. Have you ever had a situation where you were aware that what you said or did was a prompting of the Holy Spirit? An occasion where you know that if it had not been for the Holy Spirit at work in you, you would have said something that made things worse?

Get creative: Imagine that you were interviewing Stephen. What would you ask him? How do you think he would answer?

Spiritual Vision

The darkness is a bewildering place to be, and a time when we need our spiritual sight to be working well. In the story of Stephen, we find that he looked up and 'heaven opened' so that he could see the glory of God and the resurrected Christ at His right hand. No one else saw what he did for they were spiritually blind. We know that God is light and that Christ is the light of the world. What must it have been to see the purity and holiness of the light and glory of God and His son, in their Kingdom? This spiritual vision changed everything for Stephen. He already believed that Jesus was the Christ, that He died and rose again, but now Stephen's eyes were opened to Christ glorified in Heaven.

That is one example of spiritual vision at work, but we also see this in 2 Kings 6: 8-17, when the King of Syria was coming to war against Israel. To begin with, we find that God was giving insight about the Syrian actions to His prophet, Elisha, so that Israel was able to avoid danger. When the King of Syria discovered this, he sent 'horses and chariots and a great army' to Dothan, to capture Elisha.

> '...when the servant of the man of God arose early and went out, there was an army, surrounding the city with horses and chariots. And his servant said to him, "Alas, my master! What shall we do?"' 2 Kings 6:15

We can feel metaphorically surrounded by our circumstances and what we face; Elisha and his servant were literally surrounded by an enemy army. The servant saw men of war, horses and chariots, all deployed against them – against a servant and a prophet, not against soldiers. Quite understandably, his reaction was dismay, fear and an inability to find a solution to this. Elisha, however, had a different reaction to the same sight, responding:

> '"Do not fear, for those who are with us are more than those who are with them."' 2 Kings 6:16

Elisha saw the physical situation before him, but he also had a revelation of the spiritual situation which transformed his attitude and perspective. Because of this, he could testify to the younger man that there was no need to fear; that the enemy was completely outnumbered and outclassed. That could have been the end to the conversation, with the younger man expected to have conviction that what his master said was true. It would have been a learning opportunity; a chance to develop greater trust in the words of the prophet and, therefore, the words of God. However, Elisha did not leave it there.

> 'And Elisha prayed, and said, "LORD, I pray, open his eyes that he may see." Then the LORD opened the eyes of the young man, and he saw. And behold, the mountain was full of horses and chariots of fire all around Elisha.' 2 Kings 6:17

Elisha did not pray for his servant to have greater faith or confidence; nor did he command fear to flee or cry out for deliverance from evil. Out of all the things Elisha could have prayed at this point, he prayed for the young man to be enabled to see. The spiritual sight which had given Elisha peace and confidence, was what he wanted the younger man to see. Surely something that he would remember his whole life long.

The young servant of Elisha had his eyes opened to see God's armies, just as Stephen's eyes were opened to look into Heaven.

What we see informs our understanding, attitudes and reactions. We may not see the fiery chariots of God standing with us, but we trust in the word of the LORD and stand with the conviction that He is with us. We can have the spiritual sense of God's presence with us and that He is at work in the situation we face. Focusing on the physical circumstances alone does not help us respond well.

In Isaiah 8, we read that an invasion by Assyria was prophesied and God gave Isaiah clear instructions of how his response should be different to the people:

> 'For the LORD spoke thus to me with a strong hand, and instructed me that I should not walk in the way of this people ... "Do not say, 'A conspiracy,' concerning all that this people call a conspiracy, nor be afraid of their threats, nor be troubled. ... And when they say to you, 'Seek those who are mediums and wizards ... should not a people seek their God?"' Is. 8:11-12, 19

For those people will,

> '...look to the earth, and see trouble and darkness, gloom of anguish and they will be driven into darkness.' Is. 8:22

This seems so very current for the twenty-first century. If we look to the earth and follow those around us, we find ourselves on a pathway that does not lead to hope or life, just darkness of thought, emotion, attitude and perspective. Conspiracy theories, threats and troubles; seeking spiritual insight away from our God and all such things damage us and take us away from the light.

Just two verses later, Isaiah prophesied as to the coming of Christ:

'The people who walked in darkness have seen a great light; those who dwelt in the land of the shadow of death, upon them a light has shined.' Is. 9:2

What did those walking in darkness need to hear? What did those dwelling in the shadow of death need to know? That there is a light – eternal, unquenchable and victorious – that shines even in those places. Christ is the great light that we need to focus on, dwell on, abide in. The darkness of that time was real and distressing, just as it was at the time of Jesus' birth and as it is now. But we have seen the great light of salvation through Jesus Christ, by faith and through the revelation of the Holy Spirit. His light is with us and upon us. We also have the hope, the confident expectation, that one day we will see Him and live in His light, timelessly and joyously.

Reflect and Respond Ideas

Head outside: Spend some time in the sunshine just giving thanks to God and praising Him for the light of His presence and for the promise that one day we will live eternally in His presence.

Research something: Find some testimonies of those who have come to Christ. What was it that drew them to Him? What differences have they noticed between walking in the darkness and walking in the light?

Ponder further: Elisha prayed for his servant's eyes to be opened. Is this something you could pray for yourself or for someone else? How could that alter a situation?

Get creative: Part way through a day, pause and jot down thoughts that have passed through your mind so far. Which ones drag you down into darkness and which lift you into the light of God's presence? Use colour or shape to indicate the difference between the two.

TRUTH

'*emeth* (Hebrew)

'Certainty, truth, trustworthiness.'[10]

The Hebrew word for truth has a wonderful and important connection with its word for stability. The more we become bombarded with information (opinions, speculation, reports – anything delivered with authority), the more we find ourselves unsure of what to believe; but the Word of God stabilises us. It is dependable, real, trustworthy, certain. It does not contain things that are made up or faked. When our emotions have become depressed or chaotic with an information overload, we can turn to the Bible and find stability again.

Who are you listening to?

We have already seen from the story of Adam and Eve that their relationship with God (and with each other) was disrupted the moment they chose to listen to the serpent and adjust their behaviour according to what it said. They knew God's boundaries but chose to give authority to the words of someone else. We have a critical and foundational choice to make in this. Who will we listen to? Whose voice will we trust with our lives? This applies equally to Bible teaching, prophetic words, what people say about us and in dealing with temptation. We listen to numerous voices each day, and we give more attention to some based on what we believe their judgement to be like. There is a placing of authority here. Eve listened to the serpent, and as a result chose to act according to its leading rather than God's. Listening to God's voice

---

[10] James Strong, *Exhaustive Concordance*, Hebrew, number 571

leads to life, but listening to Satan leads to death, through doubt, the weakening of faith and purity before God.

Satan is the father of lies (see John 8:44) – this is what he produces; his kingdom is one of darkness and deception. If something is obviously a lie, then we can generally identify it without difficulty; but Satan is also cunning and knows how to lure us in and trap us. Deceit is such an effective weapon of his that there are repeated warnings in the New Testament about the need to distinguish truth from falsehood, so we need to understand the process. Deception works because there is something about it that draws us in, something that we want to accept as truth and therefore something that we are willing to believe.

This theme is explored in Shakespeare's play, *Macbeth*. Macbeth encounters three witches, who predict that he will become Thane of Cawdor and then King of Scotland. They also prophesy that Macbeth will never be slain by one born of woman and will never be defeated until Burnham Wood comes to Dunsinane. His best friend, Banquo, warns him against listening to these words, distrusting the source of them. He explains that those working for the darkness tell some truth in order to lure people in and to win their confidence, before leading them into the greatest possible harm.[11]

To begin with, Macbeth neither fully accepts the witches' words nor forgets them; until, through no action of his own, he is made Thane of Cawdor. A little truth lures him to consider the other parts of the prophecy – the thought of being the next King of Scotland, which he had not previously considered, suddenly fills his thoughts, seeming much closer, more possible. The throne that was not his to take filled his thoughts and his desires. Would this come to pass naturally, or should he take steps to fulfil it? The witches had assured him that no one born of woman could kill him and that no one could defeat him unless the physically impossible happened – how could a wood uproot itself and march towards him? Based on this information, there was clearly no risk to himself so there was no reason not to embark on a course that could only lead to benefit. With the encouragement of his ambitious wife, Macbeth sets out on the path of murder.

As it happens, every word the witches spoke came to pass, but the

---

[11] See William Shakespeare, *Macbeth*, Act 1, scene 3, lines 123 -126

trickery involved is revealed. Macbeth does become King of Scotland, but only briefly, for it was not his crown to take. Macbeth is killed, by a man born by Caesarian section, rather than by natural birth. Burnham Wood does come to Dunsinane, by the means of the army concealing themselves by branches so that it did appear as though the wood was moving towards Macbeth. One small truth led Macbeth to consider the tantalising offer of something that was not his to take but that suddenly appeared good and right. The witches spoke and then exited the play, allowing Macbeth's own thoughts and the input of his wife do the rest. The statements that seemed to suggest that he was undefeatable, that downplayed the possible consequences, all worked together to destroy many lives. The play finishes, as tragedies ought to, with the sense of how futile it was and how easily disaster could have been avoided had Macbeth only listened to the right voice.

Banquo's words were the wise ones. The one truth about becoming Thane of Cawdor did indeed cause Macbeth to end up in a place of tragic consequence. If anything, those words are an understatement considering what happens in the play. One murder led to further evil acts, as Macbeth attempted to conceal the original murder he had committed. His wife slowly collapsed mentally and emotionally through the weight of guilt upon her conscience. A man who was essentially decent, if weak, ended up corrupted in all manner of evil because he listened and acted upon a small truth told by those working for evil.

This play was written as a demonstration of how matters unravel when we listen to the wrong voice, with a deliberately extreme scenario to act as a memorable warning of the consequences that can result. Shakespeare clearly did this very well as the words of Banquo have stayed in my memory from when I studied the play as a teenager. Deceptions work because there is something that causes us to accept it as truth, which then leads us step by step away from the right path; we only realise we are on the wrong path someway down the line.

We see this principle at work in the words of the serpent in Genesis. The serpent said to Eve,

> "'You will not surely die. For God knows that in the day you eat of it your eyes will be opened and you will be like God,

knowing good and evil.'" Gen. 3:4-5

The first sentence is trickery. Satan knew that Adam and Eve would not be immediately struck dead by eating the fruit; but he also knew that physical death would come to them one day as a result.

The second sentence is perfectly true. In the day Adam and Eve ate the fruit, their eyes were opened; they gained the knowledge of evil. God Himself said that man had become like Him in knowing good and evil. But whilst we were made in God's image, His likeness, we were never designed to be like Him in knowing evil - it was too much for us to bear. As we have seen, it was because of this and our sin that we could no longer live eternally in Eden.

Satan told the truth, but not the whole truth. He did not explain that knowing evil would be a wholly catastrophic experience. He did not explain that disobeying God and learning of evil would cause the overthrow of everything that they knew and loved. He did not explain that they would come to know things called fear, shame, guilt, emptiness, loneliness, grief, death. He did not offer the information, and it did not occur to Eve that knowing evil could be a bad thing. How could she possibly understand a concept such as 'evil' when essentially it did not exist in her world?

Satan did not point out to Eve that she already had the full measure of God's goodness in every area of her life and that no *good* thing had been withheld from her. The only thing God had withheld from Adam and Eve was the knowledge and experience of evil. Satan knew what the outcome would be, just as the witches knew in *Macbeth*. Satan's aim was to cause Eve harm, not good; his aim was to destroy mankind. A little truth, with much left unsaid, unexplained and unquestioned, led to tragic consequences for Eve and all who came after her.

Clearly, there was nothing about the serpent that caused Eve to fear. It did not scare her; it did not make her nervous. Our adversary is *like* a lion, in terms of being a predator looking for prey, and predators are most successful when they can approach without alerting or spooking their intended prey. Satan generally starts with a subtle approach so as not to cause someone to back away – he uses a lure, an invitation to take a step towards him and away from God.

For both Macbeth and Eve, it all began with a conversation: with the witches, with the serpent.

Their thoughts and desires were then directed towards something forbidden: the crown of Scotland, the fruit that would lead to the knowledge of evil. They both justified taking the wrong path to themselves so that it seemed like the right course.

There was a lessening of the consequences of taking steps to acquire that forbidden thing – both Macbeth and Eve were told, 'you will not surely die.' The fundamental message from Satan was, and is, that it is fine to take a different path –it is not a big deal. You will not surely die.

Satan is quite happy for people to believe anything at all, as long as it is not the truth, the whole truth and nothing but the truth of the word of God. He is equally satisfied whether people believe that there is no god or many gods or an unidentified higher power out there somewhere. Failing that, let people believe that there is a God but that He is neither present nor powerful, and completely irrelevant in this modern world. Currently, there is a sense that humanity has outgrown the need for a deity or faith system to look out for us or to provide for us. We have science instead, which is used to bring the promise of a transformed life, whether through a new form of exercise, diet, lifestyle, beauty product and so on. For any spiritual needs, there is mindfulness, meditation, yoga, retreats and spiritual healing. There is no need for a deity, let alone a Saviour. It does not matter – you will not surely die.

The Con at Work

Before we go any further, it is important to note that Satan and his demons know exactly who God is – they are not in any doubt or confusion about that. In Luke's Gospel, we read of the encounter between Jesus and a man who 'had demons for a long time.' Jesus commanded the unclean spirit to come out of the man, and the response was,

> "'What have I to do with You, Jesus, Son of the Most High God?'" Luke 8:28-29

The unclean spirit could have simply said, "'What have I to do with You?'" It knew that they could not have been further apart or less compatible – like electricity and water that should never mix. But the unclean spirit knew that it was speaking to Jesus: to Emmanuel, to God made flesh. It knew it was speaking to the Son of the Most High God. There was no doubt or confusion here: the spirit did not refer to *a* god or an undefined higher spiritual power. There was no doubt or questioning of Jesus' identity, deity or authority. In fact, the demons, which had so devastated the life of a man then fearfully begged Jesus not to send them into the abyss. The demons knew without doubt that Jesus had the power and authority to do that. No doubt, no muddle and no confusion. Jesus was the Son of God Most High, with all power and authority to fulfil the will of the Father. (Luke 8:26-33)

In the very next chapter, we then read of a conversation where Jesus asks His disciples, "Who do the crowds say that I am?" The answers included John the Baptist, Elijah or one of the other prophets of old (Luke 9:18-20). In all creation, the only ones who question God's existence and authority are people. Satan wants us to doubt Jesus' identity and sovereignty, but he and all his kingdom know that Jesus is the Son of the Most High. Satan will use deception against us, to cause us to doubt the truth of God's existence, character and ability; but he never, ever believes his own lies. It is all about what he can get us to believe.

C.S. Lewis had a gift for writing books that clearly demonstrate what we face as Christians. In *The Silver Chair*, he examines the importance of knowing our true identity and not allowing ourselves to be deceived or led astray.[12] It demonstrates that the truth is a vital weapon in overcoming deception. It is well worth reading.

Rilian was the only son and heir to the throne of Narnia, son of King Caspian X. His accession to the throne should have been without contest or conflict for Narnia was at peace with its neighbouring lands, and there were no other sons or contenders to the throne. The throne of Narnia would peacefully pass to Rilian, as it ought to do.

However, Rilian became captivated, enchanted even, by a mysterious woman. Daily he rode out to meet with her and, one fateful day, he failed to return. Ten years pass without a sight of the prince. Eustace Scrubb and Jill Pole find themselves called into Narnia by Aslan,

---

[12] C.S. Lewis, *The Silver Chair* (Lions, 1992)

commissioned to find the missing prince.

Rilian had been magically enchanted by the Lady of the Green Kirtle, which caused him to forget his true identity. When found, he was living in the kingdom of the dark underworld, without natural light, under the complete control of the Lady, believing everything she told him. She had offered to win a kingdom for him in the overland area that they would rule together. The only time Rilian was in his right senses and knew who he truly was, he was held captive: strapped to a silver chair. Whilst he was deceived as to his identity and under the complete control of the Lady, he was free to go about as he pleased.

The land and throne that the Lady offered to help Rilian take by force was his own kingdom of Narnia, to which he was lawfully heir. If Rilian had only been alert and aware of who he was, he would have known that there was no need to be involved with the Lady at all. She offered what was not hers to give. She offered him what was already his. Why? Because this would give her ultimate power over him and over Narnia. Under her enchantment, Rilian would have been a puppet king, obeying her every instruction and being violent towards anyone who opposed her. She would have ruled in his name, causing destruction and oppression to others.

The Lady seemed to be a benign influence but, once identified as the enemy, transformed into a snake. Some of Satan's strategies seem to be perfectly innocent. The lure seems attractive, benign, not really anything to be concerned about, just as the Lady was in this story. No wonder that we are told so often to be alert in the Bible. For instance, in 1 Peter 5:8 we read,

> '...be sober, be vigilant; because your adversary the devil walks about like a roaring lion, seeking whom he may devour.'

In this case, being sober refers to being aware of the reality of the spiritual situation we are in; recognising that we need to take it seriously. It does not mean that we are never to have fun or to relax, but to be alert to any prompting of the Holy Spirit, wherever we are, and to respond quickly if you feel spiritual alarm bells ringing.

Be sober and vigilant. We may think that we are too sensible to make the same mistake that Eve and Adam made, or to be deceived as Rilian was. However, Satan uses lures, snares and traps against us and we are more susceptible to some than others. Only you know where you are vulnerable – only you know where past experiences have opened up wounds within you, or what would work as a lure to lead you onto the wrong path. We need to be sober and vigilant with those vulnerable areas so that we are guarded against evil.

The story of Rilian is fictitious, so let us return to Scripture and see if this has foundations there. If we were in any doubt about the need to be sober and vigilant and to exercise the truth against any wile of the evil one, we only need to look at the temptation of Jesus. He went through what we experience, and thus shows us how to respond. He did this because we need to know the right model for response.

After His baptism, Jesus was led into the desert by the Holy Spirit, where He fasted and was tested over a forty-day period (see Luke 4:1-13). Satan seriously attempted to sow doubt into Jesus' mind about things that were absolute truth. He wanted to see what he could get Jesus to buy into and where He would compromise.

1. Satan questioned Jesus' identity, even though he knew exactly who Jesus was.

2. Satan tempted Jesus to prove God's miraculous ability to rescue Him, even though he knew beyond doubt that God could rescue Jesus at any second.

3. Satan offered Jesus, the Son of God, a share in His own kingdom!

Surely this is the ultimate con. Just as the Lady of the Green Kirtle offered Rilian the throne and kingdom that were already his inheritance, Satan did the same thing with Jesus. Before the angels were even thought of, Jesus existed and was involved in the creation of everything ... What belonged to Jesus by right, Satan tried to sell to Him.

It is important to acknowledge that the truth did not change at any point: Jesus was and is and always will be the Son of God. Satan knows that, without doubt. All that was happening was Satan's attempt to confuse, cause doubt and deception.

Satan's strategies do not change. He does the same thing now as he did then. He will lie, trick and deceive in the attempt to get us to doubt our own identity and God's and to doubt God's miraculous ability and willingness to save us. Once doubt has been created, Satan will see what he can sell back to you and where you will compromise. The precise details of the temptation will vary depending on the individual, but the aim is the same – to lead us away from God's kingdom of light and truth. As we saw with Rilian in *The Silver Chair*, the Lady in the Green Kirtle offered him what was already his but via the wrong method (stealing rather than inheriting), in the wrong identity and in a way that would give her complete control over him and everything in his kingdom. She brought him into her kingdom of darkness and deceit.

This will often be done through people around us but remember our battle is against spiritual powers and not against flesh and blood. Our response should be the same as Jesus' was: the Word of God.

We need to approach this passage with the knowledge that:

- Jesus is the son of God – fully God and fully man – and Satan knows that to be true, without any doubt at all; His power and authority were never doubted by the enemy for one moment.

- Jesus had been affirmed by God the Father at His baptism. From there, He was led into the wilderness place of trial, testing and temptation.

- Jesus was in submission to God the Father in all that He did, even to the point of choosing the cross (Luke 22:39-46). We know from James 4:7 that whilst we are submitted to God, we can resist the devil and he will flee from us.

- Jesus' mission was to be the sinless blood sacrifice required to restore the children of God to relationship with Him but also to redeem the Gentile nations. There was a great victory over Satan still to be won.

The word *nasah* means, 'to test... to prove, tempt, try.'[13] This was a very real and serious time of testing or temptation for Jesus. But what was at stake? Satan wanted Jesus to sin in some way, in *any* way,

---

[13] James Strong, *Exhaustive Concordance*, Hebrew, number 5254

because then He could not redeem humanity - God's salvation plan would be blocked.

Whatever weapon Satan uses against us, we need to return to the foundation truths on which to stand and position ourselves. Just as he intended with Jesus, he wants us to sin in some way, in any way, because that impacts our relationship with God and our ability to fulfil His plans for our lives.

Any temptation or work of Satan will revolve around an area of deceit, which is why we need to have the word of God stored away in our hearts and kept in the forefront of our minds. If we consider temptations objectively as lures or 'honey traps' it is easy to see them for what they are; however, when we are in the situation of temptation, we can find that we very quickly start falling for the sales pitch of a master conman.

The temptation of Eve, which led to the first instance of human sin, the serpent asked her, "did God really say ...?" Eve listened to the serpent. She gave weight and credence to his words, then justified a forbidden course of action to herself. She did not remind herself that God had not given this to them as food. She did not go back to God and say, "this is what the serpent said to me, what is the way of truth?" We need to know what God has and has not said because this enables us to stand and withstand the enemy.

This, with the benefit of hindsight, is a very clear example of what not to do. Of course, if it were that simple, none of us would ever have any difficulty in resisting temptation. We all experience temptation, and we will all need to learn and exercise the skills to resist it. It will not be easy, because Satan knows how to offer something in a way that makes it appealing and relatively harmless. Naturally, he will continue to fail to mention the consequences and harm it will cause. We need to make sure we put those things at the front of our minds ourselves.

Reflect and Respond Ideas

Head outside: We see different places of temptation represented in these stories: Eve was in a beautiful paradise with everything she needed, Macbeth was on a journey, Jesus was in a wilderness with nothing. When you are out, consider how temptation affects us in different circumstances.

Research something: As you watch a film or programme, pay attention to the themes of trust and the truth. How many characters display integrity? Are lies told as a matter of course? What impact does this have?

Ponder further: Who do you trust and why? Equally, is there anyone you have learned not to trust? What was it that affected your trust in them?

Get creative: Read *The Silver Chair* and pay attention to the theme of deceit at work, particularly in the final encounter between the Green Lady and Puddleglum, Eustace, Jill and Rilian.

Sanctified and Set Free

In John 17, we find Jesus deep in prayer to His Father: for Himself, for His disciples then for all believers. When Jesus was praying for His disciples, He said,

> "'I do not pray that You should take them out of the world, but that You should keep them from the evil one. They are not of the world, just as I am not of the world. Sanctify them by Your truth. Your word is truth.'" John 17:15-17

We are intended to live in this world as followers of Christ, set apart by the truth of the Gospel and kept by the hand of Almighty God. This is what Jesus desired for His disciples: that they would be equipped, set apart and enabled for their time working for His kingdom on Earth. The unspoken implication is that Satan's deceptions are intended to block this work of sanctification and freedom. They are designed to lure us away from God's kingdom and to enslave us with habits and behaviour that does not honour God.

Truly coming to know the Scriptures deep in our hearts and minds opens our eyes to who God is and how He calls us to live, for our own well-being. The way of God's truth brings us into a right relationship with Him, where we increasingly want to follow and obey Him. This has the effect of sanctifying us or setting us apart as we become more like Him, and less like the world. As we become infused with the things of God, our spirit is more sensitive when we are tempted to step out of line into something that will damage us and our relationship with God.

Our part is firstly to choose the truth and refuse to compromise on that. Secondly, we need to commit to being disciplined and intentional in going to the word of God and allowing it to change us. Skim-reading does not allow this to happen. We need to spend time and concentration on it, asking the Holy Spirit to help us understand it and to change us through it. This daily process allows Scriptures to settle and be stored in your heart and mind. This is not about how much you can read at any time, but about allowing the Holy Spirit to work through Scriptures and to make them living and active within you.

Paul told the Galatians to,

> 'Stand fast in the liberty by which Christ has made us free and do not be entangled again with a yoke of bondage.' Gal. 5:1

We cannot lose our salvation once we are in Christ, but we can get caught up into things that enslave us: sin, temptation, legalism, compromise or becoming apathetic and disinterested in the things that matter to God. We are to stand fast, which suggests a determination not to fall or fail no matter how strong the storm is. We can only do this if we are clear about what brings freedom in Christ and what entangles us.

The yoke of slavery can include critical or depressive thought patterns and emotional reactions that are compulsive, persistent and seemingly beyond our control. In Christ there is freedom, so we need to be aware of any area where we live with a yoke of slavery and bring that to God. We are not helpless where yokes of slavery are concerned: through Christ we can refuse to allow them to have power in our lives and we can ask our Saviour to deliver us, set us free, release us into His liberty.

It is truth that sets us free. (John 8:31-32) Just as we saw that the light of God is active and transformative, we also read that the Word of God is,

> '...living and powerful, and sharper than any two-edged sword, piercing even to the division of soul and spirit, and of joints and marrow, and is a discerner of the thoughts and intents of the heart.' Hebrews 4:12

In the light of this passage, we return to Paul's instruction to take up the sword of the Spirit, which is the Word of God. It preserves us, protects us and empowers us. Our one weapon is truth, the Word of God, which is living, powerful, sharp enough to divide soul and spirit and capable of discerning the hidden things of the heart. Our battle is spiritual, so our weapon works in the spiritual places. As we proclaim truth, we are strengthened and set free from the things that ensnare and enslave us. As we proclaim truth, the enemy is weakened.

We are also told to put on truth as a belt. I find this intriguing as a belt is neither a weapon, nor a piece of defensive armour. The truth is compared to something that wraps around us - it keeps everything in its rightful place. Truth guards our minds and our hearts, keeping our thoughts and emotions in perspective. As truth is wrapped around us like a belt, it keeps our sword of the Spirit close to our side, whenever we need it.

This double mention of truth emphasises our need for truth in responding to the world around us and every strategy of the enemy. Satan's strategies against us will often centre on deception and distortion, so we need to be guarded against this with the opposite strategy (putting on the belt of truth) and also able to take steps against it (using the sword of the Spirit). We guard ourselves with truth and we resist the enemy with truth.

Knowing Scripture is not something we should ever opt out of – it is vital. To move this from theory into our life-blood, we use the truth of the word of God in prayer like a sword, knowing that we have authority in Christ to stand and withstand. That authority is our firepower.

We stand and withstand the enemy with the truth of the word of God. No matter how you feel, once you have been saved by the blood of the Lamb, you are *not* powerless. Acknowledging that our emotions deceive us is so crucial here. Remember that Satan has no power or authority over you *unless* you allow it. However, this is not what it feels like. If we accept his lie that we are powerless, then we will not believe that we can overcome the lies. If we accept his lie that there is no way out, that this is just how we are and always will be, then we stay trapped.

If we have not learned to challenge those emotions or how to stand in authority over the assault we face, we cannot stand against the enemy and then we believe the lie that we are powerless and helpless. We stay captive. It is important that we understand what Satan is up to so that we recognise the lies quickly and stop them from taking on a life of their own.

Lies about Ourselves

We have looked at how Satan suggests something to lead us away from God's provision and protection, which then engages our thoughts and desires. But he also uses lies to hold us captive, unable to move forward as the bold believers God wants us to be.

Satan will lie about our identity, worth and about our reason for existing- anything that will discourage us and stop us from being all we are in Christ; anything that will keep us broken instead of receiving healing; anything that will keep us stuck in bitterness, anger or stubbornness instead of pursuing all that God has for us.

Satan likes to cause self-doubt, insecurity and shame to grow vigorously within us. He tells us that we are worthless, not good enough, failing in our walk with Jesus, that we must try harder. These appear in our minds with apparent authority and the utmost credibility, which is why they are so hard to stand against. They feel completely true and we become too ashamed to tell anyone. It is only when we tell someone else what those thoughts are that we recognise that they are something to be challenged. We can then take a stand because we recognise that those words have no authority to control us, and no right to dwell within us.

Satan will encourage us to think things about ourselves that we would never think about someone else. That can be a useful test of whether the thoughts you hold about yourself are truth or not. Would you think that or say that about someone you care about?

Satan encourages us to condemn ourselves (this was useless, not good enough), to heap shame upon ourselves (I am a failure, I am just kidding myself that this could have worked, I will never amount to anything). He will suggest things that might improve all that you see as wrong about yourself, such as: trying harder, reading more Christian books, praying longer, looking to see what other people are doing so that you can copy them and so on.

Some lies can be so deeply rooted in us, we do not even recognise that they exist. They can have been part of our attitudes for so long that we do not see anything wrong with them and therefore we do not question or challenge them. If you find that you struggle with low self-worth, the chances are that there are deeply rooted lies causing that. Spend some time with the Holy Spirit and ask Him to show you the lies you believe about yourself. Dare to believe that those things are lies and that God will enable you to defeat them!

If there are deeply rooted lies, it is so good and helpful to have someone you trust walking with you as you challenge them. Write down truths that you can use so that every time a lie assaults you and feels true, you can stand against it. This can be hard to do because it is a lightning clash of the kingdoms: Satan wants to keep the yoke of slavery in place and Jesus wants you to be living in freedom, so having someone you can contact who will pray when you are standing against a lie is enormously helpful.

Lies in our Thoughts and Emotions

Emotions are powerful forces in our lives. They are part of our response to the things that happen to us and around us: anger at injustice, fear when we receive a distressing health diagnosis, heartache when a loved one is struggling. Jesus was fully human, so He knew grief at the death of His cousin; He cried out to God in anguish in the Garden of Gethsemane. It is right and necessary to be honest about our emotions before God, and to process them with our Heavenly Father. Our emotions are so often valid and need to be brought to God; but they are not a reliable guide, so they need to be handled carefully. Anger can cause us to sin so easily, as that strong emotion can cause us to react without the Holy Spirit. Our emotions can also be deceptive. We can easily feel unloved or unappreciated when that is far from true. We can easily feel that God has abandoned or rejected us; that we are failures, and so on.

Psalm 119:160 says, 'the entirety of Your word is truth…' It is our strong foundation, and one that can be trusted no matter what our thoughts and emotions tell us. Words of Scripture may not *feel* true at times, and deceit may *feel* completely accurate, so we need to deliberately choose the word of God over our internal dialogue, based on the knowledge that the entirety of the word of God is true, dependable, reliable, certain and trustworthy.

If we have genuinely done something wrong, the Holy Spirit will prompt us to deal with it; but it will be a sense of conviction that we have sinned and there will be the invitation to respond constructively through repenting and turning away from that sin. Although we have a time of feeling grief and shame at our sin, the fruit of this is constructive because it leads to repentance and restoration. The Holy Spirit never leaves us feeling condemned. This should not leave us dwelling in a mire of failure, hopelessness and uselessness. Those things indicate that we have not received restoration with God.

If the thoughts we have lead to fruits such as despair, condemnation, insecurity or dwelling in depression, then they are not from God. This can be very difficult to deal with when you are overwhelmed by powerful thoughts and emotions (for example, high anxiety). If your brain is fogged with depression on an ongoing basis then it paralyses your ability to think, weigh things up and communicate what you are experiencing.

Psalm 119 refers to choosing the way of truth, and it may be helpful to picture yourself at a crossroads when tackling thoughts and emotions. (Psalm 119:30) In depression and storms this is challenging, but there is still a choice to make. A foundational truth of the Bible is Jesus' statement, "'I am the way, the truth and the life.'" (John 14:6) There is no other way to be saved, no other way to find life in abundance and life eternal. If we do nothing else in the dark times, proclaim and keep proclaiming the truth that Jesus is Lord; that He is the way, the truth and the life in whatever is challenging. This is powerful and transformational in our circumstances. Psalm 119 also proclaims that 'Your word is a lamp to my feet and a light to my path' (verse 105). This is not just for the critical decisions of our lives, but for each day we live and every situation, we face, big or small. Keeping close to the Word of God and allowing the Holy Spirit to reveal God's will to us, keeps us on the right path.

Recognising Footholds and Strongholds

A friend once told me that she had experienced a dark time of extreme anxiety and panic attacks but could not particularly pinpoint a trigger for this. The only thing that she could think of was that a fear had come into her mind one day, which seemed to 'take on a life of its own'. A phrase which I suspect is far more telling than we realise.

Scripture says that we can 'give the devil a foothold', (Eph. 4:27, NIV). This is in the context of allowing our anger to lead us into sin, which gives Satan the opportunity to act against us. Giving something a foothold means that we are giving something room in our lives, which gives Satan the chance to move in and start disrupting things. Lies, fears and desires can also gain a foothold or take on a life of their own.

If we accept or agree with lies, then they are allowed to take root in our lives. The more we agree with those lies and accept them as truth, the more it grows and thrives – they take on a life of their own and become a controlling influence. The thoughts that we encourage do the same, so if we feed and endorse attitudes of anger, bitterness, resentment, unforgiveness, they will grow and thrive within us. They become strongholds where it is much more difficult to break the behaviours, but it is not impossible. So, we need to learn to take authority over our lives to reject any foothold of the enemy as soon as we recognise them.

Truth in the Darkness

The darkness is a place where truth no longer seems clear or certain. Lies begin to feel true, which gives them the opportunity to take hold and have mastery over us. We find ourselves in a power battle over what we believe and who we listen to.

The darkness impacts our judgement and the way we perceive our circumstances. We lose our ability to accurately weigh the risk involved and our chances of coming out of that situation unscathed or at all. We completely lose confidence in our ability to handle the situation. It is why the darkness is so frightening – it turns our secure foundations into quicksand.

In one dark time of turmoil, I saw myself out at sea in the middle of a hurricane. The ocean was tumultuous, both sea and sky were dark. It was a frightening place to find myself, but that was just what it felt like – out of my depth, drowning in a hurricane, helpless and unhelped. But in the depths of that fear, a thought arrived in my mind that completely changed my attitude. 'I bet I can put my feet down.' In the picture, I put my feet down ... and touched rock. As I did so, I looked round and saw Jesus alongside me in a rescue boat and had a sense of the Holy Spirit around me. With God the rock under my feet, I would not drown, no matter what my emotions told me. With Jesus by my side and the Holy Spirit around me, the midst of the hurricane was a safe place to be. My emotions told me one thing but the truth of God told me another. The situation did not dramatically change, but I was able to stand and withstand. We see this demonstrated well in another C.S. Lewis story.

In *The Voyage of the Dawn Treader*, King Caspian and his companions encounter a great darkness. There is some discussion about whether to keep going or whether to enter it. The human response was to avoid it, but Reepicheep, the valiant mouse, scorns this cowardly response and sees only the adventure that might be had by entering the darkness.

Into the darkness they sailed and found themselves in the place of facing their greatest fears. They could see nothing and lost the ability to think rationally. They lost all sense of direction, time and distance. They lost all sense of being safe and secure.

> '"We shall never get out, never get out," moaned the rowers. "He's steering us wrong. We're going round and round in circles. We shall never get out."'

It became a place where they felt abandoned, lost and overwhelmed. Moving from light into darkness caused them to lose confidence and courage, especially as they no longer had any understanding of their circumstances to enable them to make good decisions about where to go or what to do there. All sound, vision and thought became distorted in that place. The sailors lost faith in their leaders. They believed that they were travelling aimlessly, round in circles.

In the darkness, the crew of the Dawn Treader found that their own deep fears surfaced and, even though they were armed and brave men, those fears were powerful and traumatic. As fear filled their minds and hearts, they each became trapped in an unseen prison. For those who suffer from anxiety and panic attacks, this may be a familiar scenario whereby the mind is full of overwhelming fear, when in reality nothing bad has happened. No one was physically attacked in the darkness, there was no physical enemy assaulting them. The assault was within them, in their thoughts and perceptions. When our darkness consists of fear, it is difficult to overcome because our reasoning and perspectives become distorted. It is like an alternate reality where you cannot find your way out.

It was in this darkness, from her position on the fighting top of the ship, that Lucy cried out to Aslan:

> '"Aslan, if ever you loved us at all, send us help now." The darkness did not grow any less, but she began to feel a little – a very, very little – better. "After all, nothing has really happened to us yet," she thought.'

Having called out to Aslan, a 'tiny speck of light' appeared in front of them, which turned into a 'broad beam of light'. This light, 'did not alter the surrounding darkness, but the whole ship was lit up as if by searchlight…' In this beam of light, appeared an albatross that,

> '…called out in a strong sweet voice what seemed to be words though no one understood them. After that it … began to fly slowly ahead… Drinian steered after it not doubting that it offered good guidance. But no one except Lucy knew that as it circled the mast it had whispered to her, "Courage, dear heart," and the voice, she felt sure, was Aslan's …'

Our prayers may not immediately remove the darkness that we experience but can bring light into what we face. Where the darkness creates an inner world of overwhelming fear that distorts our thoughts, perspectives and emotions; that beam of God's light can bring us secure ground to stand on. Lucy was on the fighting top of the Dawn Treader when she cried out to Aslan. That is where we need to position ourselves in the darkness: in an attitude of fighting back against the fears and the lies in the name of Jesus, trusting that Almighty God is with us.[14]

In Psalm 139, David asks,

> 'Where can I go from Your Spirit? Or where can I flee from Your presence? If I ascend into heaven, You are there; if I make my bed in hell, behold, You are there... If I say, "Surely the darkness shall fall on me," even the night shall be light about me; indeed, the darkness shall not hide from You, but the night shines as the day; the darkness and the light are both alike to You.' Ps. 139:7 and 11-12

No matter where we find ourselves, God is with us there. He knows exactly what we are experiencing and how great the struggle is in the darkness, but He also sees everything with perfect clarity. He sees His hand holding you fast and He sees His power to destroy every enemy. He sees the end of the situation as well as the beginning. He sees the good He will bring out of the situation.

In *The Dawn Treader*, the good that came out of the time in the darkness was that the crew found one of the missing Narnian lords there and they were able to rescue him from the nightmare he had lived in the darkness for so long. Our darkness experiences can bring us into a better position to help others – to play our part in God's salvation plan.

Jesus did not pray for us to be taken out of difficult situations, much as we wish He had. Instead, He prayed that Almighty God would keep and preserve us through them. We may face a darkness repeatedly, each time struggling, each time coming out hoping that we will never face that again. Hold firm in the truth that Jesus is in that place with us and that the darkness cannot overcome the victory that we hold in Him. Hear the voice of our Saviour, saying, "Courage, dear heart," and look for the glimmer of light bringing hope and peace into those circumstances.

---

[14] C.S. Lewis, *The Voyage of the Dawn Treader*, (HarperCollins, 1992) Extracts from pp. 135-145

Reflect and Respond Ideas

Head outside: How important is the mindset in sports? As you prepare for a match or race, consider how emotions impact your readiness to compete. What lies affect you as you prepare, affecting your confidence and motivation?

Research something: Some experiments have been done to research the impact of light deprivation on people. Find out how people are affected by living entirely in darkness. What does this teach us about our need for light?

Ponder further: Have you ever experienced a thought or emotion 'taking on a life of its own'? Ask the Holy Spirit to meet with you in that and to show you how to remove its foothold in your life.

Get creative: Draw or paint Lucy on the fighting top of the Dawn Treader as the words of Aslan came to her and the beam of light shone through. You could write on Aslan's words and Psalm 119:105 as encouragement, but also listen to God's word for you in the darkness and add that on as well.

Standing in Authority

When we put on the armour of God, we are equipping ourselves with all that we need to stand and withstand the evil one. We are proclaiming that we are submitted to our God and King, that we are standing in *His* authority and that we intend to see God's kingdom come in all that we face. We clothe ourselves with the salvation and righteousness of Christ, standing in faith, in truth and in the Gospel. The Word of God is our sword and our belt. When we face spiritual opposition, we need to know the grounds by which we stand in authority against the enemy.

We are covered by the blood of the Lamb.

When we accept Jesus as our Lord and Saviour, we become adopted into the family of God Most High and the treasures of His kingdom are available to us. You are a child of God Most High, not a slave to sin and to the evil one. We are covered by the blood of the Lamb, the perfect blood sacrifice, and it is through this that we are able to approach God the Father. A spiritual shift has happened, which Satan will try to ignore and that he will try to get you to forget. He will work on your emotions and thoughts, entangling you in the sense that you are helpless and that you cannot get out of the mire you are in. This is not true.

We need to make sure that we are under His covering as we come to pray. If we have sinned in some way, then that will weaken us and it will block our communication with God, so it is important to be quick to confess, repent and be restored to God. Remember the Prodigal Son – as soon as he had repented in his heart and returned to his father, his father ran to meet him. The son was returning to a place he had no right to be, *but* he was met by his father's grace and love; accepted back as son (not as the slave he offered to be) and his return home celebrated. (See Luke 15:11-32)

There is power in the name of Jesus.

It is in the darkness, when our natural senses and abilities fail us, that we call upon the name of Jesus and listen for His voice whispering, "Courage, dear heart." The darkness may not immediately dissipate, but slowly and surely change will come.

In Philippians we read that God gave His Son,

> '...the name which is above every name, that at the name of Jesus every knee should bow, of those in heaven, and of those on earth, and of those under the earth...' Phil. 2:9-10

We are saved through our faith in Christ and we come to pray in His name – the name which is higher and greater than any other name. It is His name alone that is powerful over every enemy. In His name, we have authority to say 'no' to the enemy.

Jesus has also given us authority to act in His name: to bind the work of the enemy and to loose the things of God's kingdom. When Peter was re-named and commissioned by Jesus, he was told that,

> '"...you are Peter, and on this rock I will build My church, and the gates of Hades shall not prevail against it. I will give you the keys of the kingdom of heaven, and whatever you bind on earth will be bound in heaven, and whatever you loose on earth will be loosed in heaven."' Matt. 16:18-19

There is a boundary here set by Almighty God. The gates of Hades will not prevail against, or defeat, the church of Christ. Jesus is building and increasing His kingdom and it will not be destroyed. This will not stop Satan from stealing and attacking where he can, causing Christians to walk away. But he cannot stop the work of Christ.

The name of Jesus is so much more than a group of letters or a noun. His name, the name of Jesus Christ, is life-bringing to us. His name is full of authority and power, which causes a response in the spiritual places and changes the atmosphere around us. Praying and declaring in His name, speaking out that Jesus is Lord, is a significant action. We do need to pray in line with His will but, as we listen to the Holy Spirit, we come to learn what we are to pray and how.

Taking authority over the enemy can take perseverance.

In James we read that when we are submitted to God, we can resist the enemy and he will flee from us (James 4:7). Notice that submission to God is the pre-requisite here – we cannot resist the enemy in pride and sinfulness. In repentance and trust in God, humbly submitting our will and ways to Him, we can resist the enemy and he will flee.

Whatever is going on, we do not battle against flesh and blood, but against spiritual powers. Once we have received the revelation of the Holy Spirit about the spiritual situation or season, He will also have a strategy to share – a prayer strategy and the next step of practical action.

The forces of the enemy are anti-authority and in rebellion against God, so they will resist if they can. The chances are that we will need to tackle a stronghold or foothold more than once for it to be dealt with completely; like doing several rounds in the boxing ring until victory is established. Do not be disheartened by that but keep arming yourself and standing in truth and authority. We are told by Jesus that some things require prayer and fasting to deal with, so that may be necessary. (Matt. 17:21)

We have the victory in Christ.

We looked earlier at the fact that Satan is nicknamed the Father of Lies, not the Father of Temptations or Disease and so on. Satan is the root of all that opposes the Kingdom of God, but the focus on being the Father of Lies is telling and should highlight for us the need to know the truth of the Word of God and be equipped by it. We know that Jesus is the way, the truth and the life. In contrast, Satan is the opposite: listening to him leads to a dead-end, to deceit and spiritual death. It is all part of his plan of desolation, leading us away from Christ and all He offers us.

We may know that Christ defeated Satan at Calvary, but how do we stand on that truth in the dark times? Firstly, we can hold onto the truth that,

> 'Every good gift and every perfect gift is from above, and comes down from the Father of lights, with whom there is no variation or shadow of turning.' James 1:17

When circumstances are dark around us, we find ourselves wandering on the path of confusion, doubt and disbelief about God's heart towards us. Feelings of abandonment set in; our trust in Christ's willingness to deliver us fades. Remember that Satan is always willing to test our boundaries to see where we will believe him rather than God. We need to know and recognise the fruit of his work in our thoughts and emotions:

- Satan aims to *steal* our peace of mind and our confidence in Jesus.
- Satan aims to *kill* our hope for the future and our relationship with God the Father.
- Satan aims to *destroy* our firm foundations of faith.

In contrast, our God is the Father of lights. Remember how Lucy felt when the tiny speck of light appeared in the darkness and how the fear began to dissipate? Lucy's solid ground was being built up and restored, bringing hope, courage and the ability to see salvation at work. God's work in us is constructive: it enables us to stand firm.

God's gifts are good, perfect and unchanging: they do not tarnish or grow stale, nor do they break or lose their value. Our Heavenly Father is the only source of these perfect and glorious gifts, so we are to go to Him for all that is priceless and worth having. His gift is the truth, which equips, protects and arms us. His gift is the truth, which brings us life and light in our circumstances. He gives the good and perfect gifts of the right path and the way through the darkness. We have the gift of His presence with us, no matter what it feels like, and He alone is pure and perfect goodness and faithfulness.

Secondly, we can hold onto the truth that,

> '"No weapon formed against you shall prosper, and every tongue which rises against you in judgement you shall condemn. This is the heritage of the servants of the LORD, and their righteousness is from Me,"' says the LORD.' Isaiah 54:17

What an inheritance to have! Yes, spiritual weapons are formed against us but we are not powerless against them. The Holy Spirit can reveal to us what weapon is at work and can also show us how to take authority in that situation.

The passage gives us a phenomenal promise but also a reminder that we need to be rightly positioned before God, clothed in His righteousness and not our own. He gives us all that we need to stand. Our part is to know what He has given us and to stand in that truth, with authority.

We do have victory in Christ and we do have authority to take a stand against the evil one. We are covered by the blood of the Lamb and saved through faith in Jesus Christ. That is truth.

Reflect and Respond Ideas

Head outside: When you go out for whatever reason, picture yourself putting on the belt of truth and the sword of the Spirit which is the Word of God. 'Put on' a Scripture that is helping you live in faith.

Research something: Research some of the names of Jesus. What do they tell us about His character, majesty and power?

Ponder further: Have you ever been told something with authority that was not true? What damage did it cause? You may want to renounce the authority with which those lies were spoken and to speak out the truth in the name of Jesus.

Get creative: We have read about standing in authority. Draw around your feet (or use paint to do footprints and let it dry) then write on the reasons why we can stand and withstand. Put this somewhere you will see it as you get ready each day so you can be reminded of the truth and proclaim it as you prepare for your day.

LIFE WITH GOD

zoe (Greek)

In the New Testament, *zoe* denotes not only physical life,
but spiritual life,
which one can possess only through faith in Jesus Christ.
Eternal life refers not only to duration of life, but to quality of life.
It is a present life of grace and a future life of glory.[15]

châçâh (Hebrew)

To flee for protection, to confide in... have hope,
make refuge, (put) trust.[16]

If you were asked to give an example of a life lived with God, who would you mention? Abraham, walking in the promise; Moses, who entered God's presence; Ruth, the woman who left everything she knew to come to the God of Israel; David, described as the man after God's own heart? There are many people in the Bible whose stories we hear a lot of and who stay in our minds as having great highs of faith. Maybe you thought of Elijah, Elisha or Samuel – great prophets.

But then there is the quiet life, lived before God; someone who only gets a few sentences to mark his existence for us. Part way through a list of the descendants from Adam to Noah, we find Enoch. He was the son of Jared, father of Methuselah as well as other children, and he lived for 365 years. We might marvel at that, but this stands out in the

---

[15] Definition taken from the supplementary notes of *The Spirit-Filled Life Bible*, p. 1935
[16] James Strong, *Exhaustive Concordance*, Hebrew, number 2620.

passage for being the shortest lifespan by hundreds of years. His son, Methuselah, lived for 969 years, and his grandson lived for 777 years. So why was Enoch's life remarkable? Because he 'walked with God' in such a special and noteworthy way that, after 365 years of walking with God, 'he was not, for God took him'. (See Gen. 5:18-24) Because of his life walked with God, Enoch did not physically die on Earth but was taken to Heaven by God. This was not in a dramatic encounter, as when Elijah was taken up into heaven in a chariot. It was a life quietly and faithfully lived at God's side.

Originally, I planned to entitle this chapter, 'relationship with God,' but then I could not find the word 'relationship' being used in the Bible. It underlies the entire book, but the word itself eluded me; and, of course, relationship can mean any number of things. It denotes a connection between people or nations, but it does not necessarily involve closeness, trust, faithfulness or permanency. Life with God, walking with God, carries a different sense about it. God is life, He gave us life, and He wants us to know life in all its fullness, which we will only find in His presence. He wants us to live in this moment of grace, with the promise of glory to come. This is about living life with God: sharing, communicating, trusting, walking, resting, working together in all things. Living life with God necessarily involves a relationship of trust as we commit every part of our lives and souls to Him and allow Him access to all that we are.

We have seen God's heart for relationship with His people; His desire to be chosen and claimed by us as our own. He desires to be our Father and bridegroom: the one under whose wings we find refuge, our dwelling-place and our fortress, our shield and our song. His desire is for us to be His children; for us to be the glorious bride He longs for. God's desire was to walk with us, face to face. In the restful time of the evening, Adam and Eve would hear the voice of their LORD God, their Father, calling them to join Him. Every evening, they would go to Him and they would rejoice together in all the goodness of God and the world that He had created for them.

Once Adam and Eve had sinned, instead of responding to His voice by going to Him to walk and talk with Him, they turned away and hid from Him. God's desire to be available, present and close to us is unchanged; but sin changed mankind and it impacted the manner in which we could approach our holy, sinless God.

Listening to the enemy led to separation between man and God, but also between Adam and Eve – they were no longer in unity. Satan still works this way, causing separations in relationships of all kinds with distrust, blame, miscommunication, unresolved anger and bitterness. Before Jesus' death, only the high priest could enter the Holy of Holies where God's presence was. Even then, those high priests risked death entering that place. But that was not God's desire for His people. When Jesus died on the Cross, the veil in the Temple that separated man from the Holy of Holies was torn in two by God. Now, God promises that as we draw near to Him, He will draw near to us. Even if it does not feel as if that is true, it is. When we feel that pull to move away from God, we need to be wise to that temptation and make a choice to draw close.

As we go deeper into the Word, with the revelation of the Holy Spirit to help us understand, we draw closer to God and develop a deeper relationship with Him. It is in the difficult times that our head knowledge of God transitions into heart, experiential knowledge. It is possible to believe without any doubt that God did perform all the miracles of the Bible, and still struggle to believe that He will help in the circumstances we face. Satan's strategy here will be to isolate and separate us from God and from other believers. It is often in the darkness that we encounter God in a new way, because it is in these times that we come to the end of our own resources and ability to endure, to resolve, to see solutions. It is in these times when we cannot help but acknowledge that we need God.

Respond

Adam and Eve heard the voice of the LORD God. This two-way communication is part of the relationship that God wants us to have with Him. Have you heard God speaking to you? Take a walk with God. Give the time to Him, giving Him permission to use it as He wants to. Set aside your agendas and concerns so you can let Him guide the conversation.

Living in Covenant Relationship with God

In Eden, Adam and Eve walked with God in the cool of the evening. There was harmony, closeness and openness between them. There was no obstacle to perfect relationship and communication; there was no shame, no misunderstanding, no difficulty hearing or trying to decide if God had said something or not, no hidden wounds that caused anyone to react with defensiveness, anger or withdrawal. It was beautifully straight-forward and natural. And yet, Eve did not consult God before taking a course of action that turned out to have devastating consequences. She experienced the pull to do something apart from God and decided it was good to take that course of action; to take that step away from Him. We all live with the struggle between our eternal need for closeness with God, the enemy who will do whatever he can to block that relationship, and our own natural inclination to do things our own way.

With the Exodus, we see that conflict between passionately desiring God's intervention and involvement in our lives and mankind's natural inclinations to keep God at a distance. In Egypt, the enslaved nation of Israel called out to God for deliverance – they hoped and longed for it. But when deliverance came it challenged them in ways they had not anticipated. They did not realise that encountering their God would be a powerful, foundation-shaking, life-changing experience. Israel wanted deliverance from slavery into freedom, but their understanding of freedom differed from God's. Their interpretation seemed to involve being freed from Pharaoh's oppression into self-determination. God's idea of deliverance did indeed involve removing them physically from Egypt, but it extended so much further from that. God had no intention of getting them out of Egypt and leaving them without healing or restoration. This would be giving them physical freedom but allowing spiritual captivity, which would not bring blessing this side of heaven or eternal salvation.

God wanted His people to be spiritually free, whole and blessed and that would only come through Him. God wanted to be known by His people. He wanted relationship with them. God's plan involved Israel encountering a real, living God who had personality, will and insight into their hearts; a God who completely engaged with them, not just meeting their needs when they complained and then backing away. He wanted to be a real, known, experienced and loved presence in their lives. Israel had not expected that they would encounter a God who wanted a response from them: a response of covenant relationship. They found that they needed to learn to trust and love the one leading them with their whole hearts, minds and souls.

After many years of crying out to God, they found that He did exist; and this encounter with the Living God led to a profound undoing. They got a lot more than they bargained for. They were deeply wounded and vulnerable because of their years of slavery, and this emerged in attitudes of fearful complaint and a reluctance to trust that God would continue to meet their needs from one situation to the next. This loving of God took Israel such a long time. This is why the faith of Caleb stood out as such a shining example in later years: out of all those who went to scout out the land, only he and Joshua had complete trust and conviction that God would provide and enable them. They had undivided hearts and minds where God was concerned.

For a while, Israel was encamped where the Desert or Wilderness of Sinai met Mount Sinai. The place of challenge bordered the holy place of encounter, where Moses would meet with God. (Ex. 19:1-3). Several significant incidents took place in this location, which teach us about relationship with God.

INCIDENT ONE   The Fear of the LORD

On the mountain, the Commandments and laws were given to Moses, to pass onto Israel: this was the 'how to' of being God's blessed and chosen people rather than slaves. (Ex. 20–23)

In the wilderness, the people witnessed God's power and were afraid that God would speak to them and they would die, so they asked Moses to be their intermediary.

> 'When the people saw the thunder and lightning and heard the trumpet and saw the mountain in smoke, they trembled with fear. They stayed at a distance and said to Moses, "Speak to us yourself and we will listen. But do not have God speak to us or we will die."

Moses said to the people, "Do not be afraid. God has come to test you, so that the fear of God will be with you to keep you from sinning."

The people remained at a distance, while Moses approached the thick darkness where God was.' Ex. 20:18-21, NIV

When we think of drawing close to God, do we imagine that as approaching 'thick darkness'? This was not a metaphor, but a literal darkness. Why did God not make His presence more appealing, more friendly? Moses drew close to God, even in the thick darkness, but Israel drew back. There are several things to note here.

God was right there. He was present with them. There were the sounds and sights of His presence with Israel. At that moment, they had no doubt that God existed, that He was powerful, mighty and holy – and they trembled as a result. We might like to think that we would race up the mountain into God's presence, but that was not what God required at that point. This was before the Cross had brought atonement for our sins and Israel needed to learn some serious lessons about approaching God. God placed a barrier between Israel in the wilderness and Mount Sinai for three reasons.

Firstly, because He needed to protect His children from the things they did not understand, just as He needed to protect Moses when He passed by. His glory and holiness were such that they would reduce man to nothing - they were too much for man to bear. The boundary between Him and Israel allowed them to witness His holy presence safely. Even being at a distance was overwhelming for them! Israel needed to experience that God was all-powerful and holy as well as good and faithful.

Secondly, because Israel needed to learn how to respond to God rightly and this was part of the teaching process. There was a need for Israel to have a right fear of the LORD – to be in awe of Him and to take His commands seriously; to recognise that there would be consequences to sin. Moses told the people not to be afraid because this fear of the LORD would help them resist the temptation to sin.

Thirdly, they needed to develop the attitude of heart that Moses had in approaching God, which enabled Moses to approach and talk with Him face to face. This was a resetting of priorities and attitudes for Israel – they needed to know who their God was and how to act rightly before Him; to take His word seriously and to seek to follow that in thought and deed, with all their hearts and minds. Moses' first encounter with God was at a bush that was burning but not being consumed. Fire demands that we be circumspect and recognise the qualities that make it dangerous as well as something for our benefit (providing light, warmth and a means to cook food). This was not an invitation to rush into the loving arms of his Heavenly Father. Moses was commanded to remove his sandals because he was on holy ground. The people of Israel needed to learn that same recognition that God was holy.

God had put a boundary in place regarding the mountain of His presence that required absolute obedience:

> '"Take heed to yourselves that you do not go up to the mountain or touch its base. Whoever touches the mountain shall surely be put to death."... When the trumpet sounds long, they shall come near the mountain.' Ex. 19:12-13

We are told twice that Israel kept its distance. There was a sense in which this withdrawing indicated that Israel was increasingly and rightly aware of the power and majesty of God, and the seriousness of the consequences of sin. In this moment of seeing the manifestation of God's glory and power on the mountain, knowing that going close to it would lead to death, they were recognising that the things of God were not to be treated casually or lightly.

However, Israel also created a level of separation by refusing direct communication with God. They were not to cross the mountain boundary, but they were still to draw near to God. However, they could see and understand Moses without trembling, so it was preferable to have God's messages conveyed *via* a man. As we see next, this act of separation on Israel's part led to sin.

INCIDENT TWO   Returning to Idolatry

On the mountain, Moses, Aaron and seventy of the elders were called to meet with God: they saw God, they ate and drank before Him in a mind-blowing encounter. (Ex. 24:9-11) Then Moses continued up the mountain, into the cloud of God's glory, and received the revelation for the construction of the sanctuary. (Ex. 24:12 -18, chapters 25-31)

Whereas previously it had just been Moses going up the mountain to meet with God, this time the invitation was extended to the elders of Israel. Those trusted elders of the tribes would then be able to share with their people about what they had seen and heard of Him. Even though Moses was absent for a while, the seventy elders and Aaron could testify that they, too, had been in the presence of God and lived, as Moses had. Despite this, when Israel decided they needed a figurehead or focal point to replace Moses and God, no one spoke out in favour of waiting in trust and expectancy. The people cried out,

> "'Come, make for us gods that shall go before us; for as for this Moses, the man who brought us up out of ... Egypt, we do not know what has become of him'" Ex. 32:1

Israel moved from focusing on God (in whose presence they trembled), to a man (flesh and blood like them), to an idol (that they had made). As they did not have Moses, clearly a golden calf that they could worship instead would be perfect.

Remember that they had seen and experienced God's presence, so this was not a result of doubt about His existence or His willingness to be involved with them. They ignored the commitment they had made to obey God and deliberately acted as they saw fit, despite what they had experienced of God's glory and goodness, His holiness and help to them. In this moment, there was no holy fear of the LORD or any other kind of fear, and they collectively chose to sin. An all-powerful and awesome God, who was beyond their control, was less appealing than a homemade statue that they could worship or melt down depending on their whim. They knowingly created and embraced the lie that this idol was the one who had led them out of Egypt, and they lauded it accordingly.

When Moses returned from the mountain, the people were 'running wild ... out of control and so become a laughing-stock to their enemies.' (Ex. 32:25 NIV) Outside of God's guidelines, His people became ridiculous, pitiable. When Moses challenged Aaron, all he could manage to say in response was, "you know how prone these people are to evil;" that he was given the gold, "threw it into the fire and out came this calf!" (Ex. 32:22 and 24, NIV) The age-old response of distancing oneself from the sin, blaming others and minimising the role played. As High Priest, Aaron should have reminded the people of God's goodness and constancy, even if no one else did, emphasising the importance of worshipping God alone. Instead, he had obeyed the people and been complicit in the sin.

There were two levels of activity taking place here. God was revealing His plans and purposes to Moses but, meanwhile, His people were still divided in heart and mind. There were times and seasons when they accepted God, His commandments and His ways; but equally there were times and seasons when they entirely rejected God by choosing to worship idols as the easier option that allowed licentious behaviour. We see this pattern throughout Israel's history.

INCIDENT THREE Developing spiritual wisdom

It was following this step back to idolatry that we see signs of hope.

On the mountain, Moses stood in the gap between God and Israel, interceding for them (Ex. 32:30 –34); he saw God pass by (Ex. 34:5-7) and received the commandments again. When he came down, his face was radiant 'because he had spoken with the LORD.' (Ex. 34:29-35) This was personal relationship in the privacy of the mountainside, away from the encampment. Moses would go and spend days or weeks with God, leaving Israel behind for the duration.

However, Moses did not only meet with God over long trips into the mountains: he also had a Tent of Meeting outside the camp. Israel would come out of their tents to watch Moses go there. When God was present, a pillar of cloud would descend to the entrance of the tent and Israel would stand in front of their own tents and worship. (Ex. 33:7-11)

In the wilderness, Israel was learning how to respond. As Moses, their intermediary and leader, went into God's presence, they recognised that he did so on their behalf. Perhaps they had come to acknowledge the remarkable relationship that he had with God in order to go to that place of meeting *and live*. Israel had seen the presence of God through the terrifying signs of smoke and fire like a furnace, earth tremors, thunder and lightning, the trumpets sounding and the darkness. They knew that crossing onto holy ground would lead to death.

When Moses left the camp now, Israel responded with worship rather than seeing Moses' absence as an opportunity to rebel. A spiritual wisdom was developing here, with an awareness that Moses, as their leader, was truly acting on their behalf and that it was right to respond by also standing before God. This is a beautiful image of unity and harmony in the approaching of God: Moses in the Tent of Meeting, face to face with God; and Israel standing outside their tents in worship of the Living God. Even though they were in separate locations, as Moses responded to the call to meet with God the people paid attention and also responded by turning aside from whatever they were doing to approach God through worship.

The scenes on the mountain were ever more remarkable. As part of Moses' intercessions for the people before God in Exodus 33:12-23, he made three requests and God gave three promises in response:

Request "Teach me Your ways so I may know You and continue to find favour with You."

Promise "My Presence will go with you, and I will give you rest."

Request "If Your Presence does not go with us, do not send us up from here."

Promise "I will do the very thing you have asked, because I am pleased with you and I know you by name."

Request "...show me Your glory."

Promise "I will cause all My goodness to pass in front of you, and I will proclaim my name, the LORD, in your presence.... But... you cannot see My face, for no-one may see Me and live... There is a place near me where you may stand on a rock. When my glory passes by, I will put you in a cleft in the rock and cover you with My hand until I have passed by. Then I will remove My hand and you will see My back; but My face must not be seen."

There is an interweaving in this: God's person, His glory, His goodness and His name. When God passed by, He proclaimed His name,

> "The LORD, the LORD, the compassionate and gracious God, slow to anger, abounding in love and faithfulness, maintaining love to thousands, and forgiving wickedness, rebellion and sin."

This is how our God wanted to be known, then and now. He is God of glory, goodness and grace. However, we must not forget that He is also judge – guilt is punished, so we need to be repentant in order to receive forgiveness. (Ex. 34:6-7).

What do we learn of Moses' heart here?

His relationship with God flowed from a heart that was in a right position before God.

He approached God with complete humility, recognising that he had much to learn and that there was no point in moving elsewhere unless God's presence was with them.

He had the wisdom to recognise that he needed a deeper and greater revelation of God.

He understood that it was right for him to wait on God's timing, to fit in with God's plans. He did not go up the mountain with his own schedule. Moses waited on God, waited for His time to speak. Moses was the servant, attending the King of kings.

Within this context of being servant-hearted and having a right fear of the LORD, Moses, like Abraham, had learned that he could also ask for things from God. He asked for things that were in line with God's desires for him: to know Him better, to only go where God was and to see the glory of God. These things were for his own peace of mind and well-being as he led Israel. However, he also came before God to ask for something whenever he interceded for Israel.

 We live in a different era. We live and breathe in the light of the death and resurrection of Messiah. Our experience of God is unlikely to have involved the thunder, trumpets and lightning that signalled His presence to Israel on Mount Sinai. We approach God now through the blood of Jesus Christ, through the undeserved favour of our heavenly Father. We do not risk death when we approach God because the arms of Jesus Christ were spread wide on the Cross and He welcomes us to come as children of God, adopted and accepted.

I had to pause as I wrote that. What would our experience of worship be like, if we knew that approaching the front of a church was such holy ground that we could die? Yet, because of Christ we can enter the presence of God at any time, in any place, and live. Because of Christ, we can enter the presence of God and know that His sceptre will always be pointed towards us, allowing us to approach – no, more than that, He will drop His sceptre and run to meet us. He is the same holy God who met with Israel at Sinai, but because of Christ we can now know Him as Father as well as King. There is no more astonishing truth than this: that God Most High gave His own life and blood in order to remove the separation between us. That is how much He wanted close relationship with us.

Yes, we are under grace, but purity and righteousness still matter. We are called to be in the world but not of it, being set apart for the LORD in all our interactions. We are not to be disobedient or rebellious, to live in compromise or to settle where the honour of God is at stake. Like Israel, we need to be watchful because our hearts can be deceived into turning to idolatry. We are to love and serve the LORD our God, heart and soul; to follow His ways and to hold fast to Him. This should be our priority, our motivation and our guide. If we want to be a church that can reach others for Christ, then we need to be that set-apart people that lives out the life that God has for us in purity, integrity and with hearts that are full of love for Him because we have tasted and seen that the LORD is good, glorious and gracious.

But we can create separations, just as Israel did. We can say no, just as Israel did. We can say to God, 'this far, but no further.' We may not have cast idols in our houses, but we can easily allow barriers to exist. We can have that same attitude of preferring the theory to the reality of God; of preferring to keep Him at a safe distance rather than allowing Him close enough to interact with us, avoiding any possibility that we will encounter Him and be undone in the recognition of how holy He is and how far we fall short. This God of ours is real, present and beyond our control.

Separations can exist for other reasons, too. We may unconsciously put barriers between ourselves and God as a means of protecting a wounded place in our hearts and souls. When we recognise that we have put a barrier in place that we do not want God to cross, it is important to look at why that boundary is there. If we have trusted someone and been badly hurt, we may struggle to trust God and so put a protective boundary between us and God. We will say, 'this far and no further' because we are afraid of what might happen if He comes closer. If we have experience of someone wrongfully exerting power over us and felt vulnerable, we may struggle to let Him have access to our lives or to let Him have a say in things as we are afraid of being taken advantage of or abused again. When we recognise those boundaries, see that as an invitation from God to start dealing with them. He will be gentle and patient, walking alongside as we process the root cause for the boundary being there.

Reflect and Respond Ideas

Head outside: As you exercise or garden, use Moses' request as your prayer: "Teach me Your ways so I may know You and continue to find favour with You."

Research something: Re-read the words of God as He passed by Moses. How does this description reflect His heart's desires? (Refer back to chapter one).

Ponder further: What is your experience of trusting in God? Are there areas where you find yourself doubting His word or His ability to meet your needs? Bring those things to God and ask Him to help you with the reasons why trusting Him is difficult in those things.

Get creative: Imagine that you were one of the elders present at the meal in God's presence. Write a paragraph in character like a diary entry or a monologue describing what it was like to eat and be in the presence of God. (Ex. 24:9-11)

Dwelling in the Secret Place

As with any parent, God desires His children to grow into strong and healthy adults, into believers who are strong and mature of faith. That will always be a process, as with any child. We are always children before God – there will always be more to learn and new areas in which we need to become mature. We learn the hard way that we cope so much better when we act in the flow of the Holy Spirit, rather than when we are overloaded and run down trying to be everything to everyone.

The Bible uses metaphors to help us understand how God works in our lives. God is our Father: teaching, guiding and disciplining us where necessary. God is like a gardener or vine-dresser who tends and prunes those He loves, so that they can be the healthiest and most fruitful they can be. God is like a potter, lovingly shaping and moulding us like the clay – a process that is hands on and involves the complete attention of the potter.

We could use the metaphor of a blacksmith forging metal, which is a fascinating and complex process. As metal is repeatedly heated in the fire and beaten, the metal is shaped and the impurities are worked out. The temperature of the metal matters, and this is gauged as much by experience as by measuring. The glow of the metal indicates the heat it has reached. When it has reached the correct temperature, the metal gets removed from the fire to be beaten and shaped. With each blow, some of the metal's impurities are worked out and the molecular structure of the metal is increasingly changed so it cannot revert to how it was before. This process is repeated until the metal is the required shape and thickness; then it needs to be quenched (rapidly cooled down) so that the metal retains the new shape given. This whole process is about creating the strongest metal for the finished piece.

And so it is with us. We go through a difficult time, we grow a little in our knowledge of Christ, we stand on that truth and our faith increases a little. We then go back into the fire, and learn a bit more, take another step of faith, find a few more impurities have been removed, and our faith increases further. And repeat – all in the hands of a master blacksmith, who never takes his eyes away from what he is doing. We are strengthened, purified and forged through the challenges that require us to take those steps of faith, where we find in practice (not just in theory) that God's word is true. We come to know in practice that God does truly know what is best for us. The difficult times do not get taken away, but God promises to go through them with us:

> "When you pass through the waters, I will be with you; and through the rivers, they shall not overflow you. When you walk through the fire, you shall not be burned, nor shall the flame scorch you." Isaiah 43:2

There will be a shaping and a purifying through those difficult times which will be painful. Growing pains hurt and bewilder us, but they are part of that maturing and becoming more Christ-like.

It is as we go through these things, choosing to draw close to God, that we grow in our faith and develop a stronger relationship with Him. We learn to dwell in the secret place of the Most High. Because we now have the Spirit of God dwelling within us, this does not depend on a specific geographical location, but on the positioning of our hearts before Him and in regularly spending time with Him. This is an active, intentional clinging to God; pursuing Him through His Word and through prayer; acting on His teaching as He brings it alive in our hearts. The more it is our response to take everything to God, the better prepared we are for what we face each day. We are called to dwell in the shadow of the Almighty by being with Him wherever we are and by engaging with Him in the everyday. This is about home, the place where we live; not a hotel that we visit for a short space of time as a change from our usual routines. Wherever we are, whatever we are doing, we should be dwelling in God and in His word.

It is in the secret place, this dwelling-place with God in worship, the Word of God and in prayer, that:

1. We find our true identity, worth and purpose in Christ.

It is part of that conversation and leading of the Holy Spirit that we discover things that God placed in us, that He designed us to be. I love creating things, and it gave me great joy to recognise that I take after my Heavenly Father in this way. Something that delights my heart, also delights His.

If we are all too familiar with criticism and belittling comments, it is in our times with God that He will heal our self-esteem and show us the worth that He places on us. This is something that only God can truly restore in us. It is in His presence, that we will come to know God's delight in us and the way He created us to be. And that is the heart of our worth: that God created us, He designed us carefully and with great thought. Whatever your earthly, genetic heritage may be, you are adopted by the Father and you are His child. You are of surpassing worth to Him. His love for you was so great that He died for you, so that you could know Him and love Him. It is God alone who can truly affirm you in the depths of your soul.

And it is God alone who knows what greater calling He has designed for us. Did the fishermen at Lake Galilee have any concept of a career plan that would involve giving up all that they knew and were good at, to become disciples of a Rabbi, for which they were completely unqualified? A career plan that would involve travelling extensively, challenging the religious authorities, preaching the Gospel to thousands of strangers, performing miracles in the name of someone called Jesus who claimed to be the Messiah? God can well and truly turn lives upside down and lead us on pathways we could never have imagined.

2. We find that our plans, priorities and attitudes become more like His.

One of the great challenges of prayer is knowing what to pray. We know that God will hear us when we pray in accordance with His will; but how do we know what that is? We learn to hear God's voice and the prompting of the Holy Spirit as we spend time in Scripture. Perhaps a phrase will stand out for us as we read a passage, and we will discover that God has revealed something to us that we had not previously understood. We learn to recognise the 'nudges' that point us in a particular direction.

And it is through this process, that we learn to pray, 'not my will but yours'. This is such an act of submission to God Most High as we recognise that we do not know what is best and ask Him to act according to His will and purposes. In this, we let go of our desire for a particular outcome and ask God to work as is needful.

As we become more like Christ, our tastes may change. Our life goals may change. We may find that we want to spend or invest our money or time differently. Feeling unsettled is never enjoyable, but it is something that we can learn to pay attention to. If something we used to do no longer feels right, we need to take that to God and find out what needs to change.

Spending time in God's presence is also the place where we will find the conviction of having done something wrong that needs dealing with. There is a feeling of being 'out of sorts' and unable to settle when the Holy Spirit is calling us to deal with something, and out of love for us, that unsettling will continue until we respond.

3. We are prepared and enabled for our daily lives.

Setting time apart to be alone with God in the secret place is essential preparation for anything we do that involves other people – raising children, volunteering, listening to someone's troubles, communicating via phone, social media, e-mail; meetings, deadlines, preparing meals, shopping … We need some time set apart with God. One metaphor we find in the Bible is that we are designed to be grafted onto the vine, that is Jesus Christ. Our strength, energy and vitality is meant to flow from the Holy Spirit working in us, just as sap flows through a tree trunk to the branches bringing necessary water and minerals. We need the flow of the Holy Spirit through us as part of our natural living and being, rather than waiting until we are falling apart to seek this.

In Judges 4:4, we are introduced to Deborah, who was leader of Israel and a prophetess. She was respected by the tribes of Israel; when she spoke, others listened and responded because they knew that she was acting out of her relationship with God. They trusted her. I do not believe that she waited until she was appointed judge to begin seeking God and exercising her spiritual gifts. I believe that she was already a woman who knew the importance of dwelling in the presence of God, who had grown and matured in her relationship with God, and who had been found to be faithful in the small things long before she came to high office. She was appointed judge because she was skilled, qualified and equipped for that job and calling spiritually as well as intellectually. And then, she continued to grow and lean into God as she faced things that she could not resolve in her own wisdom and had to seek the wisdom of God to complete her work. Dwelling with God is a central and crucial component of relationship with Him.

There are occasions when we need to take a longer period of time away from our regular tasks in order to seek God. For Moses, God arranged longer times of retreat for them to spend time together – prolonged periods of time spent on the mountain are more in the nature of a sabbatical. In one case, the time on the mountain involved waiting for six days with God speaking on the seventh. Moses then continued up the mountain for another forty days. (Ex. 24:15-16).

We might not be called to something like that, but we are all called to invest in time with God so that we are focused on having Him at the centre of all we do and reminded of His presence with us wherever we go. This is never time wasted, but time invested in our wellbeing and fixing our eyes on the one who loves us completely.

4. We learn to recognise His voice and prompting.

The more we spend time walking with God as His child, the more easily we come to recognise Him speaking to us and directing us. It means accepting that we will not always get what we want, when we want it. Being strong and independent are traits that are highly admired in the world, but this puts an unrealistic pressure on us. God calls us to be like children before Him and to accept His leadership, to accept that He knows better than us. This does not make us weak people. On the contrary, it takes great inner strength to go against the ways of the world. It puts us on a different path through life that accepts that most things are out of our control and we need God to navigate us through the times and seasons of life.

The Bible says that God is our shepherd and that we, as His sheep, recognise His voice. This is a process and keeping a journal is helpful as you can jot down things that come to mind as you study the Bible, Scriptures, things that you had not noticed before, pictures that God gives you or dreams.

Dreams from God are different to ordinary dreams, and the key way I notice them is that they stay with me into the day and that there are particular moments that stick in my mind. My response is to write down what happened in the dream, to note what was of significance and any emotions that came in the dream. I can then come back to it and ask God what He is saying to me. I do the same thing with pictures. Sometimes the meaning is straight-forward and with others the meaning becomes apparent in time.

I find that nightmares can be useful as well. This is not because they come from God but because God can use them to draw us close to Him. Often, they are an indication of a deep worry or fear, or perhaps a sense of insecurity or inadequacy. I have learned to use these as a prompt to bring those things to God and invite His work in that fear or insecurity.

Reflect and Respond Ideas

Head outside: How good are you at taking directions when driving somewhere? Do you argue with the Sat Nav or whoever is directing you? Consider how you respond to the direction of the Holy Spirit.

Research something: Do some research into traditional blacksmith methods. What do you notice about the skills required and how the metal needs to be treated for the product to be sound?

Ponder further: Spend some time with Isaiah 43:2. Have you seen the truth of this in your own walk with God? Claim the promises of God in this verse to encourage you.

Get creative: On one occasion Moses waited for six days, then God spoke on the seventh. Draw yourself on the mountainside, waiting for God; then spend six minutes just waiting before God. If a distraction comes to mind, refocus on sitting on the mountainside. God may or not speak in that time but choose to set those minutes aside just to be still and invite Him to come.

Praying as Jesus Prayed

With this in mind, we can look at the Lord's Prayer with a fresh perspective. For those who were raised in a traditional church, reciting this prayer is probably a familiar process that we have repeated numerous times. But there was a first time for this prayer: a time when it had never been heard before.

The disciples had gone to Jesus and asked Him how they should pray. They were Jews, so we know that they had grown up with a strong tradition of prayer in the home and in the synagogue. They knew the Old Testament Scriptures well, so were familiar with words of praise, lament, dedication and blessing. They knew the story of the Exodus and the long season in the wilderness, returning to it every Passover. They had a rich heritage of prayer and praise, but they asked Jesus how they should pray *now*. Now that Messiah had come and walked with them, after all He had taught them, how should they approach God in prayer? Jesus responded with these words:

> "Our Father in heaven, hallowed be Your name. Your kingdom come. Your will be done on earth as it is in heaven. Give us this day our daily bread and forgive us our debts, as we forgive our debtors. And do not lead us into temptation, but deliver us from the evil one. For Yours is the kingdom and the power and the glory forever. Amen." Matt. 6:9-13

It is a remarkably concise prayer. We are not to indulge in verbose prayers for the sake of hearing our own voices or to impress others.

The Son of God taught His followers to pray: 'Abba'.

Surely this must have been revolutionary to the disciples, raised with the knowledge of our separation from God and the ordinances that stated who could go into the holy of holies and what they had to do in order to approach God Most High *and live*. Jesus' instructions did not involve going to a priest, who would put on the garments we read about in Leviticus, nor did it involve offering burned sacrifices at the temple. In fact, He did not mention going to a special place at all. Even prior to His death and resurrection, Jesus said to pray *our* Father, *our* Dad. Our Saviour's Father in heaven is now also our Father through Christ – we are no longer slaves but sons. The term Abba was and is a term of great respect, as well as a term denoting the trust of a child in a parent.[17] God's very name was, is and always will be holy, set apart and sanctified; yet He desires His children to call Him Father. These two things cannot be separated: He is eternally and completely holy, and He is always and completely our Father.

We are to pray that God's kingdom and will be established on

---

[17] Cornwall and Smith, *Bible Names*, p. 1

earth as in heaven. It makes me smile to note that we are not invited to make suggestions on what we feel God's will should be or on how that should be done! Our Father is holy right to His very name; therefore, we are to submit and release our own desires and 'kingdom building' to Him in favour of His kingdom and will.

We then bring our need for daily sustenance to Him (seven words) before focusing on our need to be forgiven and to forgive (twelve words). The fact that our prayer for daily bread is in the same sentence as the prayers about forgiveness should indicate that forgiveness is as much matter for daily attention as our need to eat. Forgiving and being forgiven is just as important as food. We ask for God's help to choose a path away from temptation and to be delivered from the evil one who means us great harm.

The final phrase puts God and us in correct perspective: the kingdom, power and glory are not ours, but His. All that Satan has sought and desired belongs to God alone; no one can bring us glorious richness of life but our God.

Relational prayer involves us bringing our all to Him, committing and submitting every aspect of our lives to Him and trusting that His plans and purposes for us are good, even if it does not look like that! We are to acknowledge that our Heavenly Father wants us to look to Him in all things; that we were never meant to live independently of Him. This is particularly counter-cultural now, when the emphasis is on independence and empowerment, being so strong that we are practically armour-plated, making our own way and pursuing our own dreams. The comparison between mankind and sheep is far from flattering to us (I have never yet heard a shepherd describe his sheep without using the word 'stupid') but it is humbling and something that we probably only recognise when we find that we cannot control everything in our lives, that we cannot do it all ourselves.

Even as adults, God is our Father and Shepherd, and we are designed to look to Him for our lives to be fulfilled and brought to completion. Eve chose not to submit her will to God's – she chose not to invite His perspective on her decision-making. We also struggle to submit our will to His, pursuing His Kingdom and His righteousness before all else. But this is where the blessing lies.

In the dark times, when words fail us, return to the Lord's Prayer and keep it simple. For example:

Abba, Father – I need help: deliver me from the evil in the circumstances I face. I declare that You are with me, listening to me and that You are acting on my behalf, whether I can see that or not.

Abba, Father – I am in need and I do not know how to get through. Give me this day my daily bread. I declare that You will provide for my needs and that You will make a way for me.

Abba, Father – I have messed up and really upset someone. Please forgive me for what I have done wrong and show me how to mend the situation. I declare that You are the way, the truth and the life in this. I declare that You can redeem this mess as I repent and invite You in.

Abba, Father - I do not know what is best in this situation. I let go of all my ideas and plans and ask for Your will to be done in this. I declare that You are the author and perfecter of my faith and that You will establish Your kingdom in this situation as I trust in You. I declare that You will guide me and make the way clear for me.

We can also return to the words of the Lord's prayer if we do not know how to pray for someone else. We can pray:

- for them to know that God is their loving Father and to know His presence with them.
- for God's kingdom to come and His will to be done in their situation; for God to use whatever they face for good.
- for God to meet their needs out of His glorious riches in Christ.
- for God to strengthen them and enable them to resist temptation or to forgive others where needed, and to deliver them from evil.

We can also proclaim the kingdom, the power and glory of God over their circumstances.

Respond

Use the Lord's Prayer to intercede for those who are in need, remembering that these words have power when we pray them in Jesus' name.

Life in the Darkness

Having a close relationship with someone involves communication but also a considerable amount of trust: you need to know that you are listened to when you speak, that those words will be taken seriously and receive a response, and that those words will be treated with respect and confidentiality. When times are dark, we tend to only turn to those we truly trust with our vulnerability, shame and weakness. It is often when things are dark that we withdraw from relationships and lose the desire to communicate with others, especially about what is truly concerning us.

Elijah was a prophet, who generally seemed to be remarkably resilient and unflustered in all that God called him to do and experience. We first encounter him in 1 Kings 17, proclaiming to the idolatrous and wicked King Ahab of Israel that a drought will come which will last until Elijah ends it. As soon as he prophesied this, God called Elijah to hide away on his own, for an indefinite length of time, in a place where there was still water to drink and ravens would bring him food. When the brook dried up, God sent him to Zarephath where a widow would provide for him. Elijah performed two miracles here, one of provision and one of resurrection. Meanwhile, the three-year drought had caused severe famine and Ahab's queen, Jezebel, had murdered many prophets of the LORD.

It was at this point that Elijah returned to Ahab, at God's command, and ordered him to go to Mount Carmel with all Israel, the 450 prophets of Baal and 400 prophets of Asherah who had the favour of Jezebel. In this famous encounter, the false gods of Israel were found to be powerless and the LORD God sovereign over all. Elijah proclaimed the end of the drought and prayed for the rains to come, which they did. All was as God, and Elijah, had said.

It was as a result of this extraordinary encounter at Mount Carmel that Elijah's life was threatened by Queen Jezebel. Suddenly, Elijah's courage failed him and his faith collapsed. He ran away out of fear for his life.

It is not clear why Jezebel's threat had such a powerful effect on Elijah. Her words were,

> "So let the gods do to me, and more also, if I do not make your life as the life of one of them by tomorrow about this time." 1 Kings 19:2

Jezebel's gods had been proven to be ineffectual at Mount Carmel, so that was a meaningless comment. The threat of assassination within twenty-four hours, however, was not an empty one.

Now this was a man who had acted courageously and in trust of God's protection of him several times before and known God's faithfulness. When filled with the Spirit of God, Elijah was filled with confidence, authority and conviction that God would do exactly what He said He would. He knew that his prayers for rain would be answered and prayed until the clouds came. He travelled in the power of the Holy Spirit, running faster than Ahab's chariot. (1 Kings 18:46) He was obedient to God in all things, even fearlessly putting himself in situations that risked his life, because such was his trust in God.

Somehow, this threat caught Elijah in a vulnerable and unguarded place of his heart, and he ran. Something caused his heart to respond out of fear rather than faith. Was it a fear of Jezebel? Something in her words? A fear of death?

If we continue with the story, we find that Elijah ran first to Beersheba where he left his servant, and then he,

> '... went a day's journey into the wilderness, and came and sat down under a broom tree. And he prayed that he might die, and said, "It is enough! Now, LORD, take my life, for I am no better than my fathers!"' 1 Kings 19:4

Jezebel's threat was assassination within twenty-four hours; Elijah travelled a day's journey into the desert. He had left all human companionship behind and withdrawn completely. This man who had run to avoid death, then prayed for death. Why? Because in Elijah's opinion, he was no better than his ancestors and those who had gone before. Having prayed this, he slept.

This was the start of a series of encounters with God. Firstly, it was in the desert that he was tended by an angel who provided food and enabled him to sleep once more. When the angel returned to feed him again, Elijah received supernatural strength to travel to Mount Horeb. Secondly, he spent the night in a cave in the mountainside, where God spoke to him, asking, "What are you doing here, Elijah?" Even though God understood what was happening far better than Elijah did, He wanted Elijah to express what was most truly on his heart. His complaint was as follows:

> "'I have been very zealous for the LORD God of hosts; for the children of Israel have forsaken Your covenant, torn down Your altars, and killed Your prophets with the sword. I alone am left; and they seek to take my life.'"
> 1 Kings 19:10, repeated in verse 14

There is a strong sense of loneliness, even bereavement in this. There was a deep need in Elijah's soul to know that God had seen his faithfulness and work on His behalf. In this moment, in conversation with the Living God, Elijah felt abandoned. This is something that goes much deeper than head knowledge and understanding. Elijah knew perfectly well that he was not the only one left - after all, Obadiah had told him that he had saved 100 prophets from death in 1 Kings 18:13. Elijah knew that God had seen all that he had done in obedience. He had recently seen God move powerfully against the false prophets of Ahab, so had witnessed that He was already at work dealing with Israel's idolatry. As God did not directly address Elijah's complaint, either on this occasion or the second, it suggests that there was something deeper going on.

A deep place of insecurity, fear and loneliness had surfaced because of Jezebel's threat. Elijah prayed for death in the desert because he felt that he was no better than his fathers. This is such a poignant statement. Firstly, it shows that Elijah had believed that he had been better than those who had gone before; better than those who had committed idolatry and come under God's wrath. Secondly, it shows us that Elijah had set himself a high standard and then, when his courage failed at Jezebel's threat, he came under shame and condemnation. He had behaved just like anyone else; he was no different and no better than anyone else. He had failed to meet his own standard and expectation.

Elijah had a powerful prophetic calling which was important, but this was the most important thing he recognised about himself. His sense of worth was so interwoven with his job that he completely collapsed when he had a moment of weakness. Whereas Elijah judged himself guilty and deserving of a death sentence, God had done nothing of the sort. God was first and foremost committed to Elijah as His son; as a man with mind, heart and soul, who needed the loving help of His Father. Elijah's underlying motivation to be better than those who had gone before had come to the surface. This allowed God to remind Elijah that he only ever had to be human.

How did God go about this? Elijah poured out his complaint before God the first time and God's response was to tell Elijah to go and stand on the mountain before Him.

> 'And behold, the LORD passed by, and a great and strong wind tore into the mountains and broke the rocks in pieces before the LORD, but the LORD was not in the wind; and after the wind an earthquake, but the LORD was not in the earthquake; and after the earthquake a fire, but the LORD was not in the fire; and after the fire a still small voice. So it was, when Elijah heard it, he wrapped his face in his mantle and went out and stood in the entrance of the cave. Suddenly a voice came to him, and said, "What are you doing here, Elijah?"' 1 Kings 19:11-13

Why did God choose such a dramatic encounter? He caused a violent hurricane that shook mountains and shattered rocks, then an earthquake to shake the foundations of the earth, then a fire. God was not in these, so why did He cause them? In this encounter, God was continuing to challenge hidden beliefs in Elijah so let us look at this in that context. Elijah did not attempt suicide - he asked God to end his life. After all, he had just been involved in the destruction of hundreds of false prophets and Elijah now judged himself deserving of the same punishment. With each mighty act of God's power, did Elijah expect death at His hands? God wanted to remind Elijah that, whilst He was and always would be the Almighty God of power and creation, He was also the God of gentleness, of loving-kindness and tenderness.

It was the 'still small voice' of God that called Elijah out of the cave. Before going out, Elijah wrapped his mantle about his face. Perhaps he felt so vulnerable and ashamed that he did not want God to see his face. Perhaps it indicates that Elijah only felt secure in interacting with others when he did so in his role as prophet. To go out just as himself, a vulnerable man with fears and weaknesses like anyone else, was too much. He had failed to meet his own expectations and standards. He went out physically, but he hid his face with the garment that signified his calling. Elijah, the man, went into the presence of the God he had served faithfully and then felt he had failed, hiding his face – the face that God knew and loved.

God and Elijah then repeated their previous conversation word for word. God allowed Elijah's deep sense of loneliness to surface so that he would accept the need for company and co-workers; not just of a servant but of a student who would be like a son to him. This time, instead of a show of His power, God responded with His instructions, which initially seems somewhat heartless. However, the instructions addressed Elijah's deeper needs.

Firstly, the instruction was to go back to the desert. Elijah had felt that it was all over for him and only death was fitting, but God's work continued for him. God never left Elijah, nor did His feelings about Elijah ever change. He was with Elijah in the isolation of the Cherith Ravine, providing food by raven delivery. He was with Elijah and the widow at Zarephath when the oil and flour was miraculously multiplied. He was with Elijah during the triumph of Mount Carmel. Every glorious moment of faith was seen by God, in the hidden place and the place of miracle. But God was also with Elijah as he ran in utter fear for his life, in the desert in complaint and exhaustion, in the feeling that all the prophets of God had been killed except for him. He was with Elijah in the cave as he slept. God was with Elijah in his moments of great faith but also in his moments of great fear, distress and condemnation. God needed His son to know that being fearful and weak were not the end of the story - they did not make him worthless. God was working in a deep place in Elijah's heart.

Secondly, the instruction was to anoint co-workers. The message here was, *you are not to continue on your own; this is not all down to you*. This was not a punishment, with a message akin to, *you are clearly falling apart, therefore I need someone else to take over*. Elijah had been working on his own for some time and there is no mention of him being discontented with this. However, *now* he recognised his need and God was ready with the solution. Elijah was to anoint three men to continue and complete what God had started through him. Hazael was to be anointed king of Syria, Jehu was to be anointed king of Israel and Elisha was to be anointed as prophet. The redemption of Israel was not all on Elijah's shoulders: God was raising up others, either with a kingly or prophetic calling, to continue and complete God's work. Elijah's part was to call and anoint these men: to impart the blessing of God upon them and to release them to do the work of God. With Elisha, Elijah also assumed the role of teacher, mentor and father so that Elisha would be ready to take on this key prophetic role at the appointed time.

God knew that Elijah needed time with Him, but He did not rush that process. Timing is very much a part of this story. There are times when we simply are not ready to listen or to engage with someone. He sent an angel to minister to Elijah's physical needs *before* He engaged with Elijah's soul need because food and sleep would bring about that readiness to talk with God. We can focus on this part of Elijah's life as a season of depression and breakdown, which is valid. But it was also a season of transition from working alone, to working with; from carrying a burden alone, to sharing the burden; from being self-contained to taking on the role of spiritual father and mentor, sharing life with another.

Elijah initially ran to hide from Jezebel, then went into the desert because he felt ashamed and condemned by experiencing fear and giving into it. What Elijah saw as the end of everything, God used for good. In God's hands, this devastating event in Elijah's life became a catalyst to provoke and release the deeper, hidden emotions that God wanted to speak into.

Elijah had suddenly experienced a profound shaking of faith and confidence: the hurricane winds and the earthquake shaking the structures and foundations of his life. In agriculture and forestry, controlled burning is sometimes necessary to clear away old growth in order to restore vital nutrients to the soil and allow new growth to come up. Some of Elijah's false confidence, pride and independence was allowed to burn, so that the new things could grow up and be established. A devastating moment became a place of healing and equipping.

When we have our moments of spiritual collapse, it is important not to allow condemnation, guilt or shame to get a foothold. I believe that Elijah ran the first time out of fear and the second time out of shame and condemnation. Satan will want you to believe that you are the only one who has ever experienced this, that you are a terrible Christian and that God is disappointed in you; that you are a failure and there is no way the situation can ever be redeemed. These are all lies to destroy you. Stand against them and ask a trusted Christian to stand with you in prayer, as they can help you to recognise the lies and to give you much needed perspective. The lies of depression always work to isolate you and cut you off from those who can help you out. You are in a covenant relationship with God. He has committed to you and He will not leave you, no matter what it feels like. If you are not sure who to turn to, ask Him to bring you into conversation with someone who will understand and be able to offer the support you need.

It is all too common to face a difficult situation and feel that God is absent - that He has abandoned us in our greatest need. Relationships take work and our relationship with God is no different. It is a covenant relationship of commitment, for richer or poorer, in sickness or in health .... Covenant relationship is the foundation that reminds us to stand in fidelity through the trials. When we feel let down by God or angry with Him, we will not naturally want to spend time with Him. Our instinct will be to withdraw and go our own way. Satan *wants* us to pull away from God in anger and bitterness. That way, we are kept separated from God and we will blame God for the whole thing, backing ourselves into a dead-end of hurt and pain. The way through is to draw close, no matter how hurt we feel. With God, as with others, this is the time when we most need to keep the lines of communication and forgiveness open; to have those painful conversations where you tell Him how you feel and how disappointed you have been.

God passing by is a dramatic event, as Moses discovered on the same mountain many years before. Here, the Scripture clearly says that as the LORD passed by there was a strong wind, earthquake and fire, but that God was not in any of these even though He had caused them. Perhaps living in the dramatic had caused Elijah to forget something important. God demonstrated His awesome power and ability to control the earth beneath Elijah's feet and the elements around him; but He spoke to Elijah as *Abba*, the Father who draws close and whispers in the ear of those He loves with complete gentleness. Elijah needed that reminder of God's tender love for him; he needed the intimate whisper to speak deeply into his heart and soul. Elijah was so much more than a prophet to God: he was a beloved, cherished child.

Reflect and Respond Ideas

Head outside: Find a tree to sit under and bring to God any moments past or present when you have experienced that same kind of collapse of courage and faith. Invite the Holy Spirit to bring you the sustenance and refreshing that you need.

Research something: We have already read of an occasion when God passed Moses by. How does this compare with when He passed by Elijah? Why do you think God responded differently to Moses and Elijah?

Ponder further: Consider these dramatic moments of Elijah's life, from Mount Carmel to the desert to the cave. Can you relate to how he felt in those times?

Get creative: Choose a scene from Elijah's life that particularly impacted you and draw that scene. Talk to God about why and how it affected you.

Praying in the Darkness

The Lord's Prayer is a model for us to bring to God our praise and needs, all within the context of His holiness and His Father-heart towards us. But it is not the only way to pray or communicate with God, as we see from the conversations between Him and Elijah. In our crisis moments, the important thing is still to communicate with God and to continue to trust that He hears us, no matter what it feels like. This can be one of the hardest things to believe because our emotions tell us that we have been abandoned, rejected and that God is not there.

The Old Testament is full of the testimonies of those who cried out to God in their dark times, who knew from experience that God heard them.

David lived many years with God's promise of kingship but also with the very real threat of violent death. He testified to God's goodness in 2 Samuel 22, saying,

> 'I called upon the LORD and cried out ... *He heard my voice* from His temple and my cry entered His ears ... *He drew me out* of many waters. *He delivered me* from my strong enemy, from those who hated me; for they were too strong for me. They confronted me in the day of my calamity. But *the LORD was my support. He also brought me out* into a broad place; *He delivered me* because He delighted in me.' v.7, 17-20 (my emphasis)

When the Israelites were being crushed by slavery in Egypt, they cried out to God with seemingly no response or change in their circumstances. Then God met Moses at the burning bush, and said:

> "I have surely seen the oppression of My people ... and have heard their cry... I know their sorrows. So I have come down to deliver them..." Ex. 3:7-8

The prophet Jonah heard God tell him to go to Ninevah and call them to repentance, but he did not want to do this. In disobedience and rebellion, Jonah got on board the first ship going in the opposite direction and ended up being thrown overboard in a violent storm. From within the fish that carried him, Jonah repented before God, saying:

> "I cried out to the LORD because of my affliction, and He answered me. Out of the belly of Sheol I cried, and you heard my voice....
>
> When my soul fainted within me, I remembered the LORD; and my prayer went up to You, into Your holy temple... Salvation is of the LORD." Jonah 2:2,7,9

When the widow's son died in 1 Kings 17:17, Elijah cried out to the LORD:

> '... the LORD heard the voice of Elijah; and the soul of the child came back to him and he revived.' 1 Kings 17:20 and 22

God heard and answered, even though it may not have been in the way expected or in the time expected. But He heard from every deep, terrifying and isolated place of darkness: the endangered voice from the battlefield, the oppressed voices from the place of enslavement, the repentant voice of a rebellious prophet from the depths of the ocean, the voice of Elijah from the home of a distraught, bereaved widow. There is nowhere we can go or be, geographically, emotionally, mentally or spiritually, where the signal to reach God is poor. The moment our hearts turn towards Him, seeking Him, the channel of communication is wide open, loud and clear.

We learn in the book of Daniel that God responded the moment he began to pray, but that the spiritual battle around him was so fierce that it took several days for the angel to reach him. (Dan. 10:12-13) That is the point where the lies of abandonment and rejection take hold, because that lack of visible or tangible result suggests that God is absent or ignoring you. More than that, it feels like proof that God is not there when you truly need Him; that faith in God is just theory and not genuinely powerful. What we experience is one facet and God sees that in every minute detail of pain and anguish; but He also sees clearly the spiritual battle going on in the background, of which we only catch glimpses. You may not see dramatic results but pay attention in your spirit. There are times in prayer when you will feel inside that your work of prayer is done, that something has changed or shifted. This is because your work of prayer is achieving things in the spiritual places, and it is important to hold onto the 'things unseen' which are sensed in faith through the revelation of the Holy Spirit within you.

This is what sets our God apart from idols – our God hears and answers. Our God is both vast and intimate; not made by any human hand or imagination, but real, living and awesome in every possible way.

Respond

Read Psalm 116, making a note of the phrases that particularly impact you.

Apply the words of faith to your own circumstances, trusting that the God who heard these words also hears yours.

FAITH

pistis ...(Greek)

'conviction (of religious truth, or the truthfulness of God...),
especially reliance upon Christ for salvation;
... constancy in such profession.'[18]

Faith, as a friend once explained to me, is 'sweaty'. His metaphor was exercise: it takes energy, effort and endurance, but the result is the building of spiritual muscle and ability over time. The difficult times are the times when our faith gets exercised. We can believe that God is the same God who performed all the miracles in the Bible but still wonder if He is going to come through for us in our circumstances. I found at one point that I believed with absolute certainty that God had parted the Red Sea and brought an entire nation to freedom, but I was not convinced that He could or would help me in the things I faced. What I had come to know in my brain through studying the Word of God also had to be learned in my heart and soul through personal experience: by putting those Scriptures to work in my own challenges. Doubt is natural – it is part of our need to process what is happening to us. But if we stay in a mindset of doubt and uncertainty, we are unable to stand in faith.

We need the faith that God is Sovereign no matter what the outcome is and no matter what our circumstances are. Faith is worked out in us over time, just as repetitions in exercise develop muscle strength over time. One of the measures of increasing fitness is how quickly you recover your resting heartrate. Do not be alarmed or feel abandoned when you go through situations that challenge your faith. Instead, change your perspective to seeing it as a faith workout that will

---

[18] James Strong, *Exhaustive Concordance*, Greek, number 4102

strengthen you, increase your resilience levels and recovery time. Each time you choose faith, stand and withstand in faith, you are strengthening those spiritual muscles.

Saved by Faith in Christ

We are only saved by our faith in Jesus Christ as the Son of God and accepting Him as our Lord. But, as John explained in his first letter, each part of the Trinity is involved in our coming to faith:

> 'For whatever is born of God overcomes the world. And this is the victory that has overcome the world – our faith.
>
> Who is he who overcomes the world, but he who believes that Jesus is the Son of God? This is He who came by water and blood – Jesus Christ ....
>
> And it is the Spirit who bears witness, because the Spirit is truth. For there are three that bear witness in heaven: the Father, the Word, and the Holy Spirit; and these three are one.' 1 John 5:4-7

Christ alone is the way, the truth and the life; there is no other way to be with the Father. This is very specific: general, vague faith in there being something else out there does not lead to victorious overcoming. Faith in Jesus Christ is born of God – it is a powerful, active force which enables us to endure and find the redemptive work of God in all challenges we face in life. We come to know this through the working of the Holy Spirit in us, who reveals this truth to our hearts. The Trinity of God the Father, God the Son (described here as the Word) and the Holy Spirit witness to us of the truth that salvation is through Christ. As we put this truth into action, it moves from being an intellectual reasoning to a heart conviction that this is true.

For the Jewish people at that time who were raised on a system of regular blood sacrifices to atone for their sin, this was a significant adjustment to their mindset about where salvation lay. It took a huge step of faith to accept the changes that the Messiah was bringing to their understanding and religious practice. For centuries, Israel had observed the strict rules and regulations given to them, with the recognition that these were necessary to be right with God and that these led the way to right honouring of such a holy and righteous God. Only the High Priest was allowed to enter the Holy of Holies in the temple, where the presence of God dwelt. But at the very moment that Jesus gave up His life on the cross, the veil that separated the people from the presence of God was supernaturally torn in two. A new way was opened up to God, and that way was and is Jesus Christ.

Following the death and resurrection of Jesus, everything had changed. Now they were entrusting their eternal salvation in the teaching that, through Christ, the atonement for sin had been made once and for all. What was now necessary was circumcised hearts not bodies, sacrifices of worship and praise, not of animals. The approach to God was now through accepting the saving grace of Christ. This faith needed to come first, with worship and obedience flowing from this.

The disciples were Jewish men who believed that Jesus was the Messiah; men who had accepted Him as Lord and Saviour. It was a process for them to learn this new way of doing things, and it was often a struggle to let go of the Judaic traditions that were no longer necessary under Christ. As we learn in Acts 10, the apostle Peter struggled over the idea of meeting with a Gentile, in his home. A God-fearing Roman centurion had seen an angel, instructing him to invite Peter to come to his household. This was an invitation that Peter, as a Jew, should have refused. However, before the messengers arrived with the invitation, God sent Peter a vision that taught him that this was not only permissible but encouraged by God. While Peter considered the meaning of the vision, the Holy Spirit told him that three men had come, instructing him to:

> "Arise, therefore, go down and go with them, doubting nothing; for I have sent them." Acts 10:19-20

Peter went, heard the centurion's story, and then preached the Gospel to him and his household. There were two layers to Peter's message. The first was the message that he himself had just learned: that God was working through all nations now and not just through Israel. The second was the Gospel message, as a reminder of what they had already heard (verses 34 to 37). What happened next was also a valuable lesson to Peter as well as to the centurion's household.

> 'While Peter was still speaking these words, the Holy Spirit fell upon all those who heard the word. And those of the circumcision who believed were astonished, as many as came with Peter, because the gift of the Holy Spirit had been poured out on the Gentiles also. For they heard them speak with tongues and magnify God.' Acts 10:44-46

The expectation was that the Holy Spirit would fall on the people of Israel ('those of the circumcision') who believed in Christ alone. The fact that Peter and his companions were astonished when the Spirit fell upon the Gentile believers of Christ indicates what a revolutionary idea this was for them. From birth and for generations, Israel had been urged to be set apart from all other nations. Now, God was doing a new thing: Jew and Gentile were united through faith in Jesus Christ as Lord and Saviour, by the gift of the Holy Spirit and the grace of God. God's will was evident and it took Peter by surprise, but he could not argue with the faith of the Gentiles or the work of God the Holy Spirit in them, as they spoke in tongues and praised God. Because of this, Peter baptised them in the name of Jesus.

This did not go down well with the other Jewish believers to begin with, who were aghast that Peter had even gone to the house of a Gentile, saying, "You went in to uncircumcised men and ate with them!" (Acts 11:1-18). Peter needed to share the whole story with them and let them think it through, testifying to the Pentecost moment of the Holy Spirit falling on these Gentile believers and how he had remembered Jesus's words about men baptising with water but there also being a baptism of the Holy Spirit.

> "'If therefore God gave them the same gift as He gave us when we believed on the Lord Jesus Christ, who was I that I could withstand God?" When they heard these things they became silent; and they glorified God, saying, "Then God has also granted to the Gentiles repentance to life."' Acts 11:17-18

This was a huge shift of attitude for the Jewish believers of Christ, and an ongoing struggle to avoid going back to living under the law when they were now under grace. The subject of being circumcised and keeping the law of Moses was a critical discussion point at the time; one which is returned to repeatedly through the New Testament. (See Acts 15:1-29). The important point was acknowledging that the blood of Christ was sufficient for salvation, for both Jew and Gentile. Jesus had come because it was impossible for mankind to live up to the standard necessary with the law.[19]

We see that with Saul, who was the least likely of believers in Christ. It took a great deal of time for the believers to trust this former persecutor, but his personal transformation was witness to the work of the Holy Spirit in his life. Previously, all his confidence of salvation had been based in his Jewish birth, training and religious observance; he found these to be justifiable reasons for pride. But then he encountered Jesus the Messiah on the Damascus road and was undone. His birth, training and religious observance had led him to zealously condemn and attack those who trusted in Jesus as Lord and Saviour as blasphemers, but he was now revealed to have been wrong. His heritage did not enable him to stand before Christ; it was no defence as he heard the voice of Jesus. Saul's confidence in the wrong things was entirely unravelled and he came to acknowledge that there was only salvation through grace. We can only imagine the humility it took for this man to admit that he had been wrong. His identity was now as a child of God through grace, not through birth. (See Acts 22:1-21)

Within that context of the awesome gift of grace, we are called to live righteously as our response; not because our salvation depends upon it, but because it is our act of worship to the God who gave His life for us. Saul was full of pride and superiority because of his heritage. Paul was full of humility and wonder at the grace of Jesus Christ who saved him and who had chosen to work through him. Paul wrote to the church at Ephesus,

---

[19] It is also important to note that what Peter had seen in the visions, heard from the Holy Spirit and saw in the Holy Spirit's work in the Gentiles, was also confirmed by Scripture in the prophecies about the coming Messiah. (For example, see Is. 56:1-8)

'For by grace you have been saved through faith, and that not of yourselves; it is the gift of God, not of works, lest anyone should boast. For we are His workmanship, created in Christ Jesus for good works, which God prepared beforehand that we should work in them.' Eph. 2:8-10

None of us has earned our salvation through our religious observance or actions. All believers, from every nation, have accepted the gift of salvation available through the sacrifice and resurrection of Jesus Christ. None of us can claim the victory for ourselves and none of us can boast that this is our achievement. If we, like Saul, are experiencing pride and superiority in our faith then we need to take a step back. Our faith is a gift of God, stirred up by the Holy Spirit within us.

I do not think that it is a coincidence that this man who once placed all his pride, confidence and conviction in his Jewishness was then called to spread the Gospel to the Gentiles. Those whom he would once have rejected or considered inferior to him were the ones he was called to love and serve, at great personal cost. And it is evident that he did not do this out of a sense of duty or to earn his salvation. He was so changed by the work of the Holy Spirit within him that his heart was passionately engaged and invested with the Gentiles. He served the Gentiles because they mattered to him. Like a loving parent, he wanted them to be well and healthy in their faith. It mattered deeply to him when they went astray because he loved them. It pained him when there were disagreements, fallings away or deceptions in the communities of believers. Whilst he could see the joy that awaited him in God's presence, he accepted a life of persecution and suffering on earth for the sake of those young believers. He described himself as being poured out like a drink offering – his act of loving worship to the God who had saved him through grace.

Pause for a moment with that truth. Our salvation was and is through faith that Jesus Christ's blood has paid the price for our sin. Living righteously is our response to that: it is the outworking of our joy and thankfulness at His grace and mercy in redeeming us. It is our act of loving worship to the one who holds us in His hand.

Respond

Give thanks for the witness of the Holy Spirit that revealed to us that we have salvation through Jesus Christ. Give thanks for the gift of faith: a powerful force and tool in the situations we face. Spend some time praising and worshipping Jesus Christ for all that He did for us at Calvary.

Maturing Faith

Our lives can sometimes be bewildering. We may have trusted and followed God for years and ended up wondering what is going on. We anticipate adventurous lives of promise, particularly when we hear the testimonies of those who have witnessed miracles or seen God move in an amazing way, and think, 'yes, that is what I want!' Yet, it never quite seems to happen that way for us so we stay open to God and go on with the ordinary jobs of the day.

Recognising God's desire for us to grow and mature is so important. His timing is perfect, even though it may not seem that way to us. There is so much that we will only understand in years to come, as we look back with hindsight. Looking at the story of Moses gives us considerable insight not only into the life and development of one person, but also into how that one life fitted into a much bigger story of nations and spiritual destiny. And that is where the story begins: it is a story of the powerful nation of Egypt and the nation of Israel. They had been peacefully living alongside each other since the time of Joseph and Israel had prospered there, becoming more numerous. (See Genesis chapters 45 – 47)

However, chapter one of Exodus begins with a change of season. A new Pharaoh was ruling Egypt who had not known Joseph and who felt no gratitude or loyalty to Joseph or his people. For this Pharaoh, having such a populous and mighty people close by was a source of fear – he felt threatened because 'Israel is mightier than we' and they could all too easily join with Egypt's enemies and fight against them. Thus, Pharaoh began a campaign to weaken this potential threat.

Firstly, he appointed taskmasters over Israel to 'afflict them with their burdens.' This would weaken the people physically and mentally; causing the weakest amongst them to struggle and die.

'But the more they afflicted them, the more they multiplied and grew. And they were in dread of the children of Israel...'
Ex. 1:11-12

Therefore, Pharaoh increased the burdens and 'made their lives bitter with hard bondage.'

As this was ineffective, Pharaoh moved to his second strategy, which was to order the Hebrew midwives to kill all male babies delivered. However, the Hebrew midwives feared God and courageously disobeyed Pharaoh, both by letting the sons live and by deceiving Pharaoh in person. When he asked why the boys were still living, the midwives claimed that the Hebrew women gave birth so quickly that they did not make it in time. (Ex. 1:15-20). Pharaoh's response was to order that all sons born to Hebrew women be cast into the river to die.

It was into this conflict that Moses was born and, in a scenario worthy of a great myth, was put into a reed basket by his mother and floated down the Nile where he was retrieved by an Egyptian princess. His mother acted as nurse and would have been able to teach the young boy Hebrew customs. (Ex. 2:1-10)

Some years later, the young Moses saw an Egyptian oppressing a Hebrew slave and killed the Egyptian. We could see this as an impulsive, hot-headed response to an act of injustice; a sudden burst of anger that caused Moses to act without thinking. Yet, verse 12 says that Moses, 'looked this way and that way, and when he saw no one, he killed the Egyptian and hid him in the sand.' From this, it is evident that Moses was fully aware of what he intended to do and took the time to ensure that no one was watching before he murdered the Egyptian. The implication is that, had he seen someone, he would not have acted. However, he was seen. The Hebrews knew what he had done and Pharaoh sought Moses' death when he learned of this. Moses fled to Midian and settled there: he married, had children and dwelt as a shepherd. (Ex. 2:11-15) It was years later when he saw a bush that was on fire but not being destroyed that he decided to 'turn aside' to see the sight, and so heard the voice of God calling him to the extraordinary role he was to play in Israel's history. (Ex. 3)

How can this story help guide us into attitudes of faith in what we face?

It teaches us that sin is not the end of the story.

Moses had murdered someone and knew he would not be protected from reprisals by Pharaoh. Even though he had grown up in the royal household, killing an Egyptian to avenge his treatment of a Hebrew was not going to be supported. He ran and adopted a lifestyle as far away from his royal life geographically and in nature as he could. God had plans for him even so. Like Paul, Moses found himself with a task of immense significance in God's kingdom which carried with it the blessings of a life walked in God's presence, but also challenges that pushed him to his limit.

It teaches us the need to discern the bigger picture.

A useful phrase in this passage is, 'There was a change of season ...' First and foremost, this was about the political change which heralded a new manner of governing, particularly in relation to the attitude toward neighbouring nations. However, it was also a change of spiritual season where Satan worked through Pharaoh to oppress the people of God.

In this instance, a situation had arisen, not because people of faith had done something wrong, but because Satan did not want the people of God to prosper. This is the first point of discernment when experiencing opposition or difficulty. Has it arisen because of disobedience or obedience before God?

We hear much of Israel's seasons of disobedience in the Bible. The book of Judges shows the alternation between obedience and disobedience depending on the leadership in place. But in this instance, there is no record of Israel adopting Egyptian religious practices, turning to idolatry or forgetting the laws of God. As a result, God had greatly blessed them. We remember that the call after the flood was to be fruitful and multiply because God's people, the nation of Israel, existed and expanded through the bloodline, not by conversion (Gen. 8:17, 9:1 and 9:7). In fact, Israel had been so blessed that they had become a numerous and mighty people. The new Pharaoh, powerful ruler of all the wealth and might of Egypt, the one considered to be a god in human form, was afraid of them. This is extraordinary.

Pharaoh feared what they could do to him and his nation should they rise against him. This was not what was actually happening, but a fear that had taken on a life of its own. Pharaoh had begun asking 'what if my enemies rise against me?' and continued to, 'what if Israel joined with them?' His response to these questions was to foresee disaster for him and Egypt: he saw no or little possibility of Egyptian success if Israel joined with another nation against him. It is interesting that it did not seem to occur to him that Israel might have joined with Egypt against a shared enemy; nor did he consider a policy that would bring stronger links of friendship between the two nations, renewing what had existed between Joseph and his predecessor. His fear was such that he proceeded to act to deal with a potential threat that might never have existed except in his own imagination.

Pharaoh's strategies of enslavement and of the mass murder of infants were signs of a deeper spiritual level at work. Satan was at work through Pharaoh. It was a spiritual battle being played out in the visible world. We saw this again later in history when Herod ordered newborns to be massacred in an attempt to end the coming of the Messiah. These were profoundly wicked acts in God's sight. In his spiritual blindness, Pharaoh considered his orders to be a justifiable response to the potential threat from Israel. Those who were of an age to work were enslaved: stripped of their rights and freedoms and treated harshly to cause a breakdown of physical health and strength so that they would be unable to fight against Egypt. However, clearly Israel lived in family groups so children were still being born to them. The second step of killing newborns would have numerous impacts. It would cause intense trauma, leading to individuals and the community to experience an internal breaking. It would eventually result in the inability of the nation to multiply and, by killing the boys rather than the girls, it would render Israel incapable of fighting against Egypt.

It is difficult to see how this could not have turned the people away from God. We read at length of how Job wrestled with his faith in God when his life was stripped back, even though he could not identify any sin that could have caused it. Israel also was not suffering as a result of sin at this point, but because Satan was at work to undo God's great blessing upon them, to disempower and disenfranchise them. Yet the Scripture tells us that the people turned to the only one who could help them: their God. And God Most High heard them.

It takes wisdom and discernment to recognise what is going on behind the scenes, and this is best done prayerfully with others. If we have sinned, then we have stepped outside of God's will and purposes for our lives so we can expect to come across the consequences of that as we step outside of His favour. However, if the Holy Spirit does not bring to mind any sin, then the opposition is coming for a different reason. Ultimately, the spiritual battle is caused by Satan's opposition to God, so if we are focused on working for God's kingdom we can expect to experience some of that opposition. When a group of Christians gather to listen to God, the Holy Spirit may well give pieces of information to different people – perhaps a Scripture to one, a picture to another – which link together to bring God's message. Having a heart that is willing to listen and respond is the prerequisite for this, rather than having our own understanding of what is going on and refusing to move from that point.

Opposition can include an attempt at enslavement and the increase of burdens upon you. Note that Pharaoh's first strategy was to exhaust Israel – to weaken them physically and emotionally so that they had no strength to oppose him, no strength to stand up for themselves or to break free. For instance, there may be increasing or ever-changing regulations and requirements to meet for your ministry that slow you down and leave you entangled. There might be relational problems within a team that wear you down and make you wish you had never started the project. There may be an attempt at personal enslavement through the temptation to do things your own way rather than God's way; something that will pay off in the short-term but a compromise that will give the enemy a foothold in you which will lead to a derailment of your mission in the long-term. Satan will attempt to kill or destroy whatever God is birthing through you.

Recognising the enemy at work and knowing how to respond takes the wisdom that only God can give, because He is the only one who sees the whole picture and who sees it with perfect clarity. He is never confused, unsure or caught off guard. He has seen the end from the beginning. No matter what Pharaoh attempted, God still blessed His people.

It teaches us that every role is significant in God's kingdom.

How do we measure or gauge our significance in God's kingdom? Do we have a structure in our mind of which jobs or ministries are most important, of which count more than others? Do we aspire to be like Moses, a great leader? Receiving an impressive call to ministry and miraculously parting seas and causing water to spring forth from rocks?

We can focus so much on Moses, the future leader who spoke to God face to face and, perhaps, his mother who put him into the basket, that we miss the extraordinary role played by the Hebrew midwives. In the course of their duties assisting labouring women to deliver babies safely, they suddenly found themselves with the ruler of the land commanding them to kill all boys. Their calling was to assist in bringing life into the world, yet they were ordered to murder. These women did not have a burning bush moment with God or a 'suddenly' moment where they were called to step up into a new role. In the course of their everyday, they were faced with a choice of staggering significance that they could not avoid: would they obey Pharaoh or God? Ultimately, the two women feared God more than Pharaoh and they disobeyed the order, at great risk to their own lives.

Because of their astonishingly courageous, God-fearing act each time a Hebrew woman went into labour, countless children's lives were saved. We only know Moses by name, but God saw each and every baby who was delivered safely by the midwives; each son who was kept from death because of their holy fear of the God of Israel.

The midwives would not have known that one of the boys that they safely delivered would one day be chosen and anointed by God to lead Israel out of Egypt. They did not have any idea that this boy, out of all the others, would be written about and read about across the world and over many centuries. He was one baby amongst many whose lives they saved in the name of Almighty God. All they knew at the time was that they could not obey Pharaoh in this matter and that they would accept whatever consequences came. The rest was up to God.

The midwives were honoured by God in three ways. Firstly, the nation of Israel was blessed with further multiplication and an increase of might. Secondly, the midwives were blessed with God's provision to them of their own households. Thirdly, the two women are honoured in Scripture. Their names were Shiphrah, which means beauty, to be bright, prolific; and Puah, whose name means splendour, light, childbearing, joy of the parents.[20] How fitting those names were before God, as these women brought His light and beauty into the darkness that surrounded the labour of the Hebrew mothers at that time, and how great the joy of the parents must have been to know that their sons were safe in the hands of those faithful midwives.

God honours those who are faithful and courageous before Him; those whose hearts are firmly rooted and established before the throne of God, rather than seeking a throne of its own. The midwives honoured God, even at the risk to their own lives. Whatever you do for God is part of His kingdom being established. We are all involved in the work of pointing the way to Christ and in bringing spiritual life to others. Our God sees all that we do in His name, no matter how hidden that is in the eyes of the world, and He knows what it costs us to honour Him.

Each one of us is a representative of God Most High so whatever we do in life, our steps of faith and integrity are of such immense significance before God that He will never forget them. Whatever our marital status, work status or spiritual call happens to be, we are all part of the body of Christ and sons of God Most High. God does not judge or assess significance the same way that we do. Many miracles were performed in the New Testament, which is wonderful. But there was also a great deal of patient enduring and carrying out of the same tasks that we do. They still needed administrators and caterers, someone to sort out the details. When Paul's letter arrived in Colossae, someone needed to ensure it was read and then swapped with the letter sent to the Laodiceans (Col. 4:16). Timothy received the instruction to bring Paul's cloak from Troas, along with books and parchments (2 Tim. 4:13). There will always be practical things that need doing in an organised and faithful manner. Doing these things for the Lord are just as important as anything else. Whatever you do, do it for the glory of God.

---

[20] Cornwall and Smith, *Bible Names*, pp. 153 and 173

It teaches us that we need to have a sense of God's timing.
Moses was, in a sense, set apart from his earliest days because of his babyhood trip down the Nile to safety, but his life showed no promise at all for decades. Indeed, there is no indication given that any prophetic word had been spoken into his life, as it was with Joseph or John the Baptist. Quite the contrary. From birth into his early adult life, all that we know was that he murdered someone and fled for his life. We can look in Acts for further information, where the apostle Stephen said that Moses 'was learned in all the wisdom of the Egyptians,' the wisdom of his adopted culture and upbringing; however, he was not yet familiar with the wisdom of the Spirit of God. (Acts 7:22) At this stage, he was not the obvious candidate to lead anything, let alone God's chosen people – a formidable responsibility!

No matter what destiny he had from the beginning, no matter what benefits he had from his palace upbringing, he needed time hidden away. He was shaped by his role, responsibilities and relationships as a husband, father and family member. Family life and community may have been something he knew little about as a Hebrew foster son in an Egyptian palace. Was he ever allowed to forget that he was found floating on the river? Was he ever accepted as equal with the other children around him? He had no compunction about killing an Egyptian, clearly revolted by the treatment of the Hebrews, yet he was not accepted by the Hebrews either. He grew up between cultures and, perhaps, uncertain of his role and place in life. When called by God, I think it is also fair to say that Moses continued that experience of living between two cultures – between the precious mountain meetings with the Holy God of Israel and the wilderness living with a people who had so much to learn.

In Midian, he simply lived an ordinary life. Through this he was shaped in his character and grew in maturity. He developed the heart of a servant as he worked as a shepherd, learning to be faithful in the small things, even though no one saw but God. Surely, in this, he was prepared for the extraordinary call on his life. For God intended Moses to be shepherd to the nation of Israel: a wayward, stubborn people who, like sheep, did not seem to recognise the need to acknowledge and thank the one leading and caring for them; sheep who were forever wandering away from the safe places and getting into trouble. This hidden time was far from wasted – it was of great value. It took time for the Egyptian ways and wisdom to fade in Moses and for him to learn God's ways and wisdom instead, just as it took Israel time to grow out of being slaves to chosen sons of God.

The hidden place can be distressing and bewildering, especially if it is viewed as abandonment or rejection by God, or even as a punishment from Him. God's timing is for a reason and that is to benefit, prepare and equip you. It is also because there are other circumstances involved that you do not see. Only God knows when and where a need will arise which is exactly where you fit in with your gifts, skills and experiences. Remember that God does not waste anything – He will use it for good. Whilst Moses was a shepherd and family man in Midian, being shaped and moulded by God, back in Egypt the oppression of Israel was causing great distress and the people were calling out to God. Moses was called in response to that cry; He was part of God's rescue plan and discipleship programme for Israel.

We can also turn this around and look at it from the perspective of enslaved Israel, waiting for God to respond. He had heard them. Not only that, but He already knew that Moses was alive and in training for the role he was to play in God's rescue plan. Any time spent suffering will be too long for us, but God has heard and He is responding. In the suffering, it is important to keep our hearts open before God so that He can keep us learning, growing and maturing even in the hardest of times. God's timing can be so difficult to accept and understand, but we see that our stubbornness and refusal to trust His ways will delay God's plans for us. God will always respond to what is in our hearts so ensuring that our hearts are right before Him, even in the suffering and bewilderment is so crucial. It is in that heart position that we mature and find the treasures of God Most High.

It teaches us to turn aside when God interrupts.

For most of us, a burning bush would certainly attract our attention and interest. It seems to be a quick and effective way to get someone's attention. However, a bush on fire was not unusual in the desert and Moses could easily have kept walking, thinking no more about it. It might have niggled away in the back of his mind that there was something different about this bush, but if he had been distracted it could have taken a while for that to register with him. Fortunately, he registered at the time that the bush was on fire yet not being destroyed and so he turned aside to look more closely. He arrived on time for the meeting he did not know he had, and God spoke.

When we are distracted, it is all too easy to notice something without ever properly thinking about it. It can take a while for me to get through the many distractions and things to do to recognise that I am feeling unsettled and restless because God is calling me to sit and listen. Even then, it can take a while for me to 'turn aside' and quieten myself to spend time with Him and tune into what He has to say.

Moses noticed a bush that was on fire, which would not have been unusual. It took a closer look to recognise the aspect that was not quite right. Out of the multitude of thoughts we have, sometimes there will be one that requires us to turn aside and serve God in some way. Asking God why we are feeling unsettled or why something keeps coming to mind can be a useful habit to develop.

I once had a friend come to mind, with a vague sense that I should e-mail, but it was by no means a strong and urgent feeling. As I could not think of anything to say, I planned to leave it for a bit so that I could think of something. That could have gone on indefinitely! However, thankfully I turned aside and began an e-mail at that moment. To start with, it was a general message; but after staring out of the window for a bit at the sunset asking God what He wanted to say, I had a picture for this friend. As I wrote this in my e-mail, a couple of points stood out strongly and I wrote those down too. It was a few days later that I heard back from her and discovered just how she had needed that message from God at that time.

It teaches us that obedience to God is costly.

In any walk of life, we can find ourselves with the decision of who to serve and obey. Shiphrah and Puah were midwives; Esther was queen. All three consciously risked their own lives as they made the choice to honour God rather than an earthly ruler. They placed their own lives in the hands of Almighty God and chose to act rightly before Him; deciding "if I perish, I perish." (Esther 4:16) All three women had the spiritual maturity and wisdom to recognise that turning away from God could save their own lives, but that they would lose something of far greater worth in their souls.

Daniel, Shadrach, Meshach and Abednego were Hebrew exiles in Babylon working in the administration and government of the day, who also repeatedly faced the same choice of who to serve and obey. Daniel and his friends put a boundary in place from the beginning by refusing to eat the food they were offered, on the grounds that it had first been offered to an idol. They had resolved not to compromise, even in something that perhaps could be seen as quite a small matter, so that they would stay spiritually strong. They worked faithfully for the King, unless the King made edicts that were contrary to God's law. In those situations, they obeyed God even though it meant death. When they were ordered to worship an idol of gold, they refused, despite the death penalty being the result – in this case, of being thrown into a furnace and burned alive. (See Daniel 3) The only way that those who hated Daniel could guarantee his downfall was to orchestrate a situation that caused him to obey God rather than King Darius. A decree was issued that for thirty days it was only legal to petition the King. Anyone who petitioned or prayed to any other man or god in that time would be put to death – this time, through being thrown to the lions. Knowing this, Daniel prayed to God at his open window as usual and was sentenced to death. (See Daniel 6)

None of these people had any control over the outcome of their acts of faith. They made their choice, knowing that the consequence was likely to be death, and then had to wait and see what the result would be. They knew that God might miraculously save them from execution or might not. These were genuine life or death decisions, yet that was not the critical point for them. Remarkably, whether they lived or died at the whim of man was less important to them than their spiritual lives before God. The critical point, therefore, was whether they would compromise where the things of God were concerned. Would they bow to idols, knowing that it was expressly forbidden by God? Would they stay silent whilst God's chosen people faced massacre? They each made the courageous decision to honour God above all else, no matter what the outcome, based on the conviction that acting rightly before God was the most important thing that they would ever do.

No matter how much we try to avoid conflict or confrontation in life, there will be times when we cannot escape it. No matter how much we are pacifists and peacemakers at heart, there will be times when we have to take a stand. This may be in making the resolution to put boundaries in with regards to your work situation, refusing to cross the line into anything that does not honour God. We are called to be in the world and not of it, which is modelled perfectly in the book of Daniel. They lived and worked in a land which did not recognise or honour the God of Israel, just as we do. They worked hard in their jobs, with integrity and commitment, but had boundaries that they would not cross no matter what the consequences. This is also what we are required to do. Daniel was given a name that honoured a Babylonian god, Bel, but his heart and worship were all focused on the one true God. He ate no food that had been dedicated to a false god, nor did he worship any man or statue. For Daniel, Shadrach, Meshach and Abednego, they knew that their decision was who to obey and honour; the consequences of that choice were in God's hands.

Reflect and Respond Ideas

Head outside: As you exercise, consider how your physical fitness and resilience has increased over time. Then consider how your faith has increased through different exercises and the impact they have had. For example, repeatedly pushing against obstacles or lifting weights.

Research something: We read of a 'change of season' in Egypt that profoundly impacted people's lives. What other Bible stories show us a change of season? Can you identify any changes of season in your own life or in the world today?

Ponder further: In what ways has your walk with Christ been different to your expectations? List your expectations and then note down the reality next to it. What has been better or worse than expected? Invite God into those things.

Get creative: Get into character as one of the midwives or one of the friends of Daniel and write a journal entry in that character as they consider the choice before them – obeying God or doing something that they knew was against His will.

Faith in the Darkness

The book of Job is an unsettling read. It covers a time of profound darkness and upheaval in one person's life. We want stories to be concluded tidily and satisfactorily and, although the story ends happily, it leaves unresolved questions; much like our own lives.

This book is a remarkable insight into the thought processes and emotions that we experience in times of suffering. Most of the discussions took place when he was on the ash heap in profound physical, emotional, mental and spiritual pain; his distress, loss, anguish and confusion were raw and real. It is a difficult book to read because of this, but it also shows just how important our thoughts and emotions are to the heart of God. These matters are not ignored or covered in a couple of verses before moving onto the happiness of restoration and miracle. In Jewish tradition, seven days were taken following a bereavement for 'shiva:' to step out of normal life to grieve, sitting with friends and family. But mourning does not fit a time-frame and this book shows that the process needs an unlimited time, it needs silence, it needs conversation and dialogue, and it needs God to speak into the situation. The book of Job is 42 chapters long, of which chapters 3 to 37 are conversations about suffering. To put that in context, the history of Joshua leading the people of Israel is 24 chapters long, and the relating of Jonah's story takes just four chapters. Our emotional and mental needs and processes matter deeply to God.

Job was a man who had sought to follow God's ways all his life and who honoured his LORD; a man who knew the favour of God in every area of his life. Then suddenly and systematically, all that he knew, loved and valued was stripped away. In Job 2:8, we find Job sitting on the ash-heap. As he sat there:

He asked why? He searched his own heart and mind, looking for a reason for this complete reversal in his circumstances. He felt abandoned by God, bereaved and confused. Job 7:17-21

He experienced hopelessness, despair and loss of purpose, without relief. "I have been allotted months of futility, and wearisome nights have been appointed to me." Job 7:3-4

He blamed God for taking away his hope and wearing down his resilience and ability to endure. "As water disappears from the sea, and a river becomes parched and dries up, so man lies down and does not rise.... As water wears away stones, and as torrents wash away the soil of the earth; so You destroy the hope of man..." Job 14:11-12, 19

He blamed God for what was happening to him. "The arrows of the Almighty are within me; my spirit drinks in their poison." Job 6:4

He was broken in spirit, as well as in body and heart. Job 17:1

He was bitter of soul and began to view death as a source of relief because he could not see beyond his circumstances. Job 3:20-22 and 6:11

During the trial, in heart-breaking grief, Job simply and understandably felt abandoned and destroyed by his own God, and that is anguish which shakes the very foundations of a believer's life. Job was a righteous man of faith, but this season cost him dearly. Early on, Job asked, "What strength do I have that I should hope? And what is my end, that I should prolong my life?" (Job 6:11). He connected his ability to hope with his own strength, and he had none left. He looked to the future and saw no reason to continue living, because he did not see how his situation could possibly change. He had not done anything differently in life, but calamity had struck him with grief and pain in every possible area of life.

We are body, mind, heart and spirit, so each of those areas will be affected when we go through difficult times. Physically, we can find that our sleep patterns, appetite and energy levels are disrupted, which in turn affect our ability to concentrate, reason, make decisions and maintain perspective. Mentally and emotionally, we can experience anxiety, despair and depression. We can feel that we have lost our identity, everything that made us who we are, because we cannot think, feel and act the way we want to or the way we normally would. There is something about depression that robs us of our ability to communicate with those around us, leading to social isolation and an inability to engage with things we previously enjoyed. Health problems that we, or a loved one, face, impact us as we go through that process of enduring, waiting for results and medical appointments, dealing with the side effects of medication. All of these affect our well-being and ability to cope with the situation before us.

No matter how hard we try to have a good attitude in the darkest of times, there are occasions where we need to bring to God all that is within us: doubts, questions, anger, fear, despair, and so on. We have times when we find that we are sitting on the ash-heap, as Job did.

In the end, Job answered his own questions, still in the season of not knowing. He renewed his trust in the Lord *before* he was delivered and restored; even though he could not see God in his circumstances and it felt like He was absent. He proclaimed,

> "I know that my Redeemer lives and He shall stand at last on the earth... this I know, that in my flesh I shall see God..."
> Job 19:25-26

Later on, he proclaimed that the Lord,

> "...knows the way that I take; when He has tested me, I shall come forth as gold. My foot has held fast to His steps; I have kept His way and not turned aside. I have not departed from the commandment of His lips; I have treasured the words of His mouth more than my necessary food." Job 23:10-12

I believe this is an example of Job receiving the gift of faith, upon which he could stand. (See 1 Cor. 12:9) He received a revelation of eternal truths, which enabled him to speak out about the ultimate victory of God. It is also a prophetic statement for this is long before Jesus came, yet Job stated the truth that "my Redeemer lives and He shall stand at last on the earth." Surely this is the power of the Holy Spirit at work in this time of darkness on the ash-heap, enabling Job to speak of the Messiah and the salvation that was to come.

Job's consolation came from becoming convinced deep in his soul of these eternal truths: that he would see God, that his Redeemer lived and that through enduring, he would be purified into gold. Job needed to recognise that it was not his fault that such tragedy had befallen him and that holding onto God during the time of devastation was worth it. He was able to state that the things of God were of greater worth than any material thing. The change was in his attitude, not in his circumstances.

In this instance, the Bible gives us an insight into what was going on behind the scenes, but this was unknown to Job. We also have the advantage of knowing the end of the story so we know that Job's words and feelings of deep despair will not last forever. We know that he will be restored to health and prosperity once more. I doubt anyone at the time (or even now) could have provided any kind of valid response to Job's questions, but as he expressed deep emotions and griefs to God, the Holy Spirit guided him into the revelations he needed to endure and overcome in faith.

As with Elijah, Job experienced a profound shaking in all that he had believed. At the end of the trial, he still believed but in a deeper and more profound way because he had come to that faith through the hurricane, the earthquake and the fire. If we take Job's story metaphorically, we see things stripped away that can be the source of our worth and sense of God's blessing: status, the respect of the community, work, wealth, prosperity, achievement, family, health. Job was left entirely vulnerable – there was nothing left but him in his rawest, most vulnerable state. He lost everything; he questioned everything and still concluded that God was God: his personal and known Redeemer.

Sometimes, life is just hard for us. There are times when just a word from God would help alleviate our sufferings and He is silent. Declarations of faith in these times of anguish have profound significance because, despite everything that is happening and how we feel in those circumstances, we have determined to push through in faith and trust regardless. That is a powerful overcoming of Satan's works against us. We always want to understand why we are going through something, to know what God is up to and why. To declare eternal truths of God's character and resurrection power despite the circumstances, no matter what the outcome, is a powerful and charged act of faith.

When Jesus failed to arrive in time to heal Lazarus, his bereaved sister Martha went to meet Jesus with reproach and hurt that He had not come when they needed Him so desperately. She spoke out her circumstances and her emotions to Jesus. She did not ignore Him or refuse to see Him on the grounds that she was hurt and never wanted to see Him again. She did not tell all her friends how betrayed she felt, staying bitter and resentful. She did not decide to respect Jesus's teachings as an interesting philosophy, withdrawing her love from him and keeping Him out of her heart. She took everything directly to the only one who could help her. In her time of grief and sense of abandonment, Martha made four declarations of faith:

1. "Lord, if You had been here, my brother would not have died."

2. "But even now I know that whatever You ask of God, God will give You…"

3. "I know that [Lazarus] will rise again in the resurrection at the last day"

4. "I believe that You are the Christ, the Son of God, who is to come into the world.' John 11:1-44

Martha believed correctly that Jesus could have healed her sick brother and His delay in coming did not change that belief. We do not always see God heal our loved ones this side of Heaven, and that is never easy to accept or understand. To have an attitude of 'even now I know' is powerful. Remember, Martha made these statements *before* Jesus raised Lazarus from the dead. She still knew that her brother would be resurrected at the end of days and that Jesus was the Messiah. This was a statement of faith but also a sign that she had received the revelation of the Holy Spirit as to Jesus' true identity. She stood before Jesus in faith that He was the Messiah. Martha made this remarkable choice to express her faith in the darkness of grief, without any hint or promise of a miracle.

For us, under God's new covenant, our strength is in Christ. We have the gift of the Holy Spirit working within us, to comfort and guide us through darkness and through storms. Our hope is in Christ: the hope of glory, the hope of a way where there seems to be no way. Our present and our future is in God's hands: the God who promises that whatever Satan means for evil, He will use for good. We look in faith to resurrection and eternal life, then declare God's ability to redeem all that we go through. We declare those eternal truths in the power of the Holy Spirit, who enables us in even the darkest of times.

Earlier in this chapter, we read these words from 1 John:

'For whatever is born of God overcomes the world. And this is the victory that has overcome the world – our faith. Who is he who overcomes the world, but he who believes that Jesus is the Son of God?'

Our faith in Jesus Christ as the Son of God, is the source of the victory that has overcome the things of this world. Persevering in faith through the trials and challenges of this world, is part of our overcoming them. As we overcome, we take hold of and receive the promises of life.[21]

Respond

As an act of faith, speak out Job's declaration over whatever darkness you face (Job 19:25-26). Then proclaim, as Martha did, that Jesus Christ is Lord (John 11:27). Use these eternal truths to release the strength of God into your soul and enable you to stand and withstand.

The Shield of Faith

Scripture says, *above all*, take up the shield of faith which protects us from the fiery darts of the enemy. Fiery darts are those untrue words of accusation that cause faith to deflate and leave us bound by shame, condemnation, guilt, fear and so on. Crossbows could fire bolts long distances. If a crossbowman fired from a castle, through an arrow-slit, they would never be seen, but the bolt would hit its mark with great force. They were the proverbial 'bolts from the blue,' which we did not see coming, but which wound deeply. We cannot stop them from being fired at us, but we can block them.

---

[21] See Revelation chapters 2 and 3, where the messages to the churches are given an area of correction and a promise of the rewards of overcoming, specifically Revelation 2:7, 11, 17, 26; 3:5, 12 and 21.

We have a choice and responsibility here: it is up to us to pray the shield of faith into position. If we leave it by our side or vacillate between lifting and lowering it, we will be hit by the fiery darts. In battle, the shield needed to be in place before the arrow hit, not afterwards. Similarly, we need to have our shield of faith raised in readiness within us; armed and protected by the knowledge that we do not face anything alone but with the help and power of the Holy Spirit within us. We stand firm, knowing that whatever other people say about us, we are created and accepted by God Most High.

We need to make that choice and keep our shield raised. We need to be vigilant in applying our faith so that it will protect us. We continually make the choice to trust God and to stand on truth as a step of faith, which gives us the steadfastness to stand and endure. This takes perseverance, just like any soldier in a training exercise. The more they put the skills into practice, the quicker their reflexes become and the quicker their recovery time is. Faith is built in the tough times; it is established, deepened and strengthened in darkness.

In the darkness, we do not necessarily experience individual wounds being sustained. It can be more like an illness where everything feels wrong and we do not know what to believe anymore. Through the gift of the Holy Spirit, it was in the darkness that Job and Martha were able to speak out the revealed truth of the sovereignty and ultimate victory of God Most High, regardless of what the earthly outcome turned out to be.

God also calls us to be in fellowship with one another: to be one body in Christ, with our different skills and strengths working together for the kingdom of God. One historical military strategy was for soldiers to stand shoulder to shoulder with their shields raised in front of them and meeting together to create a shield wall. This created strength as well as protection for the army, allowing them to push back against an oncoming force. This is a good image for the need to stand with others in prayer and faith: all facing the same direction, with the strength to keep our shields in position, standing shoulder to shoulder with our shields of faith linked.

This was the method used by the Anglo-Saxon army at the Battle of Hastings in 1066. The Normans knew that they could not successfully attack and breach the Anglo-Saxon shield wall because it created such a strong defensive position. Therefore, they used a trick to cause the Anglo-Saxons to break up their own shield wall. Instead of attacking, the Normans pretended to retreat and run away from the battle. Upon seeing this, Anglo-Saxon soldiers on the flanks abandoned their positions in the shield wall and gave chase. This weakened the Anglo-Saxon line and left themselves completely vulnerable. As the Normans turned back and attacked them, they were easily defeated. King Harold was subsequently killed and Duke William of Normandy was victorious. Had they held their positions, keeping the shield wall in place, the outcome could have been very different.

We are to have a strong shield wall of faith as Christians. This can only be done as we stand and withstand in faith with others, so we need to be wise about what the enemy is doing to deceive us, to separate us away from the group and to leave us vulnerable. I was struck by a film I saw many years ago, which spoofed superhero films. There was a team of heroes with superpowers ... or rather, what they viewed as superpowers. In one scene, the team sought out some gadgets to help them overcome the bad guys and they were given a weapon called a 'blame thrower.' When activated, it caused people on the same team to turn against one another in angry accusation. A very effective weapon! Blame, accusation, shaming and criticising others, are all weapons that cause us to break our shield wall and allow the enemy to divide and scatter us. We need to keep our shield wall strong and effective, resolving any disputes between us with the help of the Holy Spirit.

We are human. We will fall down, get tired, lose motivation and get distracted. We will have days when taking up a shield of faith to resist the evil one feels too hard, too much, too overwhelming. Firstly, we can ask God's help in stirring us up when we feel that way. We can still lift our eyes to Him and cry out for His mighty hand to show us the path of life in our thoughts and emotions. Secondly, when we are shoulder to shoulder with others, it is easier to recognise when someone is struggling and to respond with prayer and practical help. We keep going: soldiers in the faith alongside each other, cheering each other on and supporting each other when we feel tired and weak. This is all part of our shield wall of faith: building one another up, supporting each other in Godly decision-making and discernment of what is going on around each other, helping each other to heal when we get hurt. Keep that shield wall in place in your friendships and fellowship: it needs to be healthy, strong and committed.

Reflect and Respond Ideas

Head outside: Watch some team sports and focus on the strategies at work. How do you see team-mates working together to score? Where do you see something not working and why? How can we relate this to how we work together in church?

Research something: Look into the training that athletes do in order to run the different distances in competitions. How does the preparation vary between a sprint and a marathon? What does that teach us about the preparation we need for our spiritual race?

Ponder further: Have you experienced a 'blame-thrower' at work in the church? How can we respond to this in a way that leads to greater unity and a strong 'shield wall' of faith?

Get creative: Design a shield for yourself or your church. What would you have on it to represent your faith and trust in Jesus Christ as your Saviour?

HOPE

elpis ... (Greek)

Hope, not in the sense of an optimistic outlook
or wishful thinking without any foundation,
but in the sense of confident expectation based on solid certainty.... [22]

The language of hope is so common to us. We hope for things throughout each day – good weather, a good meeting, good opportunities; for desires and dreams to be fulfilled; for prayers to be answered. We hope for good things.

We have already seen that we cannot escape trials and tribulations in life. They will come. In those times, we *hope* that the trials will be over quickly; we *hope* that there will be a positive outcome; we *hope* that good will come out of it. We *hope*, but we are not *certain* of these things. We have no assurance or guarantee about the duration of a trial or the outcome. This is a 'situational hope' – our natural, general hope for a positive outcome to situations, rather than a negative one. It does not influence the outcome, but it is our preference and on what we choose to dwell. After all, the alternative is hopelessness: the belief or understanding that there are no more options, that there will not be a positive outcome, that there is no way through the situation.

So much of this can be linked to our personality and outlook on life, whether we happen to be a 'glass half full' person or not. Some people are naturally buoyant and able to see things positively. Others are more likely to catastrophise and feel that there is no way through. Having a positive, hope-filled perspective does bring life to us: it is part of our original design. However, Biblical hope takes us beyond person-

---

[22] Definition taken from the supplementary notes of *The Spirit-Filled Life Bible*, p. 1826

ality into providing us with a strong and secure position that enables us to stand and withstand the dark times. There is a need to nurture hope-filled attitudes based on something unshakeable and eternal.

We need eternal hope: hope based on the unshakeable truth of God. The fact that the definition used for 'hope' uses the words confident and solid, expectation and certainty, all indicate that we are looking at something formidable and resilient. This is the hope that sustained Job when everything was lost: the confident expectation, the solid certainty, that his Redeemer lived and that he would see God. (Job 19:25-26)

There is nothing ephemeral or weak about this hope. This is hope as a fortress, as a stronghold that gives us protection against every weapon of the evil one. This is hope as the wellspring of life that sustains us, refreshes us, and brings us all that we need to keep on keeping on. This is hope as the strength of our hearts, causing courage and determination to grow within us. This is hope that causes us to get back up off the floor and to fight another day.

Holding and Held

In Hebrews, we are instructed to '... lay hold of the hope set before us,' just as we would pick up any tangible, physical object. (Hebrews 6:18) We are told to grasp it, grip it and not let go of it. We only do that when something is of surpassing worth to us, which must be protected; or when something is vital to our very existence. Hope is not a decorative or optional item, but an essential, life-bringing piece of equipment.

The hope is there, before us. Our part is to grasp the eternal hope that we have in our unchanging, faithful God, and put it to work as a tool and protective garment in our lives.

So, where do we find this eternal hope? There are two sources that are interlinked: salvation and Scripture. Salvation through Jesus Christ is our reason for hope, and it is through Scripture that we find knowledge and encouragement about the wonders of that salvation. It is in the Bible that we find the tools and skills that we need to stand strong despite disappointment, depression and doubt.

Salvation

Basing our hope in the work of Christ is central, which is why we are instructed to 'put on as a helmet the hope of salvation,' (1 Thess. 5:8). Helmets are a critical part of armour, quite understandably, as they protect the head where all our mental and emotional processing takes place. Twice, Paul compares the protection of the head with salvation and the hope it gives to believers (here and in Ephesians 6) which emphasises the need to guard our minds.

Soldiers need to put on their helmets *before* going into battle, not part way through. They need that protection in place as soon as possible so they can focus on responding to the situation before them. Similarly, cyclists or riders put a helmet on before setting out on a bike or on horseback. During the journey, or when an accident is imminent, is too late. Praying on the helmet of the hope of salvation is preparation for whatever we do: it needs to happen before we get started on our daily jobs. It is what guards our minds from the things that cause hopelessness, anxiety, apathy, distractions and all the other things that impact our mood and attitudes every day. It is what guards our minds from temptations and anything that takes our focus away from Jesus and the things of His kingdom.

Salvation gives us the eternal perspective we need: that God is sovereign, has defeated sin and death, and walks with us in whatever we face. This needs to be the filter for our thought processes. It is human nature to begin with the problem and dwell in that situation with all the difficulties and disasters that could result; but we feel increasingly helpless if we do not have a solution or any means to guarantee a good outcome. If we choose to dwell in the hope that comes from knowing that God's sovereignty and power are at work on our behalf, we begin to release life-bringing hope into our lives.

If we take that to the next level by looking at *eternal* hope, then our hope is no longer founded on the outcome of any situation. We already have sonship, redemption and life assured in the presence and glory of God. Place this knowledge on your head as a helmet because we are not promised an easy life or a fast-track through tribulations. The apostles were clear on the need to balance out the sufferings of life now with what was to come. They wrote having experienced much suffering and correctly expecting there to be more suffering before they died. Paul wrote:

> 'The Spirit Himself bears witness with our spirit that we are children of God, and if children, then heirs – heirs of God and joint heirs with Christ, if indeed we suffer with Him, that we may also be glorified together. For I consider that the sufferings of this present time are not worthy to be compared with the glory which shall be revealed in us.'
> Romans 8:16-18

The apostle Peter spoke out blessing upon God who had brought us,

> '... a living hope through the resurrection of Jesus Christ from the dead, to an inheritance incorruptible and undefiled and that does not fade away, reserved in heaven for you, who are kept by the power of God through faith ...
>
> In this you greatly rejoice, though now for a little while, if need be, you have been grieved by various trials, that the genuineness of your faith, being much more precious than gold that perishes, though it is tested by fire, may be found to praise, honour and glory at the revelation of Jesus Christ...' 1 Peter 1:3-7

Was Peter thinking of Job's words as he wrote his letter? Both wrote of the development of something of greater value than gold, through the testing of fire refining the metal to something in its purest and most costly form. What we go through this side of Heaven is bearing fruit: a treasure that is eternal, pure, costly and glorious before God the Father. This is hope that brings life, refreshing and a reason to keep going. This is hope that develops resilience, perseverance and courage. As Peter said, this hope is a *living* hope: it is vibrant, transformative and actively working in us. If we have hope, we have reason to get up and get on with our lives. If we feel hopeless then the opposite is true: we lose motivation, energy and life.

What we hope for is the inheritance awaiting us: something that will not be corrupted, defiled or fade away. We have hope because that inheritance is secured in Heaven for us. We have hope because God's power will keep us in the meantime, until salvation is brought to its fullness.

As we suffer in His name now, we can have the solid certainty of being glorified with Him. More than that, there is a glory to be revealed in us. Paul went on to explain that now we, along with creation, wait with expectation for the eternal things. We wait for everything to be made new and glorious; free, unmarred, without corruption or decay. It is a painful waiting process, compared to the pains of giving birth. This gives us the context of the season that creation is in: it is a labouring in bringing forth life, a process that was intended to be without pain or struggle. There is an eternal knowledge that this is not how it was meant to be, but we stand in the hope that all things will be made new once more and creation restored to God's plans and purposes. (See Romans 8:18-25)

This qualifies as hope because we are trusting in something that is unseen and not experienced in its fullness: the glory yet to come as both we and God's creation are made new. We are all too familiar with things that cause suffering – that is what we see, hear about, experience. We quite naturally focus on what our immediate experience is. Paul, who experienced suffering in a variety of forms, was convinced that those sufferings were going to fade into insignificance when the glory was eventually revealed.

Death is not the end for those who believe. At that moment, we reach the finish line with all of heaven cheering us into the Kingdom of God. We wake eternally to live the life we were created for. From that moment, Satan can no longer block the fullness of God's goodness and healing in our lives. This is one race we can all win, no matter what our sporting ability is like! Satan loses and we have the victory through Christ. Praise God!

God still remembers all that His apostles suffered for His sake. He remembers all that His children suffer for His sake – it matters to Him more deeply than we can ever know. But now, Peter and Paul do not remember their sufferings. Every tear has been wiped away from their eyes by their King, the one they lived and died for. They do not relive those memories or the pain. They now live in the glory of God's presence and everything else has faded away. It was the knowledge of this and the hope it caused that anchored their souls on Earth.

In Scripture

Where do we find these reasons to hope? In the Word of God. We find the truth of salvation within its pages, in the words of Jesus and the heart cry of our God. We find the testimony of those who have gone before along with all that they have found to be true in the worst of times.

The Psalms regularly testify to the need to hope in God's word in the challenges of life, whether they were caused by sin or opposition or circumstance. Instead of basing our hope on emotional reasons, we are encouraged to base our hope on the truth of the Word of God because this is unchanging, just as God Himself is unchanging. The Bible does not ignore the trials of life, and it certainly does not make any claim for it to be easy to hope in the darkness. It is a choice, and as we make that choice, the Holy Spirit meets us and helps us go further than we could go in our own strength.

In Hebrews 6:19, hope is described as, 'an anchor of the soul, both sure and steadfast.' An anchor is used when we are pausing in a journey, either to rest or because the weather conditions demand it. The anchor prevents a boat from being swept off course, wherever the tide or current would take it. Hope is compared to a reliable anchor in our souls that holds us securely. This is a perfect image of how the gifts of God go to work on our behalf because it is not the job of the sailor to hold the boat still by hope, willpower, force or some special skill. The work of the sailor is to deploy the anchor when needed so it can fulfil its function. Our part is to put the anchor of hope into action. Once it has been released, it does its job and holds us securely in position.

Ocean water is never still: it constantly moves with the tides, currents and winds. An anchor allows a certain amount of movement for a boat or ship on the surface of the water, so we can still expect our emotions and thoughts to fluctuate. However, we can trust that we are held and that we will not be moved from that position of anchorage. A boat can only move to the extent that the anchor chain allows.

We should not be afraid of experiencing those fluctuations of thought and emotion in storms or times of shaking. In areas prone to earthquakes, architects have replaced traditional designs with structures that allow for the building to be shaken. Rigid structures are more likely to collapse, whereas structures that allow for a certain amount of movement are more likely to stand.

When we need to pause in the journey to rest or to stand firm in the storms, we need to deploy that anchor of hope. The Psalms never gloss over the darkness but are full of the choice to hope and trust in God despite it. Psalm 119, for instance, includes these verses:

'Remember the word to Your servant, upon which You have caused me to hope. This is my comfort in my affliction, for Your word has given me life.' Ps. 119:49-50

'My soul faints for Your salvation, but I hope in Your word... Forever, O LORD, Your word is settled in heaven. Your faithfulness endures to all generations ... Unless Your law had been my delight, I would then have perished in my affliction. I will never forget Your precepts, for by them You have given me life.' Ps. 119:81, 89-90, 92-93

'You are my hiding place and my shield; I hope in Your word.' Ps. 119:114

The word of God brings hope, comfort and life as the Psalmist chooses to continue following God's ways. These are not platitudes that might lift our mood. How could they be? The Psalms are full of the distress of people in all kinds of situations where they need God's help because there is no other way through. The Psalmist was holding onto the word of God because that was where he found life and reason to hope. This was his anchor, his refuge, the lifebelt he was holding onto for dear life. He was looking to God as his shield, as tangible protection from whatever was faced on Earth, because only God was and is above and beyond every circumstance.

When times are hard we need good tools, solid ground and we need clarity. We find a sure foundation and a strong anchor when we place our hope in the eternal power and faithfulness of God to bring us through the storms. We find protection for our thoughts and emotions as we put on the helmet of salvation and choose to tune our thoughts into things that are life-bringing. We find refreshing and perspective for our souls as we drink in the truth of the Word of God and let it enter every part of us.

In times of judgement, the Psalmist remembers that those times do not last forever. His pain is evident as he clearly expresses his desperation and need for deliverance. He does not hide that from God, but he chooses to hope in God's word and faithfulness. When we hope in the things of God, we can be confident that they will be fulfilled. Not necessarily in the way we expect or in the time-frame we would like, but God never stops working on our behalf. Jesus never stops being the way for us in our circumstances; He never stops being the truth; He never stops being the source of our life, eternally and in the here and now.

Having God's word hidden in our hearts is a treasure in itself. This brings us wisdom and help whenever we need it. The more familiar we are with Scriptures, the more we have stored away in our memories so that the Holy Spirit can bring them to the front of our minds when needed. These Scriptures can also then be used to cultivate mind and heart attitudes of godly hope and confidence. Having God's law in our hearts keeps us on the correct path, which gives us the confidence that we are right before Him.

Remember that your emotions will not be onboard with this to begin with. On the contrary, you are likely to find that your emotions will be dragging you down and telling you that it is not worth the effort. They are likely to tell you that there is no hope, that there is no good stuff coming and that God might come through for other people but He will not bother for you. When that happens, arm yourself and anchor yourself. Our part is to open our hearts to hope, even when our reason and logic is telling us that it is all over.

Reflect and Respond Ideas

Head outside: Head to the coast to watch the ocean for a while. Pay attention to the movement of the waves as the unseen currents and winds affect the water. Think about how you feel when you are on the water – it might be exhilarating for you, or you might get sea-sick! How do you respond to the movement in your thoughts and emotions?

Research something: Read through the whole of Psalm 119. How many reasons are given for having confidence in God and His Word?

Ponder further: Do you find the words in the Bible comforting and full of life and hope? If this is not your experience, ask the Holy Spirit to reveal the treasures of Scripture to you.

Get creative: You might want to read John Donne's short poem, *Death, be not Proud*, which confidently states the victory we have through Christ. Write your own poem, in whatever style, full of the confident hope and eternal life we have in Christ.

Hope Deferred

Holding onto hope when it seems that everything has gone wrong is one of the challenges we face. When it seems as though our trust in God was not justified and doubts flood in about His goodness and plans for us. When we hoped for something good and godly, but time after time our hopes are crushed and we find ourselves with broken, confused hearts.

Consider Joseph, the favoured son, adored and spoiled by his father, Jacob. We are familiar with many aspects of his story, but why was he singled out for favour? To understand this, we need to look back to Jacob's earlier life.

The household of Jacob was divided, full of rivalry and jealousy. Jacob wanted to marry Rachel but had been tricked into marrying her older sister, Leah, instead. Jacob subsequently married Rachel as well. This was the first point of contention: two sisters married to the same man, who loved one sister but not the other. The battleground between the sisters became the bearing of children. This was the second point of contention, for Leah had several sons but Rachel was unable to conceive. Like Sarah had done before her, Rachel asked Jacob to have children by her servant, which he did. As Leah had stopped conceiving by then, she also asked Jacob to have children by her servant, which he did. Eventually, Rachel gave birth to Joseph but died having given birth to her second son, Benjamin. Jacob had twelve sons, born to four mothers. As the children of these women grew they were aware of, and involved in, the dispute of their mothers.

Joseph was Jacob's eleventh son but he was the firstborn son of Rachel, whom Jacob loved and later lost in childbirth. This was what set him apart from all the other sons. Over time, his ten older brothers must surely have realised that Joseph was cherished in a way that they never would be. It is into this context of envy, rivalry, bitterness and resentment, that we find the teenaged Joseph enjoying the easy life whilst his brothers laboured. It seems reasonable to assume that Joseph was absorbed in his own life and all the pleasures he expected that to involve. If that was not bad enough, Joseph then had dreams of his family bowing down before him. These were not daydreams or wishful thinking, but prophetic visions of something that would be.

We may never have had dreams like that in our teenage years but, when we are young, we naturally tend to anticipate and daydream about the highlight moments of life (career and personal) rather than the difficult times we might go through to get there. We can confidently assume that life will involve certain things, without considering the possibility that those things might not happen as God has something else for us. As we go through life, we often need to adjust to what is, rather than what we expected. Joseph's experience illustrates that perfectly. Why would he envision anything other than a comfortable life, growing in status and glory? But quite the opposite happened, because his brothers had had enough. Years of resentment boiled over and they threw Joseph into a pit, planning to go back later and kill him. However, they saw some traders nearby and decided to sell their brother into slavery instead. Having done so, they splattered blood over Joseph's special coat, over that symbol of all the love that Jacob had given to Joseph and not to them, then pretended that Joseph had been killed by an animal. Joseph was taken into Egypt and sold as a slave there.

How could it ever have occurred to Joseph that his dreams would be fulfilled after the overthrow of everything he knew? That his future place of favour and status would come through the complete loss of his home, family, freedom and his rights? That this, in itself, would come through the jealousy-fuelled hatred of his brothers, who would first leave him to die and then sell him into slavery?

Joseph went from an extremely protected and privileged life, with a divine dream of his family bowing to him, to desperate circumstances that could not have been further from his expectations. He was suddenly completely powerless before his brothers in the pit and then powerless on the slave-traders' cart. For what might have been the first time of his life, Joseph was not listened to; his needs and wants were ignored. He became a commodity to trade. He not only had to work but he became the one who served others in complete obedience, not the one served.

It is difficult to imagine the kind of trauma that Joseph went through and the record of his life does not include much about Joseph's emotions or thoughts during this part of his life. Essentially, we are told the key events that dramatically changed Joseph's circumstances. Firstly, Joseph was bought by Potiphar, an Egyptian officer of Pharaoh. When Joseph spurned the amorous advances of his master's wife, she falsely accused him of attacking her and he was sent to prison where other prisoners of the king were held.

Remarkably, a pattern strongly emerges in these circumstances. As a slave and as a prisoner, Joseph was 'a successful man.' Would we ever think of combining these concepts: slavery, false imprisonment, success? In both instances, Joseph was given promotion and authority, with considerable trust placed in him.[23] We are told of God prospering all that Joseph did and working through him. It was in the darkness that Joseph found that the LORD was truly with him and this was evident to those around him. This was such an important change in Joseph's life. Previously, what had set Joseph apart was the favouritism of his father. In Egypt, he had no spectacular coat to impress others or to grab their attention or their respect. No one knew or cared that he was the treasured firstborn son of Rachel. Now, he gained attention because other people recognised that if they had Joseph with them, then God was also there.

Joseph acted with complete integrity and God prospered him in the sight of his masters:

---

[23] See Genesis 39:2, then Genesis 39:4-6 and 22-23

'And his master saw that the LORD was with him and that the LORD made all he did to prosper in his hand... the LORD blessed the Egyptian's house for Joseph's sake; and the blessing of the LORD was on all that he had in the house and in the field.' Genesis 39:3 and 5

'And the keeper of the prison committed to Joseph's hand all the prisoners who were in the prison; whatever they did there, it was his doing. The keeper of the prison did not look into anything that was under Joseph's authority, because the LORD was with him; and whatever he did, the LORD made it prosper.' Gen. 39:22-23

As everything Joseph knew was stripped away, he was most able to encounter God, most able to serve God with humility and integrity, most able to become mature in faith and attitude, and to trust God that He would bring him through at the right time. Joseph's conduct spoke volumes and it was correctly identified as God's presence with him, by Potiphar, by the prison guard and eventually, by Pharaoh himself.

Because Joseph had been imprisoned with the king's prisoners, he came into contact with members of Pharaoh's household, including the chief baker and chief butler who had both committed offences. The divine moment for release seemed to come when Joseph had the opportunity to interpret their dreams. He asked the butler to remember him when he was released and plead his case before Pharaoh. There was hope, a potential ending of the wilderness season. Yet, Genesis 40 ends with the heart-breaking crushing of this hope. It simply says, 'Yet the chief butler did not remember Joseph, but forgot him.' How many hours, then days, then weeks, did Joseph wait before he had to accept that the butler had forgotten all about him and that precious promise to speak up for him? How many times did he think, *if I just wait a bit longer the release will come ... surely God is in this so maybe today...*

Hope is closely connected to our expectations of what will be, how we anticipate that coming to pass and when it will happen. When we find ourselves heading the opposite way, our confidence begins to crumble. This can happen repeatedly as we set our hearts to building up our faith, only to find that hope and confidence crumble once more.

We question how this could be God's plan for our lives, just as Joseph must surely have done. We rarely know the duration of difficult seasons so part of the challenge is to trust God when we cannot see any way through to resolution or a positive outcome.

But God had not forgotten Joseph. The very next verse marks the next season of Joseph's life, the season that all of this preparation in the darkness was for:

'Then it came to pass, at the end of two full years, that Pharaoh had a dream ...' Genesis 41:1

This dream disturbed Pharaoh greatly, but no one was able to interpret it for him. It was once he had exhausted all his options that his chief butler remembered Joseph and his ability to interpret dreams. Joseph was able to interpret the dream, giving full and complete honour to the God who had revealed the meaning to him for Pharaoh. Once more, Joseph found favour, and this time, with Pharaoh.

'And Pharaoh said to his servants, "Can we find such a one as this, a man in whom is the Spirit of God?"' Gen. 41:38

Joseph was a man set apart from others because the Spirit of God was in him and this was evident because of the divine blessings that accompanied him. He was set apart, not by his father's favouritism, but by the favour of God.

For much of this season of his life, it is possible that Joseph did not feel favoured: I doubt he woke up in prison day after day, with the smells, the heat and the noise, thinking 'how favoured I am! God clearly loves me to place me here!' It is important that we are wise in this and do not base our view of God's love for us on our circumstances. Joseph could all too easily have seen slavery and prison as signs of God's displeasure, wrath ... perhaps even God's dislike of him. Perhaps he had moments where that felt true.

But for the most part, the story suggests that Joseph developed a relationship with God that was so strong and secure, he knew he was loved regardless of where he happened to be. By this part of the story, there is such a sense that you never got Joseph without God. Whatever filthy job Joseph did as a slave, he did it with God. If Joseph was serving at the table, the Spirit of God was there with him. Whatever responsibilities he was given, he fulfilled them with God. If a dream needed interpretation, it was God's response that was spoken. When Joseph was called to do something, you never just got Joseph. You got Joseph and the Spirit of God together, in partnership.

Joseph had chosen to serve God faithfully in every circumstance and God blessed him as he exercised and matured in using both his temporal and his spiritual gifts. Both were needed in what was to come. He was able to hear the voice of God telling him the interpretation of the dream but also the practical strategy for dealing with what was to come. In God's timing, it came to pass that Joseph was raised from imprisoned slave to second highest in the land. It was God's will that Joseph be in position for this season in Egypt, fully equipped with both temporal and spiritual skills; along with the humility, wisdom of heart and spirit to fulfil God's purposes.

Joseph's Heart

Our hearts matter to God, along with the priorities, attitudes and choices they hold. But more than that, *who we are* matters to God. If there are things within us that do not honour Him or that cause us to behave out of brokenness or pride, God will want to tackle those things.

Status was a theme of Joseph's life. Simply through his father's attitude and behaviour towards him, Joseph enjoyed a status that his older brothers did not have. He was indulged and pampered, protected from harm and exempted from the necessary labours of life. His brothers' hearts were bitter and resentful that they worked without reward or notice, whilst their young half-brother was treasured and given expensive gifts that set him even further above them. Not for Joseph the rough working garments fit for the fields, but a glorious and unique coat that was purely for show: a sign of his father's devotion, a sign that he did not have to work, a sign that he was special. In this household of brothers, Joseph was treated as a prince amongst the labourers and he acted as such. He seemed to have little empathy or concern for others and was apparently unaware of (or indifferent to) his brothers' animosity towards him.

It was in this context that he had the dreams of his family bowing down to him. As his brothers were already effectively acting as servants to him, it must have seemed very natural that one day they would bow down to him. Joseph was clearly not lacking in confidence or pride, but then he had no reason to because he was so highly valued. If we contrast this reaction to that of Mary, when told that she would become pregnant with the Son of God, we see a clear difference. Joseph bragged and boasted, telling those around him of his dream. What could be more natural than a life where people bowed down to him? But Mary had no such pride or conceit. She accepted the will of God with humility and wonder, treasuring the things she was told *in her heart*. (Luke 2:51)

From the treasured and favoured son, to slave, to convicted prisoner, Joseph went lower and lower in the social order of the day. He no longer had control over his own destiny and the easy future he had envisaged was suddenly replaced with a brutal reality. As a slave, he had to work: he had no choice in this, no rights, no voice. His past life and status were irrelevant. He had been sold by his brothers and then sold again in order to work. He had been purchased: he was owned, a possession of his master to do with as he wished. Joseph could have worked with a sullen, grudging attitude, yet the wonder is that he worked hard and honoured God through his heart attitude of integrity and service as a slave. This is an astonishing thing: this young man who had never had to work before, chose to work and to do so with diligence.

We do not know what happened between Joseph and God in the pit his brothers threw him into, when Joseph had no choice but to wait and see whether his brothers would murder him or leave him there to die; or on the cart when he was taken to Egypt against his will to be sold·like a household item. However, I suspect that God did meet with Joseph in those times and that this enabled him to approach his new life with a heart that was humble and accepting of the circumstances. I doubt he did so perfectly, but the fact that he was willing and able to do this at all is worthy of note. In slavery, Joseph put his heart into working because his heart had moved into the right place before God. God had been at work there.

He found favour in God's eyes and in Potiphar's through his work and attitude. In prison, Joseph was more hidden still, but again he found favour with God and with the guards because of his heart of faith and integrity. Joseph refused to let go of God and he refused to compromise on God's standards. Faithful service in the lowest of offices was his equipping and preparation for faithful service in the highest of offices. However, the key point is that by this point in his life, wherever Joseph served, no matter what role he was called to fulfil, he would have done so with a servant heart. That was the treasure worked out within him – a treasure that was of surpassing worth in the kingdom of God and a treasure that was of far greater worth than anything Pharaoh could give him.

Enduring

With many people in the Bible, we have a glimpse of a moment or season in their lives, but Joseph's story is recorded over many years because we need to be reminded of two things.

Firstly, that our circumstances do not indicate either God's pleasure or displeasure with us. Biblical hope is based on the eternal perspective that goes far beyond our immediate circumstances, trusting that God is at work. God's ways are not our ways. Joseph would have had no concept that God's plans for his life would be fulfilled through exile from his home, slavery and imprisonment. God works through situations that could destroy us; He works through the waiting and the enduring. Waiting seems passive, but it is both a calling and a discipline. Waiting for God's timing feels costly to us, especially when it seems to us that time is running out and that failure awaits; but there is always a reason for God's timing that we rarely understand without the benefit of hindsight. Because of that, waiting is an act of trust and determination.

Secondly, that regardless of what our circumstances are, we are called to walk and endure in integrity, faithfulness and righteousness before God. In slavery and in prison, Joseph had a choice as to whether to continue to follow God or not. He still had freewill to choose his attitudes and priorities in his heart and soul. Had he chosen to live in bitterness and reject everything to do with God, his story would have been very different; had he not resisted Potiphar's wife, things would have been different again. Continually choosing God in the darkness and enduring righteously before Him provided a remarkable environment for transformation. Joseph's heart became so focused on God alone, that he chose to hold onto God and to serve Him wherever God placed him. Yes, he wanted to get out of prison; yes, he wanted to live life in freedom and joy and he hoped for those things. But if God kept him in prison, then Joseph would faithfully serve Him there.

Joseph was able to lead with humility and wisdom in the public arena because that was how he had lived in the hidden darkness of his early adult life. He did not suddenly change his personality or character in that moment of appointment to high office. In the prison and the palace, Joseph was the same man. He rightly prized God in his life and recognised that he was being positioned in high office for purposes that were far more important than Pharaoh's.

The process of waiting and enduring is one that continually challenges us to choose God, even when we do not know what He is doing – *especially* when we do not know what He is doing. Something beyond price is worked out in us as we walk that place of struggle with God and as we repeatedly choose to:

- follow God even though our lives are not turning out the way we wanted, because we have come to know that no one else is worth following.
- let God transform our desires and our perspective on what is truly important in life.
- pursue deeper intimacy with God, as we seek His heart and purposes for us.
- stay open to God's word so that He can adjust our vision of how we see things; perhaps to plant in us a greater plan for our lives than we could have imagined.

In the long times of hiddenness, waiting in integrity, trust and hope that there is meaning and purpose in what seems to be a waste, there may come a God-moment of, 'it came to pass.' This is the moment when God has worked in your character and faith and you are now prepared for the work He has for you. Joseph held high office and his family did bow before him, as the dream had foretold, but by the time it happened he was a very different person. His heart had been changed and filled with the humility of a life lived in close relationship with God. By the grace of God, he was able to see and acknowledge that what men had meant for evil, God had used for good: not just for Joseph but for the nations of Egypt and Israel. In the times when our circumstances seem to be taking away all that God has for us, we can pray for God to redeem those times for good. Whatever Satan means for our harm and destruction; whatever he does to block God's plans being fulfilled in our lives, we can pray for God to use those things for an even greater victory against the enemy. Where we are out of options, God is still at work.

In Romans, Paul wrote:

'... we also glory in tribulations, knowing that tribulation produces perseverance; and perseverance, character; and character, hope. Now hope does not disappoint, because the love of God has been poured out in our hearts by the Holy Spirit who was given to us.' Romans 5:3-5

As we develop maturity in our faith, the eternal perspective takes on a greater weight in our responses to situations. We may not start dancing for joy the moment we face trouble, but then nor should we. However, we recognise that God is still at work and trust that He will establish something beyond worth as we endure – it is looking to a future glory that can be established. That eternal hope in Almighty God will not disappoint because what He has waiting for us in the new Heaven and new Earth will be entirely and perfectly satisfying.

Expectations

Our expectations of how God will resolve matters so often leads to false hope. If we have a godly desire, we tend to expect that God will fulfil that in a straightforward way. We can have an expectation that God will act in a particular way and at a particular time, then when He does not fit in with our plans, we become confused and bewildered.

Israel expected the Messiah to be a mighty military leader who would bring deliverance from the rule of Rome in a tangible overthrow of the secular political power of the time. This was what their desire was, what they expected and hoped for. Instead, they found that the Messiah was a carpenter, a man who associated with tax collectors and fishermen, a man who upset the religious status quo, a man riding a donkey, a man who allowed Himself to be arrested and crucified. Jesus did not change or challenge the political system, or even particularly engage with that. He did challenge religious practice where it was hypocritical and far from the humble, sincere heart worship of God that was supposed to exist.

Jesus was not on Earth to defeat the Roman Empire but something far greater and more powerful. What Israel got was what they most truly needed: a torn veil and deliverance from the rule of sin. It can be a tough discipline to learn to trust in God's ways when we feel that the way forward is obvious, but God is not taking us that way. There is much that we can only understand with hindsight.

If we hope for a particular outcome and invest our hearts and emotions in that, we set ourselves up to fall because then our joy, peace and heart-health are based on achieving that outcome; they become conditional on a particular result. If the outcome is not what we hoped for, or we wait and pray for that outcome over many years without any sign of it coming, our well-being becomes eroded. We can hope for something godly for many years, such as seeing a loved one come to faith, and still not see that fulfilled. When we lose hope, we lose motivation, interest and energy for life; we carry out tasks mechanically even though there seems to be no point to them. The health of our hearts needs to be based on something more constant than things that may or may not turn out the way we hope.

It is also sometimes necessary to differentiate between our desires and God's promises. Not all of our desires will be fulfilled, but God's promises do not fail. When God has promised, we put our hope, our confident expectation, in the character of God. In a recap of the story of Abraham in the book of Romans, we read that,

> '...contrary to hope, [he] in hope believed, so that he became the father of many nations, according to what was spoken....'
> Romans 4:18

To continue to hope, when all earthly hope is gone, is surely God's grace at work. Abraham accepted that his body was as good as dead, yet he believed that God could and would do what He promised.

When time passes without seeing the fulfilment we trust God for, we do lose courage and joy. Our hearts need hope to be healthy and whole: it is an essential component to our emotional and mental well-being. In some ways, it is important not to let whatever God promised us become an obsession, as we then struggle in the waiting. Abraham had many years of life before the promise was fulfilled and that could easily have been wasted in that waiting process.

What can we *confidently* expect? The only hope that is steadfast and of benefit is the hope that is placed on the eternal things of God. Anything else can lead to us investing emotionally and spiritually in something that can fall apart and leave us flat on our faces, wondering where God was in that.

Reflect and Respond Ideas

Head outside: Try using waiting as a discipline next time you go for a walk. For example, set an alarm so that after five minutes you must stop and wait for two minutes. What thoughts and emotions arise when you must stop and wait?

Research something: How is success defined? Think about measures of success in the workplace, in parenting, in church. How do these compare with what we learn of Joseph's success?

Ponder further: Pharaoh said, "Can we find such a one as this, a man in whom is the Spirit of God?" Gen. 41:39 Use this as a basis for prayer: seeking to be one in whom others recognise the Holy Spirit of God.

Get creative: Read through the story of Joseph's early life, creating thought bubbles to show what might have been going on in Joseph's heart at different moments. You might want to think about how we might have prayed at those moments, too. Use this to consider how his heart was changed by his experience, as lived with God.

Hope in the Darkness

When we consider hope, we often look at Abraham's time of waiting for the promise of God to be fulfilled. After all, he was the one praised in

Hebrews for hoping even though there was no earthly reason for hope. Like Joseph, Abraham and his wife, Sarah, experienced the struggle of waiting for God to do something to fulfil the promise and bring a life of fruitfulness. Abraham was prosperous and had a good life regardless of whether the promise was fulfilled or not, but there was a very real gap in his life where he expected God to act.

If we look at the story of Hagar, however, we find a very different situation. Her life was intertwined with Abraham and Sarah as they waited for God to fulfil the promise, and it impacted the course of her life.

As servant to Sarah, Hagar was with them as the years passed and the hope of the promised child faded. As Sarah was far beyond her child-bearing years, she suggested that Abraham have a child by Hagar, thus fulfilling the promise. Or so she thought. This attempt to fulfil the promise themselves, without God, had serious and long-lasting consequences.

At that time, being barren was seen as a sign that God's blessing was not upon a woman. Whilst this had not caused a problem whilst both women were childless, the pregnant Hagar despised her barren mistress. Sarah experienced deep shame, jealousy and bitterness that her own servant was able to conceive whilst she could not. The result of these emotions was that she responded to Hagar with harshness and cruelty. Once the relationship between Sarah and Hagar had fractured in this way, Hagar fled. God encountered her by a spring of water in the wilderness and told her to return and submit to her mistress. He also gave a prophetic word regarding her unborn child and their descendants. (Gen. 16:1-16)

Hagar did indeed bear a child, named Ishmael, but he was not the child of promise or the child of miracle. It was thirteen years after the birth of Ishmael that Sarah, in old age and after decades of barrenness, joyfully bore a son to Abraham.

However, the fractured relationship re-emerged with the birth of Isaac, as the teenaged Ishmael cruelly mocked his young half-brother. This time, Abraham sent Hagar and Ishmael away permanently. Abraham gave her a skin of water, but this was quickly used up. All Hagar could see in her future was the imminent death of her child and then herself. She could see no other possible options. She waited for this outcome, with sorrow and pain in her heart. All hope was gone.

It was in this state of waiting for death in the Wilderness of Beersheba, that Hagar encountered God a second time. (Gen. 21:14-21)

"Fear not ... Arise ..."

God heard the cries of Ishmael and Hagar and responded with two instructions: "fear not" and "arise." Because God was present and involved, there was no need to fear or stay sitting in the wilderness in grief and despair.

Then God confirmed the promise He had given to Hagar before the birth of her son: "I will make him a great nation." Gen. 21: 17-18

Hagar had been given a promise regarding Ishmael *and his descendants*. If Ishmael had died in the wilderness that day, God's promise would not have been fulfilled. Perhaps she had forgotten God's words or felt that they had been voided in some way; but God had not forgotten His words, His promise or them. He knew exactly where they were and went to meet them there.

When we feel hopeless and despairing in our situations, we need to know that God hears us and is involved. We need to remember that His word to us is *fear not ... arise*. For Hagar, it was an instruction to stand up physically; but it applies equally to ensuring that we arise in our thoughts, emotions and attitudes.

We say 'no' to fear: to the strong emotional response that drives our thoughts and attitude to our circumstances. We arise: we stir up our spirits to take a stand in faith and to wait for God with expectation.

We say 'no' to sitting, crying in fear, and choose to arise with the truth of the Word of God on our lips. We say 'no' to sitting in hopelessness and despair; choosing to arise in worship because God can make a way where there is no way; because when we are out of options, God moves in power.

'God opened her eyes...'

We may not find ourselves in an equivalent situation of literally not having food and water left to keep us alive. However, we can easily find ourselves in a situation of not having the emotional or mental reserves we need to keep going. Our reason does not always give us cause to hope. Once we have run out of ideas for solving a problem or can no longer see any options left, we feel that we have lost our grounds for hope. This is where Hagar was: she had no resources left to keep her son or herself alive, she had no other options.

Remember, our default position is to provide for ourselves apart from God. As we live our lives, meeting deadlines and caring for those around us, we can easily run dry spiritually, emotionally, mentally and physically. We try and operate out of a skin of water - out of what man can provide. When our reason tells us that we are out of options and there is nothing left to do but sit and cry out to God, or just cry, God can be heard.

The fact that God opened Hagar's eyes suggests that her vision had been impacted by hopelessness. The text does not say that God miraculously called a well into being, but that He opened Hagar's eyes. Therefore, in our emotions of hopelessness, we can ask God to open our eyes to see His provision.

'...and she saw a well of water.'

Hagar had a skin to put water in but nothing to go in it. She could not make water appear. But God opened Hagar's eyes so she could see a source of the life-giving waters she needed so desperately. Now that she could *see* the well, Hagar had something that she could do for herself to meet the need: she filled the waterskin and gave her son a drink. God provided the source of water and Hagar made use of it.

All human options had run out, but God made a way for Hagar and Ishmael. Hagar expected death but found life through God.

Abraham's provision was a skin of water that soon ran out. God's provision was a well of water: an abundance of water which was far more than she could drink.

God restored Hagar physically, but also emotionally and spiritually that day. It was only through the supernatural opening of her eyes that something life-bringing was found.

We can compare this with the story of Elisha and his servant. The servant could see the armies surrounding them and believed that he would be killed before the day was out. Elisha prayed for his eyes to be opened and then the servant could see the armies of the LORD around them. The supernatural vision changed the perspective from certain death to certain life, from certain defeat to certain victory. (See 2 Kings 6:8-17)

Accessing the wellspring of life in these stories came through the supernatural opening of eyes to see God's provision and to be more aware of God's presence with them. Life, hope, confidence and courage were released to them as they recognised that they were not alone, that God's awesome power and presence was with them and for them, that He would sustain them and provide for them.

Heart Health

We need something to live for, to push through for, to give us the determination to stand and withstand no matter what. Otherwise, we feel hopeless, despairing and powerless; we start to feel trapped by our circumstances and believe that there is no way out, that things will never change for the better. Lies like this open the way for suicidal thoughts to enter in: *there is no way out ... things would be better for my family if I were not here... I cannot go on ... there is nothing left for me to live for.* Being in such a desperate state of mind and heart needs support from other people, but the feeling that there is no point can stop us from talking to someone about what we are experiencing. Depression is extremely difficult to combat and is certainly not a reflection of the strength of someone's faith.

In Proverbs 18:14 we read,

'The spirit of a man will sustain him in sickness, but who can bear a broken spirit?'

If there is brokenness in our inner being, whether we see that as being in our heart, mind or spirit, then our resilience in difficult times is reduced. If we continue in mental and emotional attitudes of despair and hopelessness, then our spirits will be broken because we are not living out of the salvation that Christ won for us with His blood.

Psalms 42 and 43 are entitled, 'Yearning for God in the Midst of Distresses' and 'Prayer to God in Time of Trouble.' They are expressions of deep and desperate need. As we see so often in Scripture, there is the cry to God about the situation faced that is far beyond human control or understanding interspersed with a reminder to trust in God. The anguish of the Psalmist is evident in both passages:

> 'When shall I come and appear before God? My tears have been my food day and night, while they continually say to me, "Where is your God?"' Ps. 42:2-3

> 'I will say to God my Rock, "Why have You forgotten me? Why do I go mourning because of the oppression of the enemy?"' Ps. 42:9

When we hold to our faith in God to deliver, yet our circumstances do not seem to change as a result of our prayers, we easily wonder what our religious observance is for and whether there is any reason to hope in God. At the times when all we can do is cry, when we remember past times of knowing joy in the Lord yet feel that those times are long gone and will never come again, hope seems to be unattainable. The emotions of hopelessness and despair are clear as God appears to be absent and distant when He was needed the most. The implication is that one who believes should not have that sense of grief over the treatment of the enemy; that God should instantly deal with our challenges, thus turning that sense of mourning into victory and joy.

The passage is like a conversation within the Psalmist. The deep emotions and sense of abandonment of the soul is expressed; then there is the response given to the soul:

> 'Why are you cast down, O my soul? And why are you disquieted within me?

> Hope in God, for I shall yet praise Him for the help of His countenance.' Ps. 42:5, 11 and 43:5

This demonstrates that we can experience strong doubt and need, yet also speak into that by recognising that the help will come, no matter what it feels like in that moment or season of life. The problem and the emotions caused by it were honestly expressed and they did not suddenly dissipate. What did happen was that releasing the eternal perspective into the situation was a means of speaking life into the soul and circumstances and of preventing those negative emotions from having the final say. It was a restructuring of the problem before the strength and power of Almighty God.

Our hearts need to be strengthened because this gives us courage and resilience. Giving our souls a pep-talk is a good way to stir ourselves up to receive hope from God. However, it is also important to stir up your thoughts by remembering that whatever the situation, Jesus was, is and always will be the way, the truth and the life for you. In Psalm 27, David concluded:

> 'I would have lost heart *unless I had believed* that I would see the goodness of the LORD in the land of the living. Wait on the LORD; be of good courage, and He shall strengthen your heart; Wait, I say, on the LORD!' Ps. 27:13-14 (my emphasis).

The hope and faith that we will see the goodness of the LORD this side of Heaven strengthens our hearts and gives us confidence, courage and the ability to endure. It opens our perspective to His character and willingness to meet all our needs according to His glorious riches in Christ. Conversely, when we lose hope that God will show us His goodness, it opens the door to hopelessness, despair and depression. It may be a subtle shift, but taking our eyes away from our desires, whatever it is we long for but lack, and fixing our eyes on Jesus is critical. This is not about ignoring our desires or pretending that they do not exist; but when we experience that deep longing, we choose to entrust those desires to God. We choose to focus on His willingness and ability to fulfil what He has placed within us at the right time and in the right way. Only He sees the full picture and how our lives fit into His bigger picture. His plans and purposes for our lives will be fulfilled, as we stay close in trust and obedience.

Waiting and enduring in faith that God's goodness will be seen in our lives is crucial to maintaining the health of our hearts. It is also through the process of waiting on God – of clinging to His word, His promises and the hope we have in Him – that He strengthens our hearts and increases our courage. David is emphatic in his call to us to wait on the LORD, because He is the only one who can redeem our circumstances and use them for good. He is also the only one who can fully strengthen our hearts to endure the challenge and to walk in grace and praise.

There are times when our courage (our ability to respond with resilience and perseverance) is reduced or absent, and our flesh (our natural abilities, strategies and mechanisms) fails, leaving a space behind. This gap does not remain empty: anxiety and helplessness move in, then despair and hopelessness arrive. Then we have a harder job because we not only have the situation to deal with, but also all the negative emotions that have taken hold as a result. When we arrive at the end of our own ability, we need to quickly fill the gap with the treasures and tools of God's kingdom. The more we look to our God, Father, Son and Holy Spirit, the more we will be strengthened. Choosing that path and resisting the fears and despair-filled emotions is an act of will, but it is the path that leads to life and hope inside us because we are looking to the one who is far greater than anything we face. God is the source of our strength and courage; He is our inheritance, eternal and perfect.

We are designed to lean into our God and receive His strength – we were never meant to deal with anything on our own but to always respond out of relationship with God. We find courage because of this knowledge that turning to God invites Him to go to work for us: to create a way for us and to bring truth and life into the situation. Our courage, the strength of our hearts, comes from our King, our defender and refuge. We see this in Psalm 71, where trust and faith are affirmed in difficult times:

> 'But I will hope continually, and will praise You yet more and more. My mouth shall tell of Your righteousness and Your salvation all the day, for I do not know their limits. I will go in the strength of the Lord GOD; I will make mention of Your righteousness, of Yours only.' Ps. 71:14-16

The more we look to ourselves for a way through, the more we will experience despair. It places too great a burden upon us as we try to hold everything together ourselves and generate the strength we need to get through.

We are to go in the strength of the Lord GOD, not in our own strength. We are to go in His grace, righteousness and salvation, not our own. We are to go in His ability, understanding and power, not our own. We endure through trials as we draw ever more deeply of the resources of our God, available to us through the triumphant death and resurrection of Jesus Christ and the work of the Holy Spirit in us. Our mouths are to testify to God's righteousness and salvation continuously because there is no limit or end to the wonder of what God has given us so freely and at such cost. Our mouths are to increasingly speak out the praise of God. There is no reference here to dwelling on personal limitations but on the wonders of our God.

Joseph had no knowledge of when God would take him out of prison, or what it was all for. He may have alternated between strong faith that it was for a reason and that God would bring him through to something glorious, and strong doubt that this was all there would ever be for him. Exciting faith moments are a wonderful boost, but we need something to carry us through the dark doubt moments in the small hours of the night. When everything is stripped away, when our dreams feel crushed under foot, when it seems that this situation is all there will ever be, we hold onto the solid truth that we will see the goodness of God in the land of the living. We turn our hearts to dwelling in the house of the LORD now, and always.

Respond

We are called to be of good courage: to have hearts that are strong in our God.

As a daily exercise, resolve and commit to 'hope continually,' to praise God and go wherever you have to go that day in God's strength. (Psalm 71:14-15)

Bring to God any areas where you have felt that you had to do things in your own strength and the burdens that has placed upon you. Invite the Holy Spirit to release you from burdens that you should not be carrying and to strengthen your heart.

Memorise Psalm 73:26 so that you can declare God's provision for you at any time of the day or night:

'My flesh and my heart fail; but God is the strength of my heart and my portion forever.'

PEACE

shalom (Hebrew)

'*Shalom* comes from the root verb *shalam*, meaning to be complete, perfect, and full. Thus *Shalom* is much more than the absence of war and conflict; it is the wholeness that the entire human race seeks.'[24]

God's idea of peace is so much greater than ours. *Shalom* encompasses everything that we need to be emotionally and mentally healthy and whole. Therefore, Satan will target that as a matter of course. Anything that keeps us feeling overwhelmed, anxious and wondering whether God will come through for us, works to block what God has for us. Our lives are often busy, full of commitments and pressures.

God knows that we will struggle to know peace in our lives and so this is one of the fruits of His Spirit working in us. The fact that it is something God gives us and develops in us should indicate that it is something that we cannot generate out of our own efforts or willpower. It should also indicate just how vital it is for us to stand and withstand in life. This is not about 'happily-ever-after' moments where all the conflict has been resolved, the plot points are brought to a satisfying conclusion and all is well. God's *shalom* is designed to steady and strengthen us in the darkest moments of our lives. It is designed to bring us a wholeness in our innermost being that helps us in the shakings and upheavals of the world.

Several books of the Old Testament include the cry of God's heart

---

[24] Definition taken from the supplementary notes of *The Spirit-Filled Life Bible*, p. 1334

ringing out through the courageous and faithful prophets who heard His voice and shared His call to repent with a rebellious nation. The book of the prophet Isaiah is lengthy, alternating between passionate calls to Israel to repent and the promise of all that God will do to restore them when they do. It is here that we find a promise and description of the coming Messiah. In this, Jesus is described as the Prince of Peace (Is. 9:6). We may hear that as a nice-sounding phrase to enjoy at Christmas carol services. God came to us in flesh because mankind desperately needed the Messiah, God Made Flesh, God With Us, the Prince of *Shalom*. We, the human race, need Jesus Christ because He was, is and always will be the Prince of completeness, wholeness, health, safety, fullness, rest.

Reactiveness

We may dream of serenely travelling through life, responding with grace and humility in all circumstances, but it rarely works out in real life. Driving somewhere generally depletes reserves of peace and graciousness rapidly! When we are tired, it does not take much for someone to say the wrong thing at the wrong time and for us to lose our tempers.

When we have unresolved wounds, we can develop reactive behaviours when those areas are touched or hurt again. It can simply be that there is someone who knows how to 'push your buttons' and 'rub you up the wrong way', but it can be more than that. When we have unresolved wounds, it allows all the things that are the opposite of *shalom* to dwell within us. Instead of wholeness, soundness, rest and fullness, there are areas where we are still broken, fragmented, empty, agitated and vulnerable. It is not that we exhibit those things the whole time because we find ways to manage and carry on regardless; however, we become reactive when those wounded areas are broached.

At secondary school, we learned about the group one alkali metals on the periodic table. These are soft metals, which are easily cut with a knife. They also become increasingly reactive in water as you go down the column. At the top, there is lithium. When this is put in water, it gently fizzes and moves around a little on the surface. Then we have sodium and potassium, which are more reactive: still floating but moving more energetically, giving off hydrogen gas and perhaps a flame as well. Caesium, however, is violently reactive in water. At school, this was the experiment we watched on video (not one to do yourself in the classroom!) and I still remember watching the reaction take place. The piece of caesium shot across the surface of the water like it had been fired from a gun, and the glass bowl it was in shattered when the caesium hit it.[25]

The reaction begins the moment the metal touches the water, but the speed and violence of the reactions increase as we move down through the alkali metals. Our reactive behaviours can be like this: there is a place where we are easily wounded and the moment that is activated, we respond automatically with agitation and distress when buried emotions come to the surface. These metals are easily cut, just as we are easily hurt again in those wounded areas.

It may be like the lithium touching the water: it stirs up our emotions, leaving us agitated, and it takes a while for us to calm down again. It may be more like the caesium, with an instantaneous and violent burst of anger. These reactive behaviours happen whether we want them to or not because it is a case of cause and effect: just as alkali metals react in water, we react in a particular way when those deep wounds are hurt again.

Watching experiments online, I was struck by one where the caesium was carefully placed in a container of oil so that air and moisture could not access the metal.[26] It was separated from the elements that would cause its reactive behaviours. Where we are wounded and reactive, we need the Holy Spirit to immerse those things in oil: to bring healing, to soothe and soften those raw and rough places of our hearts and souls.

Oil is a common theme in the Bible, which we see in many contexts. Oils were common and had an array of uses, both practical and spiritual. When instructions were being given to the people for what

---

[25] See University of Nottingham video where caesium is released underwater and the reaction is filmed from several angles. Accessed 26 May 2020. https://www.youtube.com/watch?v=b2YrZNahqiw

[26] Preparation for doing an experiment with caesium, with the caesium being placed in oil. See University of Nottingham video, accessed 26 May 2020. https://www.youtube.com/watch?v=5aD6HwUE2c0

offerings they should bring for the temple, 'oil for the light, and spices for the anointing oil and for the sweet incense' were included in the list of acceptable products (Ex. 25:6). It was a staple product used:

- to create light
- to make bread
- as an ointment, to soothe, soften and moisturise
- as perfume, when scented with spices
- for anointing the living (for a particular calling, such as kingship; but also as a part of hospitality)
- for anointing the dead. (See the anointing of Jesus in Matt. 26:6-13).

Oil was also symbolic of God's blessing, as we see when Job thought longingly of past days, "when my steps were bathed with cream, and the rock poured out rivers of oil for me!" (Job 29:6) Or in Psalm 133:1-2, where the oil pouring down the head of Aaron the high priest was a sign of God's blessing, prompted by the unity of the people.

Oils sustained the body internally through food and externally through healing properties. Fragranced oils would also have been refreshing and pleasing when they were used, which would have helped lift people's moods and well-being.

Psalm 23:5 tells us that God Himself anoints our heads with oil. He anoints us for our calling. He anoints us so that we can rest from the things that cause us to be reactive and experience past hurts all over again. It is the blessing of our Father and King that shows His acceptance and love for us; it shows His tender care for us as He anoints our wounds for healing. He also anoints us with the oil of joy. This is His heart for us: to pour out the oil of His blessing, healing and joy upon us.

Where we know that we have reactive behaviours, try picturing a container of oil. Take each memory, each incident, each wound and immerse them into the oil. As you do so, pray for the oil of God's kingdom to be an ointment to your heart and mind: to soothe the hurt, to deal with the infection and all that continues to cause pain and reactiveness. Pray for the oil to bring light into your life. Pray that it will nourish those dry and brittle places within you and for the fragrance of Jesus' healing presence to be known there. Welcome the anointing of God for healing, restoration, wholeness and for all the blessings He has for you.

We will be bruised in life, but as we receive the oil of His blessing and presence we find that we can respond better rather than reacting automatically out of past hurts. Bruising or heating herbs like thyme or rosemary releases the fragrant oils, which are attractive. Similarly, when spices like cardamom are ground or heated, they release their strong fragrance, filling the room. This does not make it acceptable for people to hurt us; nor does it justify anyone's misuse of us. That is never the case. It is an example of how our responses change through the work of the Holy Spirit in us, by the grace and love of our God, who knows our pain and anguish and who does not want us to carry that our whole lives. As we increasingly become whole and healed in Christ, when people rub against us the fragrance of Christ is released rather than our reactive behaviours of woundedness. This is for our benefit and as a witness to those around us.

Healing sometimes comes immediately and sometimes it is a process over time. God's desire is to heal and restore us to wholeness. Our part in this is to keep turning to God in all things, not turning away. Facing areas of hurt and grief is painful so this can take a great deal of courage, but God is gentle as He brings healing and restoration.

Reflect and Respond Ideas

Head outside: Plant some herbs in pots or in a garden. Rosemary and thyme are very aromatic and release their scent when you rub them. Release the fragrance as you pray, remembering that God's work in you will release the fragrance of Christ to flow from you.

Research something: Look online to see the experiment with the group 1 metals being put in water. Have you ever experienced reactive behaviours in yourself or witnessed someone else being reactive? How can we release the oils of God's Kingdom?

Ponder further: Re-read the definition of *shalom*. Which part best sums up what you experience in Christ, or most want to experience in Christ? Bring it to God and ask Him to help you come to know this in Him.

Get creative: Try using some different herbs or grinding your own spices to cook something. Focus on the way the fragrances are released as you grind, bruise or heat the spices.

The Process of Healing

God desires restoration for His people but, as with any building work, it happens over time. When a structure is damaged, it needs to be assessed to find out what is still secure and what is likely to collapse; then that needs to be dealt with. The structural integrity of a building is essential: it cannot be ignored or dealt with in a rush. God does the same thing with us. He wants us to be sound in mind, whole of heart and secure in Him. With some things that we have faced, it would be too much to deal with the whole thing in one go. There are layers of pain, layers of experience, and God knows how to approach these things with gentleness so that we trust Him with our fragile places.

Returning to the story of Joseph in the Old Testament enables us to see something of this restoration process.

We looked at his story up until the time Pharaoh appointed Joseph to be his second-in-command across the Kingdom. It is tempting to take the simple view that he was taken from prison, given high position and then he lived happily ever after. However, as we continue with his story, we can see that Joseph's restoration took place in a variety of ways, over years. God was not interested in just restoring Joseph externally, in the eyes of the world. He wanted to restore the deep, inner places of Joseph's mind, heart and soul as well; to make them whole and complete in His peace.

Being appointed to high office was not a sudden, instant fix after years of God not really doing anything. Firstly, it is so important to recognise that God was just as much at work in the darkness as He was in bringing Joseph into high office. Secondly, we need to know that the season in the darkness was not a punishment. God was in both, at work in both, showing favour to Joseph in both. It does not fit with our mindset of success to see that God was present and showing blessing and favour in the darkness of Joseph's life. We see it easily in the moment when he was brought out of prison and given a great job, a big house, wealth and so on. If we use our circumstances as an indication of God's opinion of us, we will come unstuck very quickly.

We looked at Joseph's early life from the hated favourite of the family to slavery, then imprisonment. It was in this season that Joseph was enabled by God to live out what we read in Psalm 34:14:

'Depart from evil and do good; seek peace and pursue it...'

In his heart, Joseph chose to honour God in every circumstance, whether just or unjust, deserved or undeserved. When thoughts of bitterness or anger arose, Joseph made the choice to depart from evil.

This does not mean ignoring the emotions or refusing to express them before God. On the contrary, it is important that we take all these emotions to Him and allow Him access to the causes of them. However, we should not allow those emotions to lead us into sin. We are to depart from evil by turning away from any thoughts of revenge or retribution, turning away from contention and any desire to do harm to those who have hurt us. Instead, we are to do good, no matter how we feel. There was very little that Joseph had control over during that time of darkness, but he could control how he behaved towards others, towards God and towards himself.

Joseph chose to do good to the master who owned him and to the gaolers, who could easily have mistreated him. We see that he did good in three ways:

1. he chose not to rebel towards those in authority over him

2. he resolved not to do them any harm

3. he committed himself to working for their good.

Each one of these matters. He could have chosen just to do the bare minimum and with a bad grace at that; but he actively worked for the good of others. He honoured those in authority over him and treated them well.

Joseph chose to do good in his relationship with God. He chose not to depart from the presence of God, even though he did not understand why God had allowed him to be in slavery or in prison. He chose to keep his eyes fixed on his God, trusting Him with his life and acting rightly before Him.

Joseph chose to do good for himself, by pursuing wholeness and healing from God. Dwelling in a place of bitterness and anger would have harmed him and stopped him from moving on in his life. Joseph was human, so it is fair to assume that he had nights when he shouted out to God in pain and confusion at all that had happened to him. But he chose not to sin against people or against God in those moments. It is necessary to bring those emotions to God and then allow the Holy Spirit to pour out the oil of healing to soothe and surround those areas of pain.

External Restoration

In the middle of yet another ordinary day in prison, God's plan moved to the next step. Before Joseph had any idea that God was at work in a new way, God had sent dreams to Pharaoh which no one could interpret. The cupbearer had forgotten about Joseph until this moment, but now came the perfect time to mention him to Pharaoh. Joseph could not appear before Pharaoh in his prison rags, unkempt and unclean; therefore, he was able to wash and put on appropriate clothes. At this point, this was a temporary restoration that was likely to be reversed when Pharaoh had finished with him. (Gen. 41:14)

Joseph was able to interpret the dream and give glory to God through that. Immediately, there was not only further restoration but an extraordinary promotion:

> "'You shall be over my house, and all my people shall be ruled according to your word; only in regard to the throne will I be greater than you... See, I have set you over all the land of Egypt."
>
> Then Pharaoh took his signet ring off his hand and put it on Joseph's hand; and he clothed him in garments of fine linen and put a gold chain around his neck. And he had him ride in the second chariot which he had; and they cried out before him, "Bow the knee!" So he set him over all the land of Egypt.' Gen. 41:40-43

For the second time in his life, Joseph's circumstances were entirely reversed. From favoured son to the pit; then from prison to Pharaoh's second in command. There was a restoration and advancement of appearance and status, with the conferring of royal appointment and authority.

When Pharaoh appointed him to rule over his house, people and land, he did so in word and action. There was nothing stingy or half-hearted in Pharaoh's appointment of Joseph. Pharaoh conferred authority upon Joseph by:

- personally putting his signet ring upon Joseph's hand. He was given fine clothes and honoured publicly.

- publicly announcing that Joseph was second only to him; there would be no other official with equal or greater power over Joseph. This is a staggering expression of trust in this man, purely because Pharaoh recognised the power of God at work through Joseph.

- parading Joseph through the streets so that everyone would know to bow down to Joseph, giving him due honour and respect.

He gave sign upon sign to his household and his people that this was no longer Joseph, former convicted Hebrew slave, but one who was in authority over them. When Egyptians saw Joseph, they would see the shadow of Pharaoh at his back, authorising his actions and enforcing all that Joseph said and did.

These things were *external* and *public* restorations to his life. He was transformed *externally* from Hebrew slave to the second highest in the land. No longer Joseph but Zaphnath-Paaneah, who would look like an Egyptian; live, speak and act as an Egyptian. As he was given an Egyptian wife, this would presumably have extended to his home as well as his work environment.

Internally, Joseph was the same man. By this time, he was God's man, no matter what name he was given or what job he did. He was also the same man who had experienced the pit, the slave-traders' cart, the slave market, the exchange of coins for him, and so on. This release from the darkness would have brought one level of healing to Joseph, but it would not have made everything better. All those years since being sold by his brothers would have been an enormous strain and learning process for Joseph, all the while wondering what it was all for.

Throughout this darkness, God had been working out His purposes for Joseph so that he would be ready at the right time. This external restoration was a beginning or continuation of an internal process of restoration.

The Healing of Joseph

Over the seven years of fruitfulness, Joseph served God, Pharaoh and Egypt. He and his wife had two sons together, Manasseh and Ephraim. With the naming of his first-born child, Joseph declared that God had enabled him to forget what was past. With the naming of his second son, Joseph proclaimed the fruitfulness that God had brought into his life.[27] We can see these as milestones of the gradual healing that God was doing inside him: the changing perspective and emotions as Joseph considered his past and recognised contentment in his present life. All that he had learned in the darkness was bearing fruit and it brought healing into his life, over months and years. It might have been that Joseph considered that all was well at that point, but there were unresolved things that were still to be dealt with. The birth of his sons clearly enabled the hurts of the past to fade into the background, but they had not disappeared.

It is as we look at the seven lean years in Egypt that we see more of the healing and restoration process. The famine was increasingly hard in Canaan, so a group of brothers travelled to Egypt to plead for food. They were shown into the presence of Zaphnath-Paaneah, all-powerful official of Egypt, a man to fearfully honour; the man upon whom their very survival depended. How great was the apprehension of these farmers and cattlemen as they were led into the splendour and wealth of the Egyptian court and bowed face down before a man such as this? They presented their need and their plea and waited as the interpreter translated their request into Egyptian for Zaphnath-Paaneah.

In the middle of another ordinary day, administering the king-

---

[27] Manasseh means 'one who causes to forget' and Ephraim means 'two-fold increase; very fruitful.' Cornwell and Smith, *Book of Names*, p. 126 and 52

dom of Egypt, Joseph was suddenly confronted with ten brothers in the royal court, bowing before him - the brothers who had hated him, thrown him in a pit, considered murdering him and then sold him. Over the previous years, many people had bowed before him, many had petitioned him for food, but now his brothers were before him, humble, respectful, desperate. Whatever emotions had been buried, left untouched for years, now arose. Hatred, anger, bitterness... perhaps all those thoughts from sleepless nights of what he would do or say if he ever saw them again.

It is important to note what Joseph did not do at this point. He did not tell his brothers who he was. He did not launch into a speech denouncing them and throwing them out to starve. He did not forgive them, either grudgingly or freely. Instead, he accused them of being spies. Why? The object seemed to be focused on ensuring that the youngest brother, Benjamin, would be brought to him. Initially, Joseph ordered that one brother return to Canaan to fetch Benjamin whilst the rest awaited his return in prison. Joseph put all ten of his half-brothers in prison for three days, and then adjusted the plan. All but one brother could return for Benjamin.

It is interesting that the brothers identified this as a direct consequence of their actions regarding Joseph so many years before:

"'We are truly guilty concerning our brother, for we saw the anguish of his soul when he pleaded with us, and we would not hear; therefore this distress has come upon us.'

And Reuben answered them saying, "Did I not speak to you, saying, 'Do not sin against the boy;' and you would not listen? Therefore, behold, his blood is now required of us.'"
Gen. 42:21-22

As Joseph heard his brothers acknowledge their guilt, 'he turned himself away from them and wept.' (verses 23-24) In the whole account of Joseph's life, this is the first time he is recorded as weeping as a result of something happening to him. The record of Joseph's story began when he was seventeen years old (Gen. 37:2) and he was thirty years old when he went before Pharaoh (Gen. 41:46). The seven fruitful years had passed and the famine was established, so Joseph could have been around forty years old when this encounter took place. In all the trauma of his life, it is only in these encounters with his brothers, many years after they had sinned against him, that we are allowed this insight into Joseph's emotions. Hearing those who had done him such harm confess their guilt released tears and another step of healing.

But he did not reveal his identity to them, nor did he speak out forgiveness.

When the men finally returned with Benjamin, Joseph ordered a meal to be prepared for them all in his own house. The brothers had returned with gifts of balm, honey, spices and myrrh, pistachio nuts and almonds and they waited for Zaphnath-Paaneah. (Gen.43:11) Seeing Benjamin again touched a deep place in Joseph's heart and tears quickly came again. Benjamin was the youngest of the family and the one full brother to Joseph – both were born to Rachel. Had Joseph ever spent time in the intervening years working out how old Benjamin would be and what he would be doing at home? He must surely have grieved for the lost relationship and shared experiences that they should have had. Now, after all those years of separation, this young man was metres away from him and unable to recognise Joseph as his brother. Joseph went to his chamber so that he could cry without being seen; composed himself and returned to begin the meal. (Gen. 43:24-31)

By stages, Joseph was arranging the arrival of his whole family in Egypt, but he was doing so secretly and in such a way that it heightened the fear of his brothers. The brothers did not know that they were encountering Joseph. They were facing Zaphnath-Paaneah, a man who was second to Pharaoh and who had absolute power over them. They had already been accused of being spies and imprisoned. This time, when the brothers were on their way home, they were stopped and searched for a missing silver cup from Zaphneath-Paaneah's house. As the 'guilty' one, Benjamin was to face the consequence of being made a slave.

There are so many echoes to Joseph's early life here. The gifts Jacob sent with the brothers were similar to those carried by the traders who had bought him (including balm, spices and myrrh). Joseph had been sold for twenty shekels of silver and now he staged a theft of silver. Finally, Joseph introduced the threat of Jacob's other favourite son being unjustly enslaved. All those years previously, it had been Judah's idea to sell Joseph into slavery and now it was Judah who interceded for Benjamin, for,

"...he alone is left of his mother's children, and his father loves him ... his life is bound up in the lad's life..."
Gen. 44:20 and 30

Judah then offered to remain as slave in Benjamin's place.

It is a painful speech to read, as Judah explained the love that Jacob had for Benjamin – a love that Judah and his other brothers had never experienced. Many years before, their bitterness and anger over this favouritism had led them into sin, but now there was acceptance of the favouritism and repentance for the sin. By this time, Judah was older and a father himself, which brought a new perspective. He referred to Benjamin as *lad*, which suggests a considerable age difference, perhaps seeing Benjamin more with the eyes of a father or uncle than the eyes of a brother. Finally, Judah had lived all those years with Jacob's grief over Joseph's alleged death. All these things had changed Judah's heart to the extent that he would offer himself to be a slave to spare his father further pain. This was the point that broke Joseph's resolve to stay aloof. He sent his servants away and told his brothers who he was, weeping so loudly that the rest of the household heard it.

Three points that released the floodgates of tears, three signposts of healing at work, three moments that acted powerfully in Joseph's heart: the acknowledgement of guilt, seeing his younger brother once more and realising how much that separation had pained him, then Judah's request to take Benjamin's place. Each encounter released deep pain, heartache, yearning and a place that needed to be made whole. Those years of separation had changed Joseph's heart, but they had also impacted his ten half-brothers who had lived with knowing that they were the cause of their father's years of grief.

When someone sins against us, it is like we develop a place that carries the injustice, grievance and accusation within us. It is a burden that remains because the events of the past cannot be undone or changed; the memories remain and can replay, causing us to relive the trauma of what happened along with all the emotions of that time. Even if someone apologises, the past is unchanged. If Joseph had revealed himself to them in their first meeting, without those moments of tearful release and healing, he might well have spoken to them very differently – full of anger, grief, pride (along the lines of, *Look at me now! I have complete power over you - your lives are in my hands!*). It would have been possible for him to acknowledge God's intentions and purposes yet still hold a grudge against his family, desiring to harm them in revenge. In his new position, Joseph had them completely at his mercy. He had been sinned against and nothing could change or undo those years; but at this point he was ready and able to let go of all that he had held against them.

Having sent away his Egyptian staff, Joseph welcomed his brothers with the words, "Please come near to me." (Gen. 45:4) When someone has sinned against us, our natural inclination is to keep them at a distance, to cut off contact, to harden our hearts against them. That is a form of punishment in itself. Over time, the grace and power of God had been miraculously at work within Joseph, so that he could whole-heartedly welcome his brothers back into his life and confidence.

Then he released forgiveness to his brothers as he testified to God's purposes:

> "But now, do not therefore be grieved or angry with yourselves because you sold me here; for God sent me before you to preserve life.... God sent me before you to preserve a posterity for you in the earth, and to save your lives by a great deliverance. So now it was not you who sent me here, but God; and He has made me a father to Pharaoh, and lord of all his house, and a ruler throughout all the land of Egypt." Gen. 45:5, 7-8

Through having an open heart before God and seeing the fruit of God's plans enabled Joseph to speak of God's purposes and give glory to Him, freely and completely, with all unforgiveness relinquished. Joseph had heard that his brothers were grieved about their actions and that was important, but he did not want them to continue to experience that regret. Joseph could proclaim that God had sent him to Egypt as part of a calling of deliverance. Twice Joseph stated that it was God who sent him to Egypt. Twice he stated that it was to preserve lives – lives generally and their lives specifically.

Without those years in the hiddenness, living purely on God's grace and favour, Joseph would not have learned to listen to God's voice and reveal the interpretations of dreams to his fellow prisoners. Without them, he would not have learned how to be a skilled household steward, fluent in Egyptian, trustworthy and successful. Without God's hand at work, Joseph knew that he would not have found Pharaoh's favour and listening ear. After all, Pharaoh could easily have listened to the interpretation and then sent Joseph back to jail. Yet, he freely appointed him to the position of his second in command over all Egypt. A Hebrew slave and prisoner was given unlimited power, wealth and freedom to act as he saw fit! The trust and confidence that Pharaoh placed in this man was clearly the hand of God at work.

The time spent in darkness would have been enormously frustrating and painful, but during it his heart was being rooted and established before God in righteousness so that Joseph was enabled to avoid the potential pitfalls of serving in Egypt. Imagine how Joseph's life would have been if he had not served with diligence or if he had not seen any reason to resist Potiphar's wife. It was only because Joseph's heart was positioned rightly before God that he behaved with righteousness in all he did in Egypt.

Once he was raised to high position, there was the potential temptation of idolatry. His wife, Asenath, was the daughter of a pagan priest. Asenath means, 'who belongs to Neith' (an Egyptian goddess of war, amongst other things.)[28] Her father's name was Poti-Pherah, which means, 'priest of the sun'.[29]

The other potential area to fall from God's ways came from the complete power that Joseph had over many who were vulnerable and needy during the famine. In his early life, the privilege of being set apart from others had made Joseph lazy and selfish. However, he was now

---

[28] Cornwell and Smith, *Book of Names*, p. 18
[29] Cornwell and Smith, *Book of Names*, p. 152

able to handle a position of complete power and privilege with maturity and the recognition that it was for God's purposes alone. He had experienced being in the hands of others and of being helpless before them. As people came before him in need, unable to help themselves, he was able to resist any temptation to abuse or mistreat others. Joseph's priority in prison and in the palace was serving God rightly. He knew that he was in that position by God's hand alone and that God could remove him easily should he become corrupted. He did not take advantage of God's trust in him, or Pharaoh's, but acted rightly before both.

Joseph's Egyptian name has a very telling meaning:

'...saviour of the age, of the world; giver of the nourishment of life; prince of the life of the age; revealer of a secret. The concealed treasure....'[30]

If Joseph had desired confirmation of God's plan for his life, surely, he found it every time this new name was used. He had revealed the secret of Pharaoh's dream, he was a ruler with the responsibility of preserving the lives of a generation of people. It seems unlikely that Joseph spent any time in the darkness saying to himself, 'all is well, I am a concealed treasure of God,' and yet this was how God saw it. Joseph was His treasure, hidden away to be prepared for what was to come. God had allowed Joseph to be a slave, a steward and a prisoner, and Joseph had behaved righteously in these things. Joseph then used three phrases to describe the appointment he held before God in Egypt:

father to Pharaoh: this is the position of a trusted family member, who was respected, listened to and given privileges that no other person had. He desired to do good for Pharaoh, just as if he were one of Joseph's sons.

lord of Pharaoh's household: still in that position of stewardship, and who could understand that role better than one who had already been a steward?

ruler over the land: which Joseph saw as a sacred trust, ruling on Pharaoh's behalf in this matter of preserving life.

---

[30] Cornwell and Smith, *Book of Names*, p. 192

In all these things, Joseph maintained his heart attitude that first and foremost he was appointed by God. Joseph did not let wealth or position make him proud or conceited. He worked diligently for the benefit and good of others: as father to son, steward to master, ruler on behalf of, and for the benefit of, others. Regardless of his worldly position, Joseph saw himself as being under the authority and lordship of God, always answerable to Him for his stewardship.

Healing for the Brothers

We generally approach this story from Joseph's perspective - the perspective of the injured party. But what of the older brothers? These ten men had grown up in an extended family environment of rivalry and favouritism, with their mothers competing for Jacob's affections and attentions.[31] Once Joseph had been sold, we only learn of a few incidents in the brothers' lives; yet God had clearly been at work in their hearts, too, where Joseph was concerned.

From the brothers' perspective, they had simply gone to Egypt for food and somehow found themselves on the wrong side of this all-powerful Egyptian ruler, in a situation that went from bad to worse. If it had not been sufficiently terrifying to be in the presence of this powerful Egyptian, who had accused them of theft and threatened slavery; now Zaphnath-Paaneah revealed himself as their brother, Joseph - the one who knew their greatest sin and regret, the one who had every reason to revile them and demand retribution.

Their words of confession and repentance, spoken unknowingly to Joseph, revealed the changes of their hearts and had brought healing to Joseph. When Joseph called his brothers close, he released the brothers from the burden of guilt, shame and condemnation they carried because of their sin. Whereas Joseph gained peace and wholeness at this point, his brothers had a lot of healing still to do before the matter was closed for them.

After they had lived in Egypt for some time, their father, Jacob, died. The brothers' insecurity rose again: what if Joseph had only been waiting until their father died to have his complete revenge on them? (Gen. 50:15-21) Joseph had spoken out forgiveness to them which re-

---

[31] See Gen. 29:15-35 and 30:1-24

leased Joseph from the burden of holding a grudge and brought him freedom. However, the brothers had only partially received his forgiveness. Part of them did not trust that it was complete, sincere and permanent. Because they did not completely trust in Joseph's forgiveness, it allowed fear to remain within them that at any time he could change his mind and seek vengeance. Healing was needed on both sides and it took time for that process to take place, both for the one wronged and the ones who had wronged him.

If we get cut, then we know that the wound will heal over time. Time is not the thing that heals. It is the process taking place in the human body that heals, as the flesh is knitted together and made whole once more. Time was not the healer of Joseph's wounded heart; God was. Our part is to keep the wound clean and protected from germs and dirt so that it does not get infected, then to leave it to heal. Therefore, we acknowledge the hurt before God and allow Him to heal us. We choose to depart from evil every time we are tempted to dwell in the hurt or to hold a grudge. We keep the wound clean and immersed in the oil of the Holy Spirit. We choose to do good, seeking and pursuing peace: pursuing wholeness and completion in Christ.

God's presence was so evident in these events that it was not only acknowledged by Joseph but by the Egyptians who encountered him. We can only conclude that it was God's grace that brought Joseph through the darkness and the fruitful years. Healing and wholeness happened over years and through different situations: recognising that he was finally living out what God intended for him, the birth of his children, the passing of time giving him the benefit of hindsight, meeting his brothers again and the healing that God brought through that.

Respond

If there is someone in your life you struggle to forgive, trust in God to enable you. Bring those people to God. Acknowledge before Him what was done or said and how that impacted you: how it made you feel, how it damaged you, how it has affected your ability to trust / step out in faith / move on ... In forgiving, you are not saying that what happened was acceptable. You are choosing to release that person to God in prayer, so that grace can be released to you and to the one who hurt you. (As Jesus did on the cross, as Stephen did when he was martyred).

Speak the blessing of grace and peace to replace the hurt in you, and to impact the person who hurt you.

Be aware that you may need to keep choosing to forgive and keep releasing grace and peace. This is partly because Satan does not give up his footholds easily, but also because our emotions and memories take a while to be transformed. It is like a music track: once it gets activated in your memory, the same words and emotions emerge and do the same thing. This pattern needs to be disrupted once you have chosen to forgive. Do not let the track run to the end, replaying all the things that hurt you or reminding you of all the reasons to be angry, stirring up the emotions once more. Make a deliberate choice to stop the track as early as possible, because that is the choice that opens the way to healing and peace.

Ask the Holy Spirit to bring healing and wholeness into those memories and emotions. It may be that you would find it helpful to arrange time with another Christian you know and trust to pray through things together.

Becoming Complete

God's *shalom* is all about our healing and becoming whole, in all areas of brokenness and anywhere we feel that there is something lacking. In our busy lives it is all too easy to feel that things are falling apart or barely holding together; that if we slow down or take a break everything will collapse around us. So much seems to depend on us always being on top of all things.

One of the ways in which we can find the peace that we need is to recognise that we do not need to hold everything together, no matter what it feels like. Paul's letter to the Colossians begins with great affection and encouragement, expressing his desire that they should be strengthened in God so that they would be able to endure with patience and thanksgiving. He continued by talking about Jesus,

> 'He is the image of the invisible God, the firstborn over all creation. For by Him all things were created ... all things were created by Him and for Him. He is before all things, and in Him all things hold together.' Col. 1:15-17, NIV

It is in Christ that all things hold together. If we picture an archway made of blocks of stone, the one at the top is the cornerstone which holds all the others in position.[32] Christ is the cornerstone, therefore, *He* is the one who stops everything from collapsing, not us. Applying this truth to our lives is so helpful. Wherever we feel that we are the cornerstone, that we are the one who is stopping (or attempting to stop) everything from falling apart, hand over that position to Jesus as the cornerstone and proclaim that those things hold together in Him. Let Him take the strain of that.

I had this verse on my work diary so that when the responsibility began to feel overwhelming, I could quickly remind myself that all aspects of my job were held together in Christ and that He was above and before all things. It also brings important perspective to be reminded that nothing that happens to us comes as a surprise to God. He is before all things: He already has complete knowledge of what is going on, He already has all the resources we need available for us. He is always focused and on top of everything, even if we are not. Somehow it is reassuring to remember that God does not have off days like we do.

Christ is before all things but also above all things. When we look to Jesus, we are looking to God Most High. They were together before anything was in existence, working together in complete harmony to create stars, planets and all that we need. He is above all powers and authorities, whether temporal or spiritual. When we take our problems to Christ, we are returning to our Creator to ask Him to take His place in resolving that problem. We ask Him to be the cornerstone of our emotions, thoughts and decisions as we go through the difficulty and allow Him to hold us together rather than struggling on our own. When we come to the end of our own resources, we invite Jesus to fill that gap with Himself. We proclaim that He is Lord over all things, over every factor of that situation and over all those involved. We proclaim His sovereignty and authority to act on our behalf.

If we struggle with our sense of identity and worth, we look to Jesus to hold our identity and worth together; we invite Him to be the one who makes us whole, sound, healed, rested and full in that area. We proclaim that He is Lord over our identity and only He has the authority to speak into that.

If we struggle with areas of shame, inadequacy and failure, we

---

[32] See Isaiah 28:16, Psalm 118:22, 1 Peter 2:4-10

look to Jesus to hold us together in His love; bringing us the healing, wholeness and fullness that comes from knowing that we are enough in Him. Even when it does not feel true, we choose to trust that He will restore us.

Wherever we feel lacking, insufficient, not enough for whatever is going on, we can proclaim the truth that everything is held together by Christ. He fills those gaps in our understanding, our ability, our resourcing.

Whenever we reach the end of what we can do, we can breathe a sigh of relief that this is the part that Jesus Christ can fill with Himself. He is always ready to fill that gap with Himself, supplying all that we need and holding all things together.

In *Him*, all things hold together. Not in us. None of this is dependent on us knowing what to do, how to make things work, how to keep everything under control. It is Christ who holds every part of us together. He is the missing piece that makes us whole.

Becoming Sound

Healing can be a painful process, but with God it will be a constructive one. In Christ and through Christ we find wholeness once more.

Simon Peter had sworn to stand by Jesus, no matter what, yet denied Him three times, just as Jesus prophesied that he would. Despite his best efforts, Simon Peter had done something that he had never wanted to do. It was a devastating moment of recognising his betrayal of his Lord, but also of having this stark example of seeing that, for all his bold talk, he could not follow through when it mattered.

As the term 'peace' encompasses wholeness, fullness, rest, healing and so on, the opposite necessarily describes a state of brokenness. Even in his joy at the resurrection, there was much that needed healing in Simon Peter that did not simply go away just because Jesus was back. It had completely altered how Simon Peter saw himself. When we join the story, he was not attempting any kind of ministry at all. He had gone back to what was familiar in his life before meeting Jesus – fishing. (See John 21:1-19)

Jesus had known that Simon Peter would deny Him. It did not change the love that Jesus had for His friend, nor did it change the calling that was upon Simon Peter's life. However, denying Jesus had left Simon Peter broken inside. Jesus was not going to let His beloved disciple and friend embark on any kind of ministry without receiving the healing his heart needed. Any ministry carried out of a heart and mind that had been branded by labels such as 'failure', 'betrayer', 'stupid' would have been ineffective and weak. Simon Peter would not have been in a position to stand or withstand against the enemy in what he did, because he was not on secure ground. Jesus did not condemn him, but he condemned himself.

This encounter happened at the beach, whilst having fellowship. It was not a major debrief and Jesus did not go over every single thing that Simon Peter did wrong, condemning him systematically for each failure. They ate together, being restored physically, then Jesus brought His dear friend through a healing process. However, there are several elements that seem strange.

Firstly, Jesus calls his friend, 'Simon, son of Jonah', rather than using his new name of Peter, the rock upon which Jesus would build His church. (See Matt. 16:17-18 and John 1:42)

Secondly, it seems a strange approach for Jesus to question Peter about his love for Him – hurtful even. At the third time of asking, we learn that Peter was grieved by this.

Thirdly, every time Simon Peter affirms his love for Jesus, Jesus gives a sheep-related instruction: feed My lambs, tend My sheep, feed My sheep.

If we were to write a reconciliation scene between Jesus and Simon Peter, this is not how we would write it. There are no words of repentance from Peter, no words of forgiveness and acceptance from Jesus, no sense of warmth even. We are told that this was the third time Jesus appeared to His disciples after His resurrection, so there was purpose in this. As we know that Jesus is Love, the Prince of *Shalom*, we can know that His intention was to bring wholeness in this.

There is a formality to this exchange, in the repetition of the questioning and the use of 'Simon, son of Jonah'. The question and the answer mattered profoundly. Jesus knew the answers better than His friend did – after all, Jesus could see the depths of every heart and mind so nothing could be hidden from Him. Jesus knew the answers, but there was a need for Simon Peter to engage with the question in order to work through something that was important for him and his heart. At this point, he was able to respond that he loved Jesus in the sense of having affection for Him.

I think we need to see this as a huge learning curve for Peter. Peter had learned something of his own heart and spoke in the humble recognition that his love for Jesus was sincere and real, but not as courageous and faithful as he had thought. That mattered. Peter had come to recognise his weakness in speaking rashly, so he did not burst into protestations of great sacrificial love to Jesus as he might have done before the resurrection. He knew that he loved Jesus but was now able to recognise and acknowledge the limitations of that love.

However, his actions also spoke volumes. When he saw Jesus earlier that day, Peter had run to Him! That was not done out of mild affection or fondness, but out of a heart that cried out for his Lord. Even in his sense of guilt and failure, when he saw Jesus nearby there was *nothing* that would stop Peter going straight to Him.

Jesus did not doubt the love of His precious friend. He knew Peter's strengths and weaknesses and that He (Jesus) would be glorified through them.

Each time Peter told Jesus that he had affection for Him, Jesus told him to look after His lambs, His sheep. Why? Why did Jesus not speak words of loving encouragement into Peter's disappointment with himself? Why talk about sheep? Originally, Jesus called Simon Peter to follow Him and become 'fishers of men' (Matt. 4:19), but now Peter is called to a role of shepherding. That may not seem like a significant change until we remember that Jesus never referred to Himself as a fisherman. He did describe Himself as a shepherd leading His sheep. (John 10:1-16) He now called Peter to follow in that ministry of shepherding.

Peter brought the sincerity of his heart, with its brokenness and failure. He brought the confession that his love was affectionate rather than the courageous and passionate love that would die for his friend. Into this brokenness and humility of heart, Jesus called His beloved friend to walk in His footsteps. He brought words of a life that would be lived for Him. Even at this point, where Peter accepted that he would not have risked his own life for his Lord, Jesus knew that one day, Peter would give his life.

Soon after this encounter, the Holy Spirit came upon Peter and he spoke with power and authority so that many were saved. He no longer spoke rashly or with bravado, but with the words imparted to him. He was not perfect, he still made mistakes, but this area of weakness in him was made complete in Christ.

In 2 Timothy 1:7, we read,

> 'For God has not given us a spirit of fear but of power and of love and of a sound mind.'

So many verses concentrate on what our hearts need, like strength and courage; but this verse focuses on the spirit and mind. The message to Timothy was that he needed to stir up his God-given gifts and to not let the spirit of fear be an obstacle to preaching the Gospel. The spirit of fear comes from the evil one and its purpose was, and is, to create a blockage for those called to preach the Gospel. What God gives us is the spirit of power and love, out of which our witnessing should flow.

Peter was given a sound mind: a mind that had good judgement, good understanding and self-control. The spirit of fear was evicted as the Holy Spirit worked in him.

Through denying Christ, Peter had discovered that his love for Jesus was not as courageous as he thought it was, but it was not the end of his walk with Jesus or his ministry for Jesus. Whatever was lacking in his faith, love and courage was brought to completion and fullness through the work of the Holy Spirit. He was then able to step out in power and love.

Wherever we have shame, condemnation or guilt dwelling within us, we will be vulnerable to Satan attacking us and dragging us down. It is so important to bring these things to Christ, to the one who saw the whole of your life and who knows exactly how deep those wounds go. Bring to Him all the labels you bear: stupid, useless, failure, dirty, not wanted, a waste of space, mistake ... Bring the pain and the devastation of those labels and ask Him to bring healing to those places. Ask Him to enable you to receive and believe that you have a new name and a new identity because of Him: beloved, accepted, of surpassing worth.

This change of attitude may take time, but the more you reject the lies and stand on the truth, regardless of what your emotions tell you, the more established the truth will be.

It is good to commit all areas of our lives to God in prayer and to cover them with Jesus' salvation and righteousness. If you are aware of sin in your life, get it dealt with as quickly as possible. It is an open door and foothold to the evil one which leaves any believer in a weak, vulnerable position. If you are aware of brokenness in your life, find time to commit that to God for healing and restoration. We can carry wounds from such an early age, that we need the Holy Spirit to help us with them. When we are very young, we do not have the capacity to recognise when someone is speaking to us unjustly, so we can accept lies and labels without questioning them.

With anything where we feel that we have repeatedly struggled with something and not made any progress, Satan will persuade us to believe that there is no point in trying to overcome and that we should just accept that this is how life is. Stand against that lie in Jesus' name. It may be that asking someone trusted and wise to come alongside will be helpful as sometimes speaking out the difficulty releases God to work in a new way. Keeping shame, pain and struggle secret can act as a form of imprisonment; especially if we fear that people would despise us if they knew the truth. This does not mean announcing something sensitive to everyone, but to someone you know can respond with the grace and wisdom of God and who will help you draw close to the heart of God in that area.

Our struggles are real and powerful things. But God is above all that we face and is more than able and willing to bring us through to a place of wholeness, restoration and healing. In his letter to the Ephesians, Paul became carried away by the wonders of the Gospel and life in Christ. His sentences seem to get longer and longer as he thinks of something else that is mind-blowing about Christ and all that we have in Him. His prayer for the believers there was as follows:

> '...I bow my knees to the Father ... that He would grant you, according to the riches of His glory, to be strengthened with might through His Spirit ..., that Christ may dwell in your hearts through faith; that you, being rooted and grounded

in love, may be able to comprehend ... the love of Christ which passes knowledge; that you may be filled with all the fullness of God.' Eph. 3:14-19

What a prayer! Paul struggled to put the words to something that was so phenomenal and vast, so beyond price. What would it be to be filled with the fullness of God? To have a greater revelation of the riches of His glory? To grasp something more of the nature of God's love? If we seek the heart of God and desire to be more Christ-like, how much more does God want to work that out in us! How much more does God desire to reveal His heart to us and to complete us with Himself. This is the God who is able to do 'exceedingly abundantly' more than anything we ask or think. (See Eph. 3:20)

The peace of God does not wait until our circumstances are perfect. Paul talks about finding the ability to be content in all circumstances, which is remarkable considering the beatings and incarcerations he suffered during his ministry. Paul modelled a life lived with an eternal perspective. He knew that he was likely to die for his faith and, by the grace of God, he had peace about that. He was content that his life and death were in the hands of God, whose timing and purposes were perfect.

Through the work of God the Father, Son and Holy Spirit, Paul had found what it was to be rooted in God's love and strengthened in God's might. This had so transformed and enabled him that he prayed passionately for Timothy to know these things too, so that he could also withstand the works of the evil one, so that he could run the race to the end and so that he could be sound in mind and spirit whatever he faced.

Reflect and Respond

Head outside: Have a barbecue or picnic with friends and use the opportunity to think what it would have been like for Peter and Jesus to have that time together after the trauma and drama of the crucifixion and resurrection. Invite Jesus to meet with you and bring you healing where needed.

Research something: Choose one of the apostles and look at their lives before and after Pentecost. Where do you see them changed by receiving the spirit of 'power and love and of a sound mind?'

Ponder further: Use Paul's words in Ephesians 3:14-21 to pray for other believers: perhaps people you know but also believers who are in danger of persecution, those who find it difficult to follow Christ in their workplace and so on.

Get Creative: Draw a stone archway. On each stone, write on an area of your life that needs to be held together or made complete in Christ, then write Jesus on the cornerstone. Use this to commit each element to Jesus and invite Him to hold all things together. Declare Col. 1:17 over each area, trusting God to handle all these things.

Putting on our Shoes

It is out of this *shalom* of God, which passes all understanding, that we go out into the world: full of God, complete in God, perfect in God. When Jesus first preached in the synagogue, he stated that the prophecy of Isaiah 61 was fulfilled in Him: that He was the one who would set captives free, enable the blind to see and the deaf to hear. As we find our healing and completeness in Him, so we are to live that out and minister to others as we have the opportunity.

Before Jesus went to Calvary, we find Him gathered with His disciples. Jesus knew that He would die soon and needed to do all that was necessary for His beloved friends before that happened. He was secure in the love of His Father and in His ultimate destination, which was to be gloriously restored to His Father in heaven. In this state, Jesus got up from the dinner they were sharing and prepared to wash the feet of His friends. It is difficult to imagine the astonishment of the men as their Lord did this. All but one seemed to be speechless at this action. As ever, Simon Peter was not lost for words and objected twice to Jesus washing His feet. It did not fit with what he thought was right and proper for their Lord and Rabbi. (See John 13:1-17)

Jesus did not do things without reason. When He did something unexpected, it was often a teaching point or part of challenging an attitude or behaviour. The same is true of this incident. The disciples were challenged by their Rabbi taking on a menial role. They were unsettled by Him coming to them as a servant. Jesus was teaching them that they were also to be humble and to serve even to the point of washing feet, just as He had done. However, when we read Jesus's response to Simon Peter's objection, we discover that there was clearly a deeper spiritual significance in this. Jesus responded, "If I do not wash you, you have no part with Me."

Jesus was preparing those who were to continue His work and ministry on Earth after He had returned to the Father. This literal foot-washing was a symbol of being part of Jesus' ministry and of being joined with Him. It mattered that Simon Peter have his feet washed by Jesus, but it was not necessary for his hands or head to be washed. So why the focus on feet?

The Bible says,

> '... how beautiful upon the mountains are the feet of him who brings good news, who proclaims peace, who brings glad tidings of good things, who proclaims salvation, who says to Zion, "Your God reigns!"' Is. 52:7

At a time when journeys were often by foot, those who travelled would probably arrive with hot, dusty and sweaty feet, which is why offering hospitality involved someone washing the feet of guests and anointing them with fragrant oil. Jesus washed His disciples' feet so that their feet would be beautiful in the bringing of the Gospel and proclaiming the glad tidings of life and peace in Christ.

In the light of that, we can return to the instruction in Ephesians 6 to put on the shoes of the readiness of the Gospel of peace: the shoes of the good news of wholeness, restoration, healing and of completeness in Christ. But why *shoes*? Was that the only item left that Paul could think of?

Shoes equip us for movement, for action. We put on our shoes when we intend to step out of the home and go somewhere. It is an intentional act of preparing to move and do something. We put on our shoes to exercise outside, whether walking, running or cycling. Our shoes are functional and designed for different purposes: slippers for the house, work shoes, exercise shoes, party shoes, walking boots, summer sandals, winter wellies. Therefore, the shoes of the readiness of the Gospel of peace speak of us being mobilised, properly equipped, ready to take the good news out into the world in whatever situation we find ourselves.

We may feel that shoes are the least important part of the armour of God, however, consider going through a day without wearing shoes. Without shoes, we would notice every piece of grit we walked on; the roughness would irritate us, making us uncomfortable and miserable. Toes would frequently be stubbed, and we would experience the weather conditions more: whether cold, wet or hot. Shoes provide a protective layer between us and the immediate surroundings, neutralising some of the things that would quickly trigger misery and complaint.

Paul wrote of the shoes as being part of our armour: part of our protective, defensive clothing. One of the problems of the uniform in World War 1 was the inadequacy of the boots for the consistently wet conditions. They did not give sufficient protection against the climate or the conditions, leading to cases of trench foot, which could not easily be treated on the battlefield. The boots mattered. Having boots fit for and appropriate to the task improves the efficiency of the taskforce as they are less likely to damage the feet and allow sure-footedness for the mission.

The whole point Paul was making with the metaphor of the armour of God was that we need to submit to God so that we can resist Satan – so that we can stand and withstand every attempt of the evil one to separate us from God and destroy us. We stand and withstand the evil one in the shoes of the Gospel of peace.

Peter would not have been able to do this before he had his healing encounter with Jesus. Satan would have been able to block Peter whenever he wanted, simply by bringing the guilt and condemnation of his failure back to break him all over again. Because of the healing he received, Peter was full of the grace and peace of God, Father, Son and Holy Spirit. No longer broken, but sound and whole. He had the shoes of the Gospel of *shalom* on his feet – with every step of the race, he gave thanks for the healing of Christ which enabled him to endure even to martyrdom.

We need to put our shoes of the Gospel on so that we are ready to proclaim the Gospel of *Shalom*. We are called to *bring* and *proclaim* the good news that "our God reigns!" Wherever we go, we bring and proclaim God's *shalom*, His kingdom and His reign.

We are called to walk in shoes of wholeness, restoration and healing. We are called to walk with the Gospel message of wholeness, restoration and healing wherever we go. That is God's plan for us. The more we allow God to heal and restore us, the more we take His grace and peace into difficult situations.

Reflect and Respond Ideas

Head outside: If you can do so safely, walk outside barefoot for a bit. How does it change the way you walk and how fast you go? How far do you get before you need to clean your feet and put on appropriate shoes? As you put on your shoes, give thanks for the protection of the shoes of the readiness of the Gospel of peace.

Research something: Research shoes to find out what the requirements are for different activities. ie army boots for different conditions, climbing shoes, hiking boots, and so on. How do they enable the wearer to be equipped and prepared for their task?

Ponder further: Where do you need to be prepared and equipped with the Gospel of shalom – to be enabled to walk in His peace and wholeness? Wash your feet and use that time to ask God to anoint them with His *shalom*.

Get creative: Consider the places you go. Design your own shoes to wear in those places. On your design, write a prayer for those you encounter to welcome and receive the Gospel of *shalom*.

Grace and Peace Be With You

It is wonderful to consider just how much we learn of God's desires in the Bible. He desires us to know Him as Prince of *Shalom* and to know the blessing of being made whole and healed in Him. We see this when God gave instructions on how the priests were to speak blessing over Israel:

> "The LORD bless you and keep you; The LORD make His face shine upon you, and be gracious to you; The LORD lift up His countenance upon you, and give you peace." Num. 6:24-26

In two places, there is a reference to the blessing of God's face being turned towards His people. This was a sign of His favour and engagement with them, a sign that He was watching over them and ready to listen. There is something special about making eye contact with someone because it reassures us that we have their full attention. There is the blessing for God to show grace to them and to give them peace (wholeness, fullness and so on). There is the blessing for God's protection and provision to be with them.

The speaking of blessing was known to be a powerful act in the Old Testament, so these words were of great significance. Speaking out blessing was speaking something into being. Both Peter and Paul prayed blessings on the recipients of their letters, at the start and finish. For example, Paul's letter to the Galatian church begins,

> 'Grace to you and peace from God the Father and our Lord Jesus Christ...' Gal. 1:2

Peter's letters follow the same practice of beginning with,

> 'Grace and peace be multiplied to you in the knowledge of God and of Jesus our Lord ...' 2 Peter 1:2

These are not just lovely words or a conventional greeting of the time. Grace and peace can so often seem like nice words that we use but that do not mean very much in practice. However, the letters of the apostles were always written out of a desire to encourage and strengthen other believers so that they would endure to the end, holding fast to their faith in Christ Jesus. For them, as for many now, this meant living for Christ despite persecution and the threat of assault and death. Therefore, we should read these opening and closing lines as a recognition of what all believers urgently need every day to persevere in faith.

It is also important to remember that there is life in what we speak, so speaking out blessings of grace and peace releases those things over fellow believers. It is a powerful thing to do. If we pray nothing else for our brothers and sisters in Christ, we should speak these blessings over them as a means of releasing the tools that they need to run the race to the very end. Indeed, the final verse of the Bible is, 'The grace of our Lord Jesus Christ be with you all. Amen.' (Rev. 22:21) After the extraordinary and complex revelations given to John about the end times and the world to come, John prays for the grace of Christ to be with us. We need to pay attention to this call to pray for our fellow believers to know the grace and peace of our God.

Again, this is something that only God can provide. Whatever hobbies we have or holidays we take, there is a place within us that can only be brought to peace by the grace and presence of God.

As Joseph did, we need to learn to depart from evil and do good, in heart, mind and deed; we need to seek and pursue peace. His testimony came as he walked with God in all circumstances and endured for the promise of God upon his life. He could testify with his whole heart, his healed and restored heart, that God had preserved many lives through him as a result. That trauma had been redeemed, and many lives were saved.

Respond

Firstly, make the prayer personal to you: *May God's grace and peace be multiplied to me today, as I work / parent / minster / settle to sleep / face this difficult situation / drive ...* Give thanks that God desires to fill you with His grace and peace and that these words have power to change you.

Secondly, become a person of blessing: intentionally speaking life, grace and peace into the lives of those you encounter. To help you, keep one of the Scriptures of blessing with your phone or computer so that you can pause and speak blessing over the people you have messaged.

JOY

rinnah (Hebrew)

A shout of rejoicing; shouting; loud cheering in triumph; singing. Zeph. 3:17 literally says that God will dance over His beloved people with singing or a shout of joy...[33]

What brings you joy? Before going any further, jot down the things that bring you the greatest joy in life. Maybe it is spending time with friends, favourite places or activities, sunshine and blue skies. Give thanks for those things and the people who release joy into your heart.

What kills your joy? Jot those things down too. It might be driving or trying to get your children to do their homework; management meetings where nothing gets resolved or finding that household mess is getting extreme. There may be places you go that feel oppressive or people that are emotionally draining. There may be practical steps to take for approaching these things, so bring them before God.

When times are tough, joy is an emotion that often seems out of reach, something that is reserved for special occasions. We will experience grief in our lives and many of us have some experience of depression and spiritual heaviness. We find that we get run down and overwhelmed by the daily tasks of our lives. Joy is something we would often love to experience and find strength in, but how is it to be grasped?

---

[33] Definition taken from the supplementary notes of *The Spirit-Filled Life Bible*, pp. 777-778

The Source of Joy

In two contexts, we learn that joy is given and produced in us by God. Joy is listed as a *fruit* of the Holy Spirit: a gift and result of God at work in our lives. (Gal. 5:22) Isaiah 61 teaches that God's desire is to exchange our mourning for the oil of joy, which speaks of it being an *anointing* upon us. God Himself wants to anoint us with His oil of joy.

Joy is not solely for the extroverted optimist. In fact, it is little to do with personality type at all. It is everything to do with salvation. The greatest joy is knowing that, ultimately, we are safe and secure and that when we are in Christ all is well. This is the eternal view and it is needed. It is how Paul managed to be content even when facing horrendous persecution. He knew that even if the worst happened on Earth, he would still know the restoration of all things in Christ.

Grafting is a process that works well with apple trees. It involves cutting a stem of one variety, that is good but could be improved, and inserting it into a cut edge on the root stock of a host plant, which is a stronger, more resilient variety. As the cut edges are held together, the graft continues to grow the apple of one variety, whilst benefitting from the strengths of the host plant. We do not lose our personalities when we are in Christ, we become grafted into Him and He enables us to be the best version of ourselves through His strength and resources. We are grafted onto the true vine, which means that we take on the characteristics of the host plant – we become more like Christ.

As with many things, we can know this as a fact yet not experience a release of joy because of it. But our God is a joyful God, a singing God, a rejoicing God. It is one of the most astonishing truths of the Bible that our God rejoices over each one of us! He finds joy in us. We were created to join with the joyful, exuberant fellowship that was known by the Trinity in the beginning. At the end of the book of Job, God asks Job whether he was there at the creation of the world, 'when the morning stars sang together, and all the sons of God shouted for joy?' (Job 38:7) The creation of the world was not marked with a solemn Sabbath, but with joyous shouts and songs of celebration! So, as we are grafted into Christ, we should then find that we are becoming more like God in His joy. We can invite the Holy Spirit to make us more like Christ in this and to anoint us with the oil of joy.

We rejoice, not because our circumstances are perfect or because we are in denial about what we face, but because of the eternal truths that we have in Christ. In Isaiah 61:7, God promises that His people will have *everlasting joy*, which we Gentiles share in with the Jewish people because we are grafted into God's kingdom. Isaiah responds to God's promise by stating,

> 'I will greatly rejoice in the LORD, my soul shall be joyful in my God; for He has clothed me with the garments of salvation, He has covered me with the robe of righteousness... For as the earth brings forth its bud, as the garden causes the things that are sown in it to spring forth, so the Lord GOD will cause righteousness and praise to spring forth before all the nations.' Is. 61:10-11

In Ephesians 6, we are called to put on a breastplate of righteousness and a helmet of salvation. However, here, Isaiah rejoices because God Himself has covered him in salvation and righteousness. Righteousness means that God Himself has made us right before Him: what we could not earn or achieve, God freely gave us out of His love, grace and mercy at Calvary where He paid for our sins. We were saved once and for all by accepting Christ as Lord and Saviour; our eternal life is assured. But salvation and righteousness are also worked out in us as we walk through life with the Spirit helping us become more like Christ.

Putting on the armour is a daily process of deliberately focusing our hearts on kingdom qualities and receiving them as our covering. He covers us with the robe of righteousness, but we also choose to put on the breastplate of righteousness by setting our hearts to conform to His will and expectations. We rejoice because we were saved and made righteous at Calvary, but we can rejoice every time God saves us. We can rejoice when we are driving and God alerts us to a hazard we had not spotted, or when He stops us from saying something tactless or hurtful.

These elements all come together in Isaiah 61: joy, righteousness, salvation and praise. Our right response to righteousness and salvation is rejoicing and praise. This is true all the time and not just when everything has come together in our circumstances.

Reflect and Respond Ideas

Head outside: Go to a garden and look at the different stages of growth with the plants. As those things are growing, give thanks that God will cause righteousness and praise to spring forth before all nations. (Is. 61:10-11)

Research something: Research the grafting process to see what growers aim for and which plants it works for. What traits come from the host plant? What is wanted from the plant that is grafted on?

Ponder further: What is your personality like? When was the last time you experienced joy? Does it feel like joy is something that other people experience?

Get creative: Create a map showing what leads you to the destination of joy and what leads to the destination of depression or heaviness. Use this to remind you of the need to turn back when you find yourselves heading the wrong way.

The Choice to Rejoice

We do not rejoice because things have fallen apart in our lives. We rejoice because of the eternal and unchanging truths of who God is and because He is with us in whatever we encounter. We rejoice not because we can perform miracles, but because our names are written in the Lamb's Book of Life and we are forever held by God Most High. We rejoice because He sees and hears us in the darkest times and is working on our behalf. We rejoice because God can and will use things for good, as Joseph recorded in his life. We rejoice because that is such a blessed relief! Satan does not get the final say, God does. When a believer dies, Satan loses. Yes, we grieve but victory is always in the hands of God.

As we persevere through the tough times, the Holy Spirit can inspire songs within us that help us through and focus our minds on God. As Psalm 40 says:

> 'I waited patiently for the LORD; and He inclined to me ...
> He has put a new song in my mouth – praise to our God...'
> Ps. 40:1-3

Ideally, praise would flow from us, spontaneously, at all times – perhaps it does for some! Not all of us have personalities that are naturally expressive. I love the beginning of Psalm 45, where the sons of Korah found themselves inspired to rejoice and boast in awe of the King:

> 'My heart is overflowing with a good theme; I recite my composition concerning the King; my tongue is the pen of a ready writer.' Ps. 45:1

How wonderful if the people of God had hearts overflowing with a good theme – so delighting in the King of kings that our praises to Him poured from us; so full of the worship of God that our hearts and minds had no room for bitterness, gossip, discontent or distraction. One day, we will be in the presence of our God and our hearts will naturally overflow with praise, worship and adoration. It will not be difficult, an effort, an act of will or an act of determination. It will not be boring or go on too long. We will not wish that we could sing better and hit the high notes. It will be a natural response to being in God's presence.

This side of heaven we will have moments, as the sons of Korah did, when our hearts are stirred, touched and anointed to praise and worship God. I suspect that the 'ready writer' was the Holy Spirit, moving the hearts of the men and placing the words on their tongues. However, looking through the Psalms is a quick way to ascertain that rejoicing, praising and singing are often decisions as much as spontaneous acts of joy. Psalm 63 says,

> 'When I remember You on my bed, I meditate on You in the night watches. Because You have been my help, therefore in the shadow of Your wings I will rejoice. My soul follows close behind You; Your right hand upholds me.' Ps. 63:6-8

Referring to the watches of the night reminds me of the guards who would keep watch over the city and how we, too, need to keep watch over our minds in the darkness. Lying awake at night is often the time that fear and despair can overwhelm us. This Psalm reminds us of the need to focus our minds on God during the night. The help of God is compared with being hidden by His wings: we stand on the truth that we are protected, concealed, held safe by the Almighty God who never slumbers; and because we can dwell in that place of refuge, we can sing even in the darkness. That positioning of soul is essential. As we choose to focus our thoughts and emotions on God and who He is, we come back into that positioning of dwelling within the realm of God's protection and love. As we cling to Him in the depths of our beings, He upholds us.

Singing out loud is good but singing inside is also good for us. Having a worship song running through our minds is helpful in many situations when singing aloud is not appropriate. Praise and worship has a transforming effect within us: our emotions may not be in the mood to begin with but focusing on God can bring about the change we need. Singing praises to God builds faith in us and encourages those around us. It is a means of expressing our trust in God.

Whether we sing in our hearts or out loud, praise and thanksgiving should be part of our expression of joy in Christ and to Christ. Even this act of praising flows from an infilling of the Holy Spirit! It flows from God the Spirit through us back to God.

It sounds wonderful. It also sounds very far from life experience when things are hard. In the darkness, joy and praise can be all but impossible to get into. Why? Because they are strongly contested in a way that seems very reasonable. Why would we want to praise God when things are hard? Isaiah 61 tells us that Christ came to replace the spirit of heaviness with a garment of praise. This is one of those verses that prompts in me the response of, that sounds great – how does that happen?

It is interesting that we have the image of a *garment* of praise, a metaphor of an outer covering, which is to replace the *spirit* of heaviness, something that can infuse our minds and hearts, weighing us down in a subtle but highly effective way. Feeling a heaviness inside slows us down, reducing our energy, motivation and sense that things can change for the better. It is not something that we are supposed to live with. The spirit of heaviness is something to be recognised and rejected in the name of Jesus. It also suggests that, through Christ, we can choose to clothe ourselves with praise. It is a replacement process: we renounce the work and presence of the spirit of heaviness in us and choose to replace it with the garment of praise as a covering and protection against that heaviness. We choose to speak out, sing out, play out, dance out our worship of God and to rejoice in His victory over darkness.

In Acts 16, we learn that Paul and Silas had been severely beaten and arrested in Philippi, sent to prison with their feet in the stocks. Many of us would see that as grounds for crying out to God in complaint at the injustice of being arrested for carrying out our God-given mission. We would certainly see it as an excellent reason not to praise or worship. However, Paul and Silas saw this as an opportunity to pray and sing, with the other prisoners listening. We do not know if they expected a miraculous rescue or were simply continuing their practice of prayer and praise in every circumstance. I suspect the latter. However, at midnight, when they were praying and singing,

> 'Suddenly there was a great earthquake, so that the foundations of the prison were shaken; and immediately all the doors were opened and everyone's chains were loosed.'
> Acts 16:26

Out of all the methods God could have chosen to deliver the two men, he chose something dramatic – an earthquake that shook the area and the opening of *every single* cell door. Why? God could have used a method that was discreet, allowing Paul and Silas to sneak silently away without anyone knowing anything about it. Instead, He used a method that was noticed by everyone. All the prisoners knew that this had happened while the two men of God prayed and praised. Awakened by the earthquake, the jailor intended to kill himself at the shame of all the prisoners escaping, but when assured that they were all still there, he 'called for a light, ran in, and fell down trembling before Paul and Silas,' asking how he could be saved. He was under no illusion about the cause of these frightening events. He went to Paul and Silas, not any of the other prisoners. The two men shared the Gospel to the jailor and his household, with the result that all were saved and baptised that very night. The jailor called for a light in the prison and received the light of Christ into his life, setting him free from spiritual imprisonment and death.

Most of us will not experience imprisonment for our faith, but the principle still applies to any spiritual imprisonment we face. Taking imprisonment as a metaphor, consider the earthquake and opened doors that result in the spiritual places as we praise God! Whatever has caused us to feel imprisoned in our souls or in our circumstances is shaken violently when we sing out in faith, leaving us free to move once more. Praise is a powerful weapon against the enemy. The outcome is in God's hands, the choice to praise is in our hands.

Praising to Victory

Praise as a powerful weapon is seen clearly in the story of Jehoshaphat, King of Judah, in 2 Chronicles 19 and 20. The story began with a challenge from God. As Jehoshaphat returned to Jerusalem from battle, he was met by Jehu, a man bringing a word from the LORD. Jehu said,

> "...should you help the wicked and love those who hate the LORD? Therefore the wrath of the LORD is upon you. Nevertheless good things are found in you, in that you have removed the wooden images from the land, and have prepared your heart to seek God." 2 Chron. 19:1-3

Having just seen Ahab, King of Israel, die in battle as prophesied, Jehoshaphat took this word seriously and resolved to act on it. Getting rid of the idols in his nation was a good start and his heart was focusing in the right way to honour God, but there was more to be done in his attitudes, priorities and leadership. He gathered his people and set judges over them who would administer cities in holy fear of the LORD, ensuring that they would not take bribes or show favouritism in their rulings. He appointed priests to "act in the fear of the LORD, faithfully and with a loyal heart." (2 Chron. 19:9) In this way, Jehoshaphat began to restore godly foundations to the administrative and religious structures of the kingdom of Judah, by appointing men who feared the LORD and by emphasising that his expectation of them was godly service. This was not about giving an external appearance of obedience whilst allowing abuses of power. The king wanted to appoint men whose *hearts* were set on honouring God.

This was all good. What happened in response to this restoration of Judah before God? The people of Moab, Ammon and Syria set out to declare war on Judah. (2 Chron. 20) Yet again, we see the familiar story that hearts turning towards God and actively seeking to be set apart for Him lead quickly to opposition. When warned of the great multitude coming against him, Jehoshaphat was afraid, despite both himself and his army being tried and tested in battle. He was a soldier and had been willing to join with King Ahab of Israel when asked, as long as the prophets of the LORD endorsed that. (2 Chron. 18:1-9). Jehoshaphat was clearly not a coward or afraid of warfare – quite the contrary. But he had the experience, wisdom and humility to recognise quickly that whatever military response he could muster would not be enough against the combined forces of three nations.

The prophet, Jehu, had affirmed God's pleasure in the way Jehoshaphat had sought Him and destroyed the idols, and the king's faith was further built up by knowing that God had miraculously delivered him from death in the recent battle against Syria. (2 Chron. 18:28-31) Therefore, the king took action in two ways: he personally began to seek the LORD and he called his people to fast.

'Then he gathered his people together at the house of God, and Jehoshaphat led them in prayer.

"O LORD God of our fathers, are You not God in heaven, and do You not rule over all the kingdoms of the nations, and in Your hand is there not power and might, so that no one is able to withstand You? ... If disaster comes upon us ... we will stand before this temple and in Your presence ... and cry out to You in our affliction and You will hear and save."'
2 Chron. 20:5-9

All Judah, including the children, stood before the LORD. All generations were involved and engaged in this process of seeking the LORD. How much would that have impacted the young ones to be present at such a critical time? The adult instinct is always to protect children from danger and anything that would cause fear. I am writing this during the coronavirus lockdown when children across the world are all too aware of the situation – it cannot be hidden from them, we could not stop it from impacting their lives, and it has caused anxiety and fear in them as well as in adults. The children of Judah would have been aware of the threat of the opposing army, especially once the adults began fasting as a response to the royal command, and so the decision was made to include them at this gathering. No one was to stay home. The children witnessed the fasting of the adults around them, they were present as their King prayed aloud before his people to the LORD of their fathers and they were present in the waiting.

Most importantly, they were also then present as the Spirit of the LORD came upon Jehaziel showing that God had heard them and would deliver them. This was not reported to them after the event in a child-appropriate summary: they heard it for themselves.

> 'Then the Spirit of the LORD came upon Jahaziel ... "Listen, all you ... Thus says the LORD to you: Do not be afraid nor dismayed because of this great multitude, for the battle is not yours, but God's."' 2 Chron. 20:14-15

The people had collectively brought their fear and helplessness before God through their prayers and fasting, and God began by telling them that there was no need to fear because the battle was His, not theirs. The enemy had risen against them because of Jehoshaphat's desire and work to restore a righteous nation before the LORD; therefore, God would defend His people. This provided the necessary context for what was to come. There can be a great sense of responsibility and burden that comes when we face opposition: we feel the obligation to bring about resolution for ourselves and those affected by it. For King Jehoshaphat, his actions to establish righteousness were for the benefit of his nation in the eyes of the LORD; but it looked as though that decision was going to lead to Judah's destruction instead. He could have called his advisors together and done all he could do to ready the people, but instead, he 'set himself' to seek God. And God responded to him and the people with the message, *this is My battle, not yours; this is My responsibility and obligation, not yours; I am your King and I will lead you.*

Instructions were given to them, along with promises from the

LORD:

1. "Tomorrow go down against them. They will surely come up by the Ascent of Ziz, and you will find them at the end of the brook before the Wilderness of Jeruel. You will not need to fight in this battle." 2 Chron. 20:16-17a

Firstly, they must leave the place of God and the relative safety of the walled city, and deliberately go to approach the enemy. They were not to wait for the enemy to arrive at their gates and attempt to repel this attack. They were to go out as they were, outnumbered and outclassed, and go towards the enemy. They were not to sit by passively whilst God did everything for them at a safe distance. God promised that they would not have to fight, but they did need to be armed and present in the place of battle, facing the enemy.

The information God gave was specific: the enemy would approach from one direction so Judah was to encounter them at the place appointed by God. The clarity of these instructions left no room for misunderstanding. Not following them would therefore be a case of unbelief (*this was not from God*), lack of trust *(He will not come through for us)* or disobedience *(I know better and the end of the brook is not the right place to be; besides, why go tomorrow? We need more time to prepare.)*

2. "Position yourselves, stand still and see the salvation of the LORD, who is with you, O Judah and Jerusalem.'" 2 Chron. 20:17b

We see again the importance of being rightly positioned and being able to stand in that place of danger, trusting that God will fulfil His promise. To take this step of faith would take immense courage and conviction, because they knew that they did not have the military strength to defeat the opposing army. If God did not come through for them, they would be slaughtered. In that position, God told them that they will *see* the salvation that He had promised: He wanted them to witness His miraculous victory and they could not do that by staying in Jerusalem.

3. "Do not fear or be dismayed; tomorrow go out against them, for the LORD is with you." 2 Chron. 20:17c

The instruction here spoke straight into their thoughts and emotions: Judah was not to allow fear or dismay to take a foothold because the LORD was with them. Whilst this would be easier said than done, it was a vital instruction because between hearing the word of the LORD and responding the following day, there would be a gap of several hours. Those would be the hours when doubt and fear would strike; the little whisper of, 'did the LORD really say that?' would arrive, prompting the consideration that perhaps it was just Jahaziel's imagination, or that he was kindly trying to make everyone feel better. Perhaps Jehoshaphat had ordered him to 'hear from the LORD' about going into battle, knowing that his army would not want to go to certain defeat and death. It is during the night that you lie awake and the thought of the imminent battle looms large, with all the recognition of the opposition's strengths, victories and numbers; then the painful acknowledgement that you cannot compare with them and there is nothing you can do about it.

How valuable, then, that the whole community were present to hear and to respond together before night fell. As Jehoshaphat bowed low before God, so did his people and they worshipped the LORD together. The priestly tribe of Levi then stood up to 'praise the LORD God of Israel with voices loud and high.' What a scene that must have been: a nation on its knees in worship of God, with faces to the ground. Men, women and children with hearts overwhelmed that the Almighty God of the universe had spoken to them personally and had promised to deliver them; their hopeless despair turned to thankful relief and hope. The Levites standing among them singing and shouting out the praises of God. Instead of spending the night in fear, they went to their beds in worship and praise.

Early the following morning, they gathered once more to hear the king encourage them:

"'Hear me, O Judah and you inhabitants of Jerusalem:
Believe in the LORD your God, and you shall be established;
believe His prophets, and you shall prosper." And when
he had consulted with the people, he appointed those who
should sing to the LORD, and who should praise the beauty
of holiness, as they went out before the army and were

saying: "Praise the LORD, for His mercy endures forever."'
2 Chron. 20:20-21

The word of the LORD had been given, now it was time to step out in faith. The vanguard, forming the frontline of troops, consisted of the worshippers chosen by the king and the people. Their one job was praising and declaring God's mercy, faithfulness and holiness. Interestingly, this was not part of God's instructions to them: He had said nothing about taking a worship group with them. So why was this done? The army could have gone alone. However, it was clearly a significant and deliberate action on the part of the king, who consulted with his people before choosing those who should be in the praise squad. The people were in agreement on this: yes, the army was going and they would go out heralded by the praises of God. Why? I believe it was an outward expression of their joyful confidence in God's existence and deliverance. Had they gone out in fear, they would undoubtedly let the armed men go first, anticipating trouble.

We should note that one group of worshippers were specifically appointed to focus on the beauty of holiness. Enemies had risen against Judah because the king and people were returning to being a holy people before God Most High: returning to lives of purity, sanctity, righteousness and being set apart for Him, renouncing all other gods and idols. Judah's decision to pursue and live in the beauty of holiness had led to opposition, so it was a very intentional act to proclaim this as they marched out towards their enemies. The message was clear: despite the intimidation and threat of massacre, the people would still choose the beauty of holiness before the one true God. Not as a quiet, inner resolution, nor as a valiant effort at appearing brave, but as a loud, clamorous riot of sound! Judah was not going to silently creep towards their enemies, hoping not to be seen or invite trouble. No – Judah was going out in praise and exultation of their God and they wanted everyone to know it. The army of Judah followed the worshippers with hearts uplifted and strengthened by those who went in front.

'Now *when they began to sing and to praise*, the LORD set ambushes against the people of Ammon, Moab, and

Mount Seir... and they were defeated.' 2 Chron. 20:22 (my emphasis)

God's action against Judah's enemy is directly and unequivocally linked to the praises of His people that morning. Unbeknownst to them, the *moment* they began to praise as they set out in obedience and faith, God fulfilled His promise to them. He did not wait for them to praise for a certain length of time or wait for them to arrive. The critical factors were their obedience and their heart positions of praise, delight and trust in Him. When the men of Judah arrived at the appointed place, they found that the opposing armies had destroyed each other. There was nothing left to do but gather the spoils of war.

'Then they returned ... to Jerusalem with joy, for the LORD had made them rejoice over their enemies. So they came to Jerusalem, with stringed instruments and harps and trumpets to the house of the LORD.' 2 Chron. 20:27-28

The emotion of joy is mentioned specifically as Judah returned to Jerusalem in victory and praise, but the joy had begun the day before in the darkness when they had heard the voice of the LORD. The joy of victory would not have come without the earlier actions in the despair and hopelessness when:

- they all recognised their inability to resolve the situation.
- they sought the LORD with prayer and fasting, on their own and corporately.
- when the Spirit of the LORD came upon one of the prophets, and they listened and worshipped with thankful, faith-filled hearts.
- they maintained their faith as they were obedient to God's instructions.
- they praised and worshipped the LORD together when the word was given and as they followed God's instructions – all *before* the victory had happened.
- they went out to face the enemy in praise of God, armed for

battle.
- they stepped out in the faith that God would go before them and do all He promised.

This course of action opened the way to victory – a victory that was clearly not won by man, but by God. It took faith, humility and courage; but how great was their joy when the victory was won! It is as though the moment they heard God's voice and started to praise and worship it began to fill a reservoir of joy and the moment of victory was when the joy overflowed and flooded out.

I wonder if God smiled at that moment, watching His children sing and dance back into the city, racing to be the first to share the miracle of what had happened but so excited that they could barely get the words out ... smiling at their wonder and joy, and smiling because He knew that the far greater victory had taken place the previous day, when they chose to turn to Him and trust in Him in the darkness. It was easy for Him to defeat their enemy, but everyone has free will to choose to turn to Him or turn away from Him: everyone has free will to trust Him or not. The greater miracle was for the people to turn to Him, trust Him and step out together in unity, in faith and praise.

Reflect and Respond Ideas

Head outside: Take a journey of victory: walk or run with the knowledge of God's victory over the evil one. In your heart, speak or sing praise to God, declaring that He has overcome every power of hell.

Research something: Read this story in full and pay attention to the leadership skills of the King and the willingness of the people to follow his lead. Pray for church leaders and those they lead to be full of the Holy Spirit.

Ponder further: Which worship songs have particularly spoken to you in difficult times? What truth did you need to hear from them? Have you experienced a change in your attitude as you worshipped God?

Get creative: Compose a song of praise to our God. It does not need to be written down or professional, just let your heart overflow with the things you love about Him.

Finding Joy on the Barricades

Joy in the LORD takes an eternal view. In the dark times, it may be possible to experience the emotion of joy and keep a smile on your face, but it is probably not what happens. Yet, Paul and Silas genuinely were in prison when they sang praises to God, with no guarantee of a positive outcome or a miracle coming their way. They sang anyway because God was still God. In prison or in freedom, they praised God Most High. With Paul, we know that his attitude of praise was the same whether he was free or in prison. If God had not miraculously freed him that day, he would have continued to praise. Paul was fully aware that he was likely to die for his faith and indeed, one day, God did not save him from death. Paul praised anyway, because he was convinced that the one he lived for was worth all his praise and adoration and that one day he would stand before his King. Nothing on Earth compared with what was to come in God's presence.

Having that attitude is quite something. Paul was not superhuman; he was not immune from a conflict of emotions or will. He loved God and knew that his physical death would bring him into the presence of the one who had saved him, so he had chosen to live in that eternal view whereby he looked past physical death into the perfect love of his Father. But Paul also loved those he had seen come to faith and being separated from them was his main source of grief. He wanted to be with them, personally seeing their faith, standing alongside them and helping them to run the race well. His letters are full of information because he wanted to do everything he could to encourage those he loved and to cheer them on.

Yet even Paul may have experienced moments inside when he felt that he was on the barricades spiritually – that he had established a place to stand and withstand in faith, no matter what the enemy did in response. When you feel that you are on the barricades, holding on for dear life, shout out the triumph and victory of God. Exult in His sovereignty over your circumstances; boast of all that He has done and all that He is.

We see this approach in the book of the prophet, Habbakuk. It is only three chapters long but is full of the things on his heart and the interactions between him and God. It begins with Habbakuk bringing his burden before God: a burden for the iniquity, injustice and corruption of Judah. His heart was broken by what he saw around him; all that caused oppression and pain, and all that was against the will of God. He brought his pain and need to the only one who was able to speak into that; the only one who was able to work in a situation that was entirely beyond his control.

> 'O LORD, how long shall I cry, and You will not hear? Even cry out to You, "Violence!" and You will not save. Why do You show me iniquity, and cause me to see trouble? For plundering and violence are before me; there is strife, and contention arises. Therefore the law is powerless, and justice never goes forth. For the wicked surround the righteous; therefore perverse judgement proceeds.' Hab. 1:2-4

Habbakuk's sense of frustration and helplessness is clear here, flowing from the feeling that God had not heard him despite his cries to Him. He was so aware of the lawlessness, wickedness and strife around him that he could not ignore it and he was impatient to see God at work in the situation. He longed to see the people restored to godly living.

As a prophet, Habbakuk not only brought the burden he carried for the nation to God but also listened for His response. God had heard him and revealed His plan to him: the unwelcome news that Judah would be invaded. This was not the outcome that Habbakuk had hoped for and we hear him try to make sense of this, adjusting to what he has heard. He worked through what he knew about God and what he had seen of people, asking why things were as they were.

> 'Are You not from everlasting, O LORD my God, my Holy One? ... O LORD ... O Rock ... Why ... why ...' Taken from Hab. 1:12-14

He arrived at the conclusion that he should continue to fulfil his calling before God, even without hearing the answers to his questioning of why:

> 'I will stand my watch and set myself on the rampart, and

watch to see what He will say to me, and what I will answer when I am corrected.' Hab. 2:1

Habbakuk knew that his role was as a watchman and a prophet. The role of watchman involves being observant, noticing activity before others and alerting others. This role relates to the security and well-being of the community so it is an on-going responsibility. Spiritually, the same principles apply, except that in this sense the 'watchman' is sensitive to what is going on behind the scenes and so can recognise things of spiritual concern before others or recognise a change of season before others.

As a prophet, Habbakuk's role was to dwell in that place of closeness to God so he could listen to His voice. In response, the prophet interceded before God for the people, then spoke out God's words to the people. Habbakuk had the humility to recognise that his understanding was limited and that his attitudes would be changed by God's words. Having made his decision on acting this way and positioning himself to watch and listen, God gave him the vision of what would be. In a lengthy part of the text, there came a revelation about the wickedness of those who had been violent, plundering other nations, exalting themselves, making idols and so on, and the woe that would befall them.

Habbakuk's response to this further revelation was to stand in the position of intercessor between Judah and God. When the protective city walls have been breached by sin, God calls for an intercessor to stand in that gap in prayer. (Ezek. 22:30) The intercessor experiences some of God's grief at the sin of the people but also some of God's desire for restoration as this stirs them up to pray. Habbakuk saw Judah's sin and the consequences that would result. This led him to pray for Judah in what was to come:

'O LORD, I have heard Your speech and was afraid; O LORD, revive Your work in the midst of the years! In the midst of the years make it known; in wrath remember mercy.' Hab. 3:2

It is important to note that he did not pray for God's wrath to be turned away at this point. An intercessor needs to recognise what is in line with God's will. Judah had not held to the covenant with God, despite knowing the consequences of that for generations. Habbakuk recognised that he was not to pray for judgement to be swept away, as this was the means of calling the people to repentance. However, he did ask God to hold mercy alongside His righteous wrath and asked God to 'revive [His] work in the midst' of those consequences: to open the way for redemption and restoration through the trial that was to come. In his prayer, Habbakuk spoke about God and prophesied about the Messiah (in verse 13). He was also honest about his personal response, which was one of fear at what was to come and fear that he might not fulfil his role before God. (Hab. 3:16)

It was important to him to continue in that place of prayer but also the place of praise. His next response was to write a hymn of faith. He resolved to rejoice in God, no matter what was now and what was to come. It was both a song to be set to music by the chief musician for use in public worship and a personal proclamation of faith from the barricades that God was sovereign over all.

> 'Though the fig tree may not blossom, nor fruit be on the vines; though the labour of the olive may fail, and the fields yield no food ... yet I will rejoice in the LORD, I will joy in the God of my salvation. The LORD God is my strength; He will make my feet like deer's feet, and He will make me walk on my high hills.' Hab. 3:17-19

Habbakuk decided this whilst he was still in dark circumstances, knowing full well that the darkness of those times would not only continue but get much worse before they got better. He knew that God needed to bring the people to repentance and that his role was to stand firm in faith and obedience before God.

How did he do this?

1. He chose and prepared his place to stand: no matter what destruction came upon the nation, represented by the failure of the fig tree (an image for Israel), the vine, the fields and the flocks, he resolved to rejoice in God. In the deprivation and grief to come, he would stand in a heart attitude of praise to God, focusing on the eternal and unchanging truth of His goodness and greatness.

2. His words were filled with faith, conviction and determination, without wavering doubt or anxiety. He stated, '*I will* rejoice', then followed with statements about God: He *is* my strength, He *will* make my feet like deer's feet, He *will* make me walk on my high hills. In other words, Habbakuk chose to take a stand on the truth that God was and would continue to be the strength he needed, and that God would make his feet sure in all the difficult, sheer terrain that was to come.

3. He made God's promises personal to him: the LORD God is *my* strength. He resolved to find joy in God's promises to him, no matter what hardship he faced.

This act of resolution, this act of self-discipline and will-power is important. Our will does not automatically choose God, so we need to exert authority over it and bring it into submission. Joshua gave Israel the choice about who they would follow, stating that "as for me and my house, we will serve the LORD." (Josh. 24:15) That is a decision we make when we come to Christ, but it is also a decision to make in the tough times when you are at the crossroads of faith and doubt. Standing in the middle in indecision is not a good place to be, but it is a very natural place for us to find ourselves. Our lives will continually bring us to this point each time we face a set of circumstances that require us to step out and trust God: faith or doubt? Which way will you go this time?

Pause for a moment and consider whether you have made that resolution or whether you need to make it again. Our faith can easily waver and God knows that. It is good to recognise if we have gone back to sitting on the proverbial fence, because we have been hurt or battered in our circumstances and especially when we do not know how long the season will last. If, or rather, when we set off down the path of doubt, as we easily do, that is not the end of the story. Remember that you can stop at any time and choose to make a stand in faith. Where we position ourselves spiritually in our will and attitudes is so important as these inform our behaviour in the darkness.

The book of Habbakuk demonstrates the vital steps of bringing to God the things that break our hearts, that cause us grief and confusion. Current world events can be overwhelming, so our response should be to take them straight to the one who sees all and who is able to work in those situations. However, we need to recognise that our very natural desire is for the challenges and difficulties to be magicked away, not to hear that the situation will worsen first. The trouble was that God's people had turned to wickedness and did not want to turn back to God. God wanted to reach those people and to see them restored to relationship with Him, because He knew what damage wickedness would do to His children. Habbakuk listened to God and was troubled by His words because God's plans were not what he hoped for, but he had the spiritual maturity to ascertain how to keep his feet securely in faith despite that.

Habbakuk had gone before God with a heart set to understand and to seek the LORD in the breakdown of the world around him. That should be our response too as we hear about world events and what is happening in our own nations. Our response is to go before the LORD and to listen to Him, then to pray as He leads.

This process is a necessary one in our walk with God: presenting our concerns and our burdens for the world around us or for our personal circumstances. The sheer number of Psalms indicate how important it was to express the burden or concern *and* to express faith in God. If we look at Psalm 57 as an example, the words were written by King David to a tune entitled, 'Do Not Destroy!' Not something that we come across in our worship music today! But they had music that was written specifically for occasions when the people were crying out for mercy and deliverance. The Psalm begins with a heartfelt cry for mercy at a time when David's life was threatened, but these words of desperate need are interspersed with words of faith:

'Have mercy on me, O God, have mercy on me ... I cry out to God Most High...

He sends from heaven and saves me, rebuking those who hotly pursue me... *Selah*

God sends His love and faithfulness.' From Ps. 57:1-3, NIV

The word *selah* is a word for musical direction, indicating that this was a place to pause and consider; a moment to lift up and exalt God.[34] David paused at that moment in order to alter his thinking from the very natural attitude of desperate fear to the eternal perspective of recognising God at work. He reminded himself that God had delivered him before and would do it again, and that those who sought his life would face the judgement of God. It was not David facing the situation alone; it was not one man, outnumbered by numerous other men. It was David and the Living God together. He paused and considered his circumstances in the light of this fact. He paused, lifted up and exalted the one who delivered him, the one who was involved in the situation with him. He then remembered the love and faithfulness of God as well. The Psalm concludes with a rousing stirring up of faith and resolution:

'I will praise You, O Lord, among the nations; I will sing of You among the peoples. For great is Your love, reaching to the heavens; Your faithfulness reaches to the skies. Be exalted, O God, above the heavens; let Your glory be over all the earth.' Psalm 57:9-11, NIV

This process enabled David to be steadfast in heart: steadfast in courage, strength and allegiance to God. As with Habbakuk, David set his will to sing, praise and declare the greatness of God's love, faithfulness and glory over all created things. He recognised that he needed to awaken his soul and his desire to praise and sing of the goodness of God. He needed to stir himself up on the inside to respond in this way. In the darkness, David chose a path that would invite and release God's glory. Whatever our spiritual calling, we will all have this need to choose how we focus heart and mind in the dark times. We will all have times when we need to resolve with determination that we will praise God in the darkness.

This resolution to praise and rejoice in God because of who He was and is and always will be is a vital step in experiencing joy as an

---

[34] Cornwall and Smith, *Bible Names*, p. 163

emotion in the darkness. The emotion of joy tends to follow the resolution to praise, no matter what the circumstances are and no matter how you feel about it. The stirring up of determination, will and faith come first, the feelings follow on.

Reflect and Respond Ideas

Head outside: If you get the opportunity, stand in a gateway or gap in a wall. If it was your job to guard that place and the people in your area from evil, how would you pray? What skills would you need to stand firm in that place?

Research something: Spend some time reading the introductions to different Psalms. Who wrote them? In what circumstances were they written? What was the tune called? What does this reveal about how needs, heartache and praise was expressed?

Ponder further: What makes you fearful in your walk with God? Has He ever asked you to do something that left you worried that you would not be able to fulfil that task? Use Habakkuk's statement of faith or the words of David in Psalm 57 to encourage your heart.

Get creative: Use lego or boxes to create a barricade of faith. Label your barricade or draw on your faith statements or slogans.

The Joy of the LORD is our Strength

We tend to take this phrase as a useful word of encouragement, and rightly so. Joy is a powerful weapon against the enemy. (Neh. 8:10) Therefore, it is also true that when we lose our ability to experience and stand in the joy of the LORD, that we become weak and unable to stand in our time of challenge, or even in the ordinary ups and downs of life.

But what is the context to this statement? In the book of Nehemiah we read of his project to rebuild Jerusalem's walls and gates. The physical destruction was a sign of reproach upon Israel, a sign that they had rebelled against God. The physical rebuilding was mirrored by a spiritual rebuilding, as they witnessed God's protection of them in the vigorous opposition they faced. They learned that their God was great and awesome, both in theory and in practice. However, there was more spiritual rebuilding and restoration to come.

In chapter 8, the children of Israel were summoned to the Water Gate, so that Ezra the priest could read the Law to them. From morning until midday, the Law of Moses was publicly read and they listened attentively. Men were appointed to teach and help the people understand. As they were drawn back into the character and Law of God, Israel came under deep conviction: they bowed before the LORD in worship, mourning and weeping. The passage then continues:

> 'And Nehemiah... said to all the people, "This day is holy to the LORD your God; do not mourn nor weep." For all the people wept, when they heard the words of the Law. Then he said to them, "Go your way, eat the fat, drink the sweet, and send portions to those for whom nothing is prepared; for this day is holy to our Lord. Do not sorrow, for the joy of the LORD is your strength."' Neh. 8:9-10

In this time of repentance and sorrow, they are instructed to be strengthened physically and emotionally through taking joy in the LORD. At this point we not only need to ask *why* but *how*.

They needed to learn alongside this that it was possible and right to find joy in the LORD: that through His word they would be set free and know the favour of living rightly before Him. As they were convicted and undone by the recognition of sin, they could be assured that they would be strengthened by finding joy in the LORD. And the source of their joy? 'They rejoiced greatly, because they understood the words that were declared to them.' (Neh. 8:12) The Word of God brought the conviction of their sin and faithlessness, but the Word of God also brought them the hope that this was not the end of the story. Because of the loving-kindness and faithfulness of God, repentance would lead to restoration, a new start and a future glory.

Israel was to be strengthened emotionally and mentally by having an attitude of hope in the restoration to come and by showing generosity to others. Their physical well-being also mattered, as they are instructed to 'eat the fat' and 'drink the sweet' – they were to *feast* not *fast*. This reminds me of the story of Hannah in 1 Samuel 1, where she poured out her heart of grief and pain before the LORD over her infertility. Eli, the priest, instructed her to go and eat because the LORD had heard her. She did this in faith, for there were no miraculous signs or angelic visitations. But she cast aside her mourning and went her way in peace; she ate and restored herself physically.

There is a time to fast in our desperate times. Fasting shows our heart's desire to draw closer to God, to know His good and perfect will for us, but also our desire simply to hear from Him in our circumstances. However, I think it is important to note that we are not trying to prove something to God. It is us recognising that something extra is needed to break through a situation. I have found that fasting leads to hearing God's voice more clearly. But it is equally true that there are times to eat, as an act of trust that God has heard and is responding, even if we have not yet seen that.

Israel was commanded to celebrate the feast of Tabernacles, which commemorated the days when Israel lived in tents in the wilderness. (Neh. 8:17) The feast took place after the final harvest of the agricultural year, and it would begin and end with a day of sabbath rest. For seven days they were to rejoice before the LORD. They were commanded to step outside of their normal routine by living in tents and to focus their days on being joyful and rejoicing in their God. (See Leviticus 23:33-44) In Nehemiah we read that there was 'very great gladness' each day of the feast as the Law was read (Neh. 8:17). The people remembered the LORD's goodness to Israel in another set of circumstances when they had sinned, and they remembered God's provision for them in the wilderness. Then and only then did they have a time of confession, fasting and repentance. They changed their garments for sackcloth and dust on their heads as an outward sign of an inward state.

If you are experiencing struggle because you have sinned or forgotten God's ways, then go back to the word of God and His commands. Bring before God the areas where you know that you have sinned and seek His forgiveness, being prepared to change your behaviour. Wait with the Holy Spirit for a while and invite Him to show you anything that has come between you and God. The Psalmist says:

> 'I will extol You, O LORD, for You have lifted me up,
> and have not let my foes rejoice over me.... Sing praise
> to the LORD, you saints of His, and give thanks at the

remembrance of His holy name. For His anger is but for moment, His favour is for life; weeping may endure for a night, but joy comes in the morning.' Ps. 30:1, 4-5

Repentance comes with grief and remorse, but the knowledge of our salvation and the hope of restoration with God bring joy. We are to be a people who praise in prison and on the barricades; a people who find joy through repentance and salvation. The spiritual victory comes first, rather than the physical victory in our circumstances. As with Jehoshaphat and his people, the most significant miracle took place before the enemy was defeated, as their hearts rejoiced in God in the darkness. Isaiah wrote,

'Behold, God is my salvation, I will trust and not be afraid; for YAH, The LORD, is my strength and my song; He also has become my salvation. Therefore with joy you will draw water from the wells of salvation.' Is. 12:2-3

Isaiah knew that his sense of security and well-being were based in his acceptance of the salvation of God: not as a one-off event but as a continuous, daily process, just as drawing water from the well was a daily need. Maybe we need to get in the habit of approaching the tap with joy, recognising that we can come before the Living God at any time, in any place, and know that He will hear us as our hearts are turned to Him. Each time you drink water, know that in Him there is refreshing, salvation and cleansing from sin. Perhaps we should speak words of blessing and praise to the God who gave us the water that we need to live now and the salvation we need to live eternally, just as we would say 'grace' before a meal.

Isaiah recognised that his strength and his praise flowed from his appreciation and recognition of the greatness of God's salvation; from fixing his eyes and his mind on all that God was and is. This link between strength and song would not be a coincidence. Singing out praise of God increases our strength or courage of heart because it reminds us of the greatness of God and His ability to save us. What we know theoretically in our minds needs to be infused with the dynamic, powerful faith that God is mighty to save, and that process takes place as we praise Him.

We see this important link between strength, repentance and salvation later on in Isaiah when he spoke out the words of God, saying:

"In returning and rest you shall be saved; in quietness and confidence shall be your strength." Is. 30:15

Whenever we find that we are in a position of weakness through doubt or disobedience, we need to return to that position of repentance and receiving salvation once more. Trusting God with confident expectation is our position of courage. We have a choice to do this. In this passage, God explained what was needed for salvation and strength, but Israel would not respond to Him. They refused to return to God, they refused to position themselves rightly before Him. We have free will in this.

Praise, worship and declaring the might and victory of God are found throughout the lives of those who have gone before us. Paul and Silas praised God in prison and the people of Judah praised God as they faced defeat in battle. Habakkuk knew that there were difficult times to come and so resolved to praise as part of his preparation for that. Nehemiah and the people rejoiced as part of the process of being restored to relationship with God. They came to know and understand that praising God was a meaningful act because it altered their own ability to endure and stand in faith. It also had an impact on the situations around them. Praise, using our words and voices to speak out the character and power of our God, is powerful.

Choosing to rejoice is taking a stand in the victory of God before and during difficult situations. We do this as an act and declaration of God's ability to see us through whatever we face, no matter how long it takes. As we do so, God strengthens us and provides the resilience we so desperately need. And yes, it is through persevering in God's strength that we come through to victory. What had already been proclaimed in faith, becomes a shout of triumph as the victory is seen.

Victory songs in the Bible are a recap of the event, remembering what the disastrous circumstance was and the miraculous deliverance that God brought about that, in human terms, was impossible. For example, the songs of Moses and Miriam in Exodus 15 and the song of Deborah in Judges 5 are long passages that tell the story. These songs were an immediate response of praise in the moment, but they were also a means of remembering all that God had done for them and of fixing the details of the event more fully in their minds. Their souls rejoiced because they had been strengthened, settled and made secure in God Most High; they rejoiced because they had endured through to victory.

If we return to Nehemiah, we read of the dedication of the restored wall which was done with great style. (Neh. 12:27-43) All the Levites were brought to celebrate,

> '...with gladness, both with thanksgivings and singing, with cymbals and stringed instruments and harps.' Neh. 12:27

The Levites and priests purified themselves, the people, the walls and gates. Then Nehemiah appointed two thanksgiving choirs, which would take opposite routes around the wall. It must have been quite something: the instruments, the singing, all the people and leaders gathered. Verse 43 gives the sense that Nehemiah had run out of words to describe the occasion, for it says:

> 'Also that day they offered great sacrifices, and rejoiced, for God had made them rejoice with great joy; the women and the children also rejoiced, so that the joy of Jerusalem was heard afar off.' Neh. 12:43

Somehow, the words *rejoicing* and *joy* seem insufficient to describe what was actually experienced that day: it was something that must have gone far beyond words. They were over-flowing with joy because the spiritual reproach had been lifted from them. The spirit of heaviness that had filled them from the time of rebellion, during the exile and then returning to the holy place of Jerusalem to find it in ruins, had been cast out and replaced with a garment of praise. Through spiritual and physical restoration, the reproach of God had been lifted, the spirit of heaviness cast out and the lightness of soul restored.

Respond

Use Isaiah's words to encourage you to rejoice in victory as an act of faith.

'Behold, God is my salvation, I will trust and not be afraid;'

I rejoice that God is my salvation in all that I face now. I proclaim that I will put my trust in Him to bring this situation through to resolution. I rejoice in God's power and might to handle all that concerns me. In the name of Jesus, I renounce the foothold of the spirit of fear; replacing it with my inheritance in Christ: a spirit of power, love and of a sound mind.

'...for YAH, The LORD, is my strength and my song;'

I rejoice in the strength of my God, who is with me now. I rejoice that my God is Almighty and able to equip me with all that I need to endure and persevere to victory. I welcome His strength to enable me to resist any apathy, unbelief or despair I experience. I welcome the Holy Spirit to bring a song into my heart, so that I can praise God.

'He also has become my salvation.'

I rejoice that I am saved by the blood of the Lamb. I also rejoice that Jesus is my salvation in this situation and in all things that I face. I rejoice that He is my Saviour, my Rescuer, my Deliverer, my Protector and Refuge. I rejoice that He is with me, completing me and filling me with His strength. I give thanks that He will show me the way through to life.

'Therefore with joy you will draw water from the wells of salvation'. Is. 12:2-3

I rejoice that God provides wells of salvation for me and that I can come at any time to be filled with all the refreshing and sustenance of His Kingdom. I bring before God anything that is blocking me from receiving His gifts today: repenting of any sin and resisting all works of the evil one, particularly any spirit of heaviness. I rejoice as I open my arms to Him to receive all that I need.

REST

manuchah ... (Hebrew)

Resting place; place of stillness...
Menuchah is greatly soothing, comforting and settling,
as in Psalm 23:2,
He leads me beside the waters of *menuchah*
[the waters of quietness].[35]

One hot summer, I was sitting on a wall in the garden reading. I looked up at the trees nearby and saw a squirrel lying along a thin branch with its arms and legs hanging over the sides in what seemed to me to be a precarious manner. Initially, I thought it must be ill and watched it for a while with some concern, expecting it to fall. Eventually, I realised that I was watching a sun-bathing squirrel. It was deeply relaxed, contented and safe, enjoying the moment. What seemed dangerous and precarious to me, was this squirrel's place of complete rest.

The ability to rest is so dependent on how we feel and how we perceive our situation. If we feel secure and that all is well, rest is easy. The squirrel had no fears of falling, it was not haunted by the past or worried about the future, the weather was great, so it relaxed completely in the sunshine.

It is all too difficult to achieve a balance between the energetic activities of running the race and pursuing Christ, and also resting in God. God provided a model of six days work, followed by a day of Sab-

---

[35] Definition taken from the supplementary notes of *The Spirit-Filled Life Bible*, p. 996

bath rest. However, for many of us, the Sabbath involves a considerable amount of work as we prepare and lead services in the morning and evening. Family commitments do not cease because it is the Sabbath, and often Mondays arrive with a sense of, 'where did the weekend go?' We feel far from rested.

Our lives will always involve challenges and difficulties. We will all know grief, heartbreak, illness and insecurity at some point simply because we live in a fallen world and we experience things that God never intended for us – poverty, illness, death and so on. We will inevitably find ourselves in situations that feel, that are, precarious: situations with a risk of falling or a risk of failing. It is a part of life that we cannot avoid.

In the darkness, rest is what we desperately need but find so difficult to grasp. It is opposed by fear, insecurity, doubt and our past wounds. We become overwhelmed and lose our bearings. We find it impossible to access the waters of quietness. In the darkness, we need to use our spiritual vision more than ever; trusting not in our natural understanding but in God's perspective. When we are out of our own resources and beyond our own ability to overcome, we need the provision of God.

The question is, how can we respond to our situations, thoughts and emotions so that we can experience the rest of God whatever the context?

Setting God Before Us

Rest and worry are incompatible yet worrying is a common state for many of us, despite Scripture telling us repeatedly not to worry. In one passage of Scripture alone, Jesus uses the phrase "therefore, do not worry" three times as He explains why it is not necessary. (Matthew 6:25-34)

Instruction: "Therefore, do not worry about your life, what you will eat or what you will drink; nor about your body, what you will put on."

Reasons not to worry:

1. "Is not life more than food and the body more than clothing?"

2. "Look at the birds of the air, for they neither sow nor reap nor gather into barns; yet your heavenly Father feeds them. Are you not of more value than they?"

3. "Which of you by worrying can add one cubit to his stature?"

Jesus puts worries about our provision into perspective: there is more to life than food and appearance, to impressing other people and worrying about what they will think of us if we do not wear the 'right' thing. He calls us to trust in God's loving provision for us and in the knowledge that we are of great worth to our Father.

Question: "So why do you worry about clothing?"

Reasons not to worry:

4. "Consider the lilies of the field, how they grow; they neither toil nor spin; and yet I say to you that even Solomon in all his glory was not arrayed like one of these. Now if God so clothes the grass of the field, which today is, and tomorrow is thrown into the oven, will He not much more clothe you, O you of little faith?"

Jesus points out that God provides food for the birds and gives flowers beauty, even though they have done nothing to earn those things and are quickly gone. Mankind holds a special place in God's heart – the whole of creation was made for mankind, Christ died to redeem mankind, the whole of the Bible is written to sustain and save mankind. It also puts human standards into perspective to consider that the wealthiest king in all his finery was unable to match the God-given glory of a lily, quietly and unobtrusively growing in the fields.

Instruction: "Therefore do not worry, saying, 'What shall we eat?' or 'What shall we drink?' or 'what shall we wear?'"

Reasons not to worry:

5. "For your heavenly Father knows that you need all these things."

6. "... all these things shall be added to you."

7. "... tomorrow will worry about its own things."

Jesus reminds us that our God knows our needs. He reminds us of eternal perspective – that worry is never constructive, so the best approach is to focus on seeking God and His kingdom in each moment we live, trusting Him to meet our needs. We will never escape troubles but we can learn how to manage our response to them, dealing with one day at a time and continually expressing our trust in God to meet our needs.

Based on Matthew 6, two themes emerge in the ability to rest regardless of the circumstances: trust and whole-heartedness.

Previously, Jesus had taught that we cannot serve both God and riches. Doing so is equivalent to serving two masters: it introduces a conflict of loyalty and a weakening of focus, intent and prioritising. (Matt. 6:24) This changes how we read this passage as we can recognise that Jesus was continuing to address this prioritising of acquisition and the divided heart attitude when we serve two masters. The challenge to us is to recognise that we have become divided in heart, serving two masters.

Because we are called to serve God alone, we can trust Him alone to provide for us. Our trust in Him needs to surpass our own achievements, careers and income because there is a danger that our sense of identity and worth will become caught up in those things. If we trust too much in our ability to provide for ourselves then we will struggle all the more if something happens to disrupt those things; for example, if we face redundancy. When we talk to others, so much of our conversation revolves around what we do. If asked how your week has been, the answer is generally 'busy' with a run-through of tasks that needed completing. It is not that those things are not valid or are untrue, but an indication of where our focus generally lies. There is something about 'doing' and about demonstrating ability that provides a certain validation, even if we are not aware of it.

God wants us to know and believe deep in our souls that we are of incomparable worth to Him because we are His image-bearers, His children. Labour was part of Adam and Eve's perfect existence in Eden so it is evident that work is something God intended us to have and do.

The message is that our sense of value and our identity must not be in our work or income. We must not forget that God is our provider and the one for whom we work. The birds do nothing towards food production, nor do they fill storehouses at harvest so that there is food in the lean season. The lilies in the field do not spin wool for garments to provide clothes for themselves or anyone else; they do not make anything to sell or barter with. Birds need to actively seek food to survive but lilies are entirely stationery! They simply stay in the place they were planted, growing and then flowering in season. Yet, God provides all that they need so they can fulfil their design and purpose.

We could turn this around to remind ourselves in situations where we are fearful that God will not provide for our needs: *I am of greater value than the birds – God will provide for my need for food. These flowers created by God bear a greater glory that the wealthiest person on earth; how much more will He clothe me!*

Instead of seeking to build our own kingdom of possessions, accolades and things that will impress those around us, Jesus calls us to seek God's kingdom as our priority, trusting in God's provision for our daily needs. When Jesus sent out seventy-two followers, He instructed them to take nothing with them and to trust God to provide everything. It was an act of obedience to a clear instruction from the Lord. So often what Jesus asks of us is a means to refine our hearts into purer gold before Him. Those He sent out were to rely on God the Father to provide for them in every possible way. How many of them struggled with that? Perhaps in a culture where offering hospitality was so much a part of life it was easier to trust that they would find food and shelter on the journey, but we prize independence and self-provision so much now. We do not want to be a trouble to anyone; we want to pay our own way and provide for ourselves. It is costly to look to others for basic provision. It takes humility, a swallowing of pride.

Jesus sent His followers out on the path of dependence and trust, and that needs to be our heart attitude, too. We may never be called to leave all our material possessions behind, but we are called to have hearts of humility, dependence and trust in our God. Trusting God to meet all our needs is not easy in practice because it feels risky and unsafe. It is something we learn over time as we discover His faithfulness and intervention in our lives. The more we learn that through experience, the more we trust. Our part is to be whole-hearted in putting God before us in our priorities, desires, commitments and plans, serving and worshipping Him alone.

Reflect and Respond Ideas

Head outside: Go out bird-watching and remind yourself that God provides for each bird. Then remind yourself that you are of greater value before Him and speak out your trust in His provision and love for you.

Research something: Research consumer habits to see what things are currently popular why. What does this tell us about our desires, lifestyle choices and priorities? What do the advertisements for those products promise us?

Ponder further: In what ways can we seek first the kingdom of God?

Get creative: Sketch, paint or create a collage of a bird or lilies. Look closely at God's design and workmanship, giving thanks for His creation. Give thanks for His care of all that He has created.

Secure in the Storms

Storms occur in life, in our thoughts and emotions, in our circumstances. We tend to see this as a metaphor now, but in the Bible they were generally literal storms. There are several storm stories from which we can draw help.

STORM ONE   Matthew 8:23-27

The disciples were caught in a violent storm and panic naturally ensued because they were in mortal danger of capsizing and drowning. The weather was out of their control, as was the action of the boat. Even though they were experienced sailors, their own natural resources were insufficient to deal with their circumstances, so fear and panic took hold. In this moment of peril, Jesus was with them, but He was asleep.

We might often face difficult situations and wish or pray that Jesus was right there with us – physically and tangibly; but I doubt we ever wish that He would be present *and sound asleep* in those circumstances. So, what do we learn from this?

1. Despite Jesus's physical presence, the storm still raged.

Surely with Jesus in the boat there should be no storms! How easily we feel in our storms that we have been abandoned because the storm exists and persists despite our belief in Jesus being present with us in all we face. The men were fearful even though Jesus was with them. His presence with them was not in doubt because they could see Him and touch Him, but it did not prevent the danger nor did it make it go away. Jesus was still undeniably present.

2. Jesus was present but not engaging with them in the storm.

That is not what we see or expect to see in action movies. In the desperate situation, the hero or heroine steps up, fully engaged with what is going on. After all, they are the star of the show; the reason we watch, knowing that no matter what apocalypse the world is facing in the movie, the star will save the day. We expect the hero or heroine to run toward the danger, rescuing people as they go; we expect to see them take charge of the situation, giving instructions to those around them. Active, present, engaged, in control, knowing what to do, heroic. But not Jesus, not here.

There is something about that which jars with us. It is not how the story should go! When we experience profound desperation, without any means to save ourselves, the hero of the story should not be asleep. We want him to be awake: fully alert, focused and taking charge of the situation. But Jesus was not engaging with them in what they were going through. Why not? Jesus did not do things without a reason, without something for His beloved disciples to learn.

It revealed to them that they did not believe that His presence alone was enough to keep them safe in the storm.

The fact that Jesus slept peacefully despite the storm was not interpreted as a sign that the fishermen could rest securely in the storm themselves. They did not see it as a model for their own behaviour. In that moment, the human perspective was that they had a full grasp of the situation (dire and certainly going to end in death) and Jesus, God

Himself, was not only oblivious to this but that He did not care about what happened to them.

If the disciples could feel that knowing that Jesus was physically in the boat with them, how much more can we experience that when we trust in faith that He is with us? How quickly and easily do we assume that Jesus is sleeping and has not noticed how desperate we are or that He simply does not care? God knows that we experience fear for a whole host of reasons; He knows that it is a part of human experience outside of Eden where we live in a world of war. It is because of this that He wants us to learn how to trust Him, even in our moments of greatest desperation.

The disciples were men of faith but some of them were also men of the sea. For fishermen, a violent storm in a fishing boat must have been top of the list of great fears. God does not allow us to go through situations that trigger our great fears without good reason. His desire is that we live without those fears that hold us back from living as He intended us to. His desire is that we live in complete trust in Him. Jesus brought them into this so that they could learn His sovereignty over their greatest fear. These men were also in a transition process in their attitudes and responses to situations: moving from their perspectives and judgements as fishermen to viewing situations from the perspective of co-heirs of the Kingdom of God and as partners in Jesus' Isaiah 61 ministry.

When the disciples woke Jesus, pointing out that they were going to die and accusing Him of not caring about their lives, Jesus responded by saying, *'why are you fearful, O you of little faith?'* The response of having 'little faith' here can seem wounding, but the disciples were still learning what Jesus had complete conviction about. Jesus was able to rest in the storm because He understood that He had authority over the storm. He also knew His time had not yet come to die and that the disciples were perfectly safe with Him. He was secure.

The disciples would come to learn about using spiritual authority just as they would come to recognise the spiritual timing of their lives. They would come to understand that their eternal lives were safe with Christ, but this was all a work in progress – another step on the way to stronger faith.

STORM TWO   Matthew 14:22-33

Here we have another occasion of the disciples experiencing a fierce storm. This time, Jesus was not present with them – He had made them go on without Him so He could spend some time alone in prayer.

Reading the Gospels can raise awkward questions of why Jesus took the course of action that He did. He allowed his beloved friends to go out onto the water when He knew that they would find themselves in danger. So, what was happening here?

This is the second storm that Matthew recorded: the first with Jesus physically present and the second when He was not. Jesus has taught them how to pray out of relationship (the Lord's prayer). He has taught them that God will meet all their needs. He has modelled walking with God the Father in partnership and personal relationship. Significantly, in the previous storm Jesus taught His friends that He had authority over the wind and the waves. In educational terms, it seems reasonable to see this second storm as a temporary removal of a support structure to see how someone manages to apply teaching on their own.

So how does the story play out?

During the fourth watch of the night, presumably after several long, dark hours of being in the swell of the currents and at the mercy of the strong winds, the disciples saw someone walking towards them. Returning to storm conditions without Jesus, after hours of weather conditions and darkness that could leave any fisherman feeling queasy and somewhat superstitious, the disciples automatically assumed that an already terrifying situation was about to get much worse. After all, no one could be walking out towards them except a ghost or some demonic entity. Fear can be a paralysing experience; one that left the disciples struggling to respond in faith that God would protect them from whatever they faced. It did not occur to them that help was on its way.

Into this comes the relaxed voice of their Rabbi, saying, 'cheer up, no need to panic, it's Me!' Walking on the water, in a fierce storm. Out of the vast expanse of the Sea of Galilee, Jesus knew exactly where to find His friends. He knew that they were frightened, in despair and need; He knew that they needed His presence with them. He came straight to them and spoke these eleven words:

"Be of good cheer!"

Into the darkness comes the instruction, command, encouragement to be cheerful – in good spirits, hopeful, positive, upbeat. Being told to cheer up when your world is falling apart is the last thing we want to hear. Is it humanly possible to face disaster and experience cheerfulness? So, why did Jesus begin with this? They could be 'of good cheer' because:

"It is I..."

Jesus was there and that changed everything. Jesus, their friend, rabbi and Lord was coming to them – not another threat or danger looming out of the storm, but someone loved and needed. This was followed up with another instruction or command:

"... do not be afraid."

Was Jesus reassuring them that they did not need to fear 'ghosts' or any evil spirit at work, or that they did not need to fear the physical storm? He does not specify because there was no need for the disciples to be in a state of fear, full stop.

Being of good cheer in a storm is, perhaps, not something we can force; but something that develops the more we discover God's presence with us in the storm. Between the first and second storms, the behaviour and responses of the disciples had changed very little: they were unsettled, afraid and desperate in both. However, what we see of desperate panic in these stories is not evident later in their lives, even as they face violent death. Increasingly, they had the attitude of belonging to God's kingdom and that there was a glory to come which would make the sufferings of the world seem like nothing. This attitude was not suddenly there. It came over time as they grew in the grace and knowledge of Jesus Christ, through the revelation of the Holy Spirit.

The storms of life can cause behaviours to arise in us that God wants to work in. We may not fear ghosts, but there are plenty of other things that we can fear. Such as the fear of being vulnerable, seen as unable to cope. How do we respond in situations that leave us feeling at risk?

Perhaps we react out of a need to escape in whatever way possible:

- physically leaving a situation, walking out – perhaps walking away from a church or job
- withdrawing emotionally and refusing to engage with the situation – such as being physically present in a relationship, whilst cutting off all communication with that person
- attempting to find another place to exist, through using alcohol or drugs to create a space where no one can reach you.

Perhaps we react out of the need to control in whatever way we can:

- refusing to be vulnerable
- putting self-protective measures in place
- an 'attack mentality', using defiance or anger to deflect people from the vulnerable place within us.

At Gethsemane, Peter went for this latter response – he turned to a response of anger and defiance, using his sword in an attempt to assert some control over the situation.

But in the physical storm, this was not an option. The disciples were in a boat, in the middle of the sea. There was literally no option to walk away or to escape from the situation. The disciples could not rely on their own ability to save themselves, nor could they change their circumstances by their own skills. They had to see it through without any guarantee of the outcome. The disciples feared the physical storm and they feared the supernatural that could lurk there; yet, again Jesus showed them that He had authority over the storm by walking on the water through it. He was not afraid.

We are to have a good attitude *because* Jesus is there. We can say 'no' to the fears that emerge, whatever they are, *because* Jesus is present and *because* He has authority in our circumstances.

Seeing Jesus changed everything for Peter. Immediately we see a difference to the previous situation. His words to Jesus were not ones of fear or reproach (don't you care what happens to us?) or seeking resolution (rebuke the storm! Rescue us!). In fact, Peter's words were nothing at all to do with the storm. The storm was no longer the focal point; it was no longer registering in Peter's mind. From the moment Jesus identified Himself to them, He was Peter's complete focus. Peter said,

"Lord, if it is You, command me to come to You on the water."

This is a total and remarkable transformation in everything that had gone before. The complete and consuming fear he had experienced in his circumstances was instantly replaced by the desire to be with Jesus, wherever He was. If Jesus was out there on the waves, then that was exactly where Peter wanted to be.

Just moments before, the boat had seemed entirely inadequate to keep them safe and alive, yet even so there was absolutely no way that any of the disciples would have got out of the boat because it was all that stood between them and drowning. Suddenly, though, the boat was irrelevant as a place of safety and a solid place to stand. Jesus was out on the water and so Peter wanted to be with Jesus – as close as possible. Any distance between him and Jesus was unnatural and unbearable. He did not even consider the danger of drowning any more, because his desire to be with Jesus outweighed the fear of death itself.

Uncharacteristically, Peter did not launch into action here but first sought and waited for confirmation that it was Jesus and for His command before stepping out. He then stepped out of the boat and walked on the water, as Jesus did. He acted entirely out of spiritual knowledge and understanding in this. His heart responded to the presence of Jesus with the *desire* to go to his Lord, with the *faith* to reach Jesus and remove any distance between them (regardless of what the laws of nature said was feasible) and seeking the *clear command* to go.

All the time his eyes were fixed on Jesus, acting out of his spiritual conviction of all that was possible with Christ, he walked confidently. But the sound of the continuing storm interrupted Peter's focus and took his eyes away from Jesus and onto the conditions. He listened to his reason, which told him that it was impossible for him to walk on water, then he listened to his logic tell him that he would sink and drown. He sank spiritually, emotionally and mentally first. His faith (his confident trust in Christ's ability to keep him) decreased and so he did indeed begin to sink physically. The worry entered when he paid attention to the natural laws rather than God's laws. When we keep our souls focused on Jesus, no matter what, we can keep walking on in faith without sinking into worry, doubt and unbelief. The passage ends with Jesus getting into the boat with His friends and the wind ceasing as of that moment.

It was in the storm that Peter had this momentous experience of walking on the water, just as Jesus did. How utterly mind-blowing! Peter did something contrary to all the laws of science, just as Jesus did. These were things that Jesus desired His friends and followers to know: that out of the outflow of faith in their hearts, they could do what He did. That happened in the storm, not in a supervised practice exercise on calm, shallow waters. The storm itself was not a good thing – it was genuinely a frightening and dangerous situation. But God can and will use those situations to show us His power, glory and ability to cause our faith to rise up within even those dark times.

In some ways, the encounter with Jesus was so remarkable that the calming of the storm becomes secondary. I think this is primarily because we tend to relate this to metaphorical storms rather than to a real storm at sea. We focus on our own experiences of sinking faith so we look to see what Peter did right (wishing we could have that courage and faith) and what he did wrong (hoping we will learn from his mistake and keep our eyes on Jesus). However, if we were on a boat far from land and Jesus literally stilled the storm we were in, I suspect that we would start from that. The wind and the waves obeyed Jesus.

It was in the storm that the disciples saw more of Jesus' power and authority at work and that enabled them to identify Him as the promised Messiah. We see this again in our next storm.

STORM THREE   Jonah 1:1-16

The book of Jonah demonstrates this in chapter one, as the prophet rejected God's instructions to go to Ninevah and decided to '...flee to Tarshish from the presence of the LORD.' (Jonah 1:3) This attempt to rebel against God and to escape from His presence failed. The LORD sent a 'mighty tempest on the sea, so that the ship was about to be broken up.' (Jonah 1:4)

Amazingly, Jonah slept through the storm whilst the fearful sailors called out to their gods and threw cargo overboard to lighten the ship. Jonah's calling as a prophet involved being sensitive and alert to the voice of the LORD so that His message could be passed onto other people. However, Jonah was oblivious to the violent storm that hurled the ship around to the point of destruction. He completely failed to recognise God at work. He knew that he was outside of God's will and heading in the wrong direction, yet he was at rest in the mistaken belief that he had escaped the presence of God (and therefore any consequences to disobedience) and had successfully avoided fulfilling God's command. Those sharing the boat with him experienced the consequence of his sin before he did; they recognised that there were supernatural powers at work and that it was a response to sin.

Jonah only became aware of the consequences of his sin when he was awakened by the captain demanding that he cry out to his God:

> "What do you mean, sleeper? Arise, call on your God;
> perhaps your God will consider us, so that we may not
> perish." Jonah 1:6

Interestingly, the sailors were the ones who recognised a spiritual cause for the storm and cast lots to discern whose fault it was. Jonah's disobedience was rightly revealed to be the cause of the storm. Initially, the sailors had been afraid because of the violence of the storm, but the fear increased when they discovered that Jonah had fled from the presence of the LORD and He had caused the storm. Having tried to row to shore and failed, they reluctantly followed Jonah's suggestion to throw him into the sea and the storm ceased at that moment.

> 'Then the men feared the LORD exceedingly, and offered a
> sacrifice to the LORD and took vows.' Jonah 1:16

We do not know how many different gods the sailors had prayed to in the hope of the storm being stilled; but we do know that only one God heard them and answered their plea for help. The storm itself caused one response of fear, because they could capsize and die. However, the stilling of the storm caused another type of fear: the holy awe that comes from encountering the power and authority of God at work; the kind that brought Isaiah to his knees with the recognition that he was a sinful man in the presence of the holy God. In that moment, Isaiah cried out,

"Woe is me, for I am undone! ... For my eyes have seen the King, the LORD of hosts." Is. 6:5

These storms, literal or metaphorical, shook those present out of any semblance of security or control over their circumstances or lives. Through crying out to God, people encountered His power and it brought them to their knees. They caught a glimpse of the awesome King, the LORD of hosts.

In Mark's telling of the first storm we looked at, we find out that the disciples responded to the calming of the storm with fear.

'And they feared exceedingly, and said to one another, "Who can this be, that even the wind and the sea obey Him!"'
Mark 4:41

Their lives were now safe and they knew they could take charge of their journey once more. But the supernatural stilling of the storm created a new question for them. Who was this with them who could control the elements? They knew Jesus as their friend and rabbi, but now they were recognising that they were in the presence of *God*. Being in His presence, encountering His sovereignty over the winds and the seas, shook them as profoundly as the storm did. They had caught a glimpse of the King, the LORD of hosts.

Straight after this, we read about Jesus encountering a man who lived in the storm of demon possession. He had been bound by the people but had broken those shackles and chains; he cried out and cut himself with stones. Jesus cast out the unclean spirit that tormented him. As the people came to see what had happened, they found this man 'sitting and clothed and in his right mind. *And they were afraid.*' (Mark 5:15, my emphasis.) They too had caught a glimpse of the King, the LORD of hosts. In this instance, the whole city 'begged' Jesus to leave the area. (Matt. 8:34) Having a demon-possessed man near them was one thing; having the Son of God near them was another.

The storms caused people to need God's help and, when it was received, it provided a situation for those people to either accept and follow Jesus or ask Him to depart from them.

STORM FOUR   Acts 27

In Acts 27, we find Paul under arrest and, as a Roman citizen, he was entitled to have his case heard in Rome. The voyage to Rome took several stages and the weather conditions were making this trip rough.

When they reached the south of Crete, Paul advised that they remain there due to the dangerous weather conditions. However, everyone else was in favour of sailing on and the centurion listened to them instead of Paul. (Acts 27:9-12) As their current location was unsuitable for staying over winter, the desire was to press on and complete their journey. The soft, south wind that blew seemed to confirm the view of the majority that it would be safe to continue. However, as they sailed, 'a tempestuous head wind arose.' (verse 13) Over the next days, turning into weeks, they were 'exceedingly tempest-tossed' so they lightened the ship (verse 18) and eventually, when it was so dark that they could neither see sun nor stars, all 'hope that we would we saved was finally given up.' (verse 20)

Paul is not recorded as being in a state of desperation or fear, although he may well have experienced these emotions. However, he was able to speak with faith and conviction about the outcome of the storm once he had heard what God had to say about it. After fourteen days of this tempest and the fear, hopelessness, powerlessness and desperation it caused amongst those on board, Paul spoke to them:

> "And now I urge you *to take heart*, for there will be no loss of life among you, but only of the ship. For there stood by me this night an angel of the God to whom I belong and whom I serve, saying, 'Do not be afraid, Paul; you must be brought before Caesar; and indeed God has granted you all those who sail with you.' Therefore *take heart*, men, for I believe God that it will be just as it was told me. However, we must run aground on a certain island." Acts 27:22-26 (my emphasis)

Twice, he encouraged everyone to 'take heart' – to be courageous, to stand firm and to withstand in the storm, to have confidence and conviction that the word of God was trust-worthy and true. There were two aspects to God's message.

Firstly, that Paul himself would not die in this storm because God's purposes for him were not yet complete. It was God's will that Paul appear before Caesar in Rome so that would come to pass. Understanding God's purposes and timing for their lives was key in the disciples' response to difficulty. They knew that they would physically die at some point and, for them, it was probable that they would be martyred; but they also knew that this would only happen when God allowed it, just as Jesus only died at the moment He allowed it. Before that time came, they endured the difficulty for the sake of the Lord and kept fulfilling their calling to preach the Gospel and disciple those who believed. Paul belonged to the LORD and served Him alone; his life was in God's hands. That was a foundational principle in his attitudes, behaviour and faith.

Secondly, God also 'granted' survival for all others on the ship with Paul. This granting of survival to everyone onboard suggested that Paul had been in prayer interceding for them. No one could opt out of the situation. Through seeking God in it, Paul was able to bring God's promise of survival and an awareness of what the solution would be. The people were given grounds for hope based on the word of God. They then had to trust that Paul spoke the truth, based on what they knew of his spiritual authority and integrity.

Paul was a spiritually mature apostle of Christ at this time, but the storm still happened and continued for weeks. It was a serious, life-endangering situation, and Paul treated it as such. Yet it was not a sign that he had sinned, that his faith was poor or that his prayers were ineffective. Storms happen. Paul was not guaranteed pleasant voyage conditions! Perhaps it was an attempt of Satan to stop Paul from getting to Rome, thus blocking God's plan for the Gospel to be preached to Caesar; perhaps it was simply a meteorological event. It is not clear either way, but God was still sovereign over the situation and when He sent an angel to Paul, Paul listened and acted upon that message. His faith was not so battered by the storm that he doubted this word or questioned God's faithfulness or commitment to him. He trusted.

In the storm between Crete and Malta, after fourteen days of fasting, Paul instructed the people on board to eat. Fasting was part of the waiting and the desperate need for help. But once Paul had heard from God and been assured of the survival of everyone onboard the ship, he,

> '...took bread and gave thanks to God in the presence of them all; and when he had broken it he began to eat. Then they were all encouraged, and also took food themselves.'
> Acts 27:35-36

They were eating as a sign of trust that God would deliver them as He had promised. This reminds me of the process of taking bread and wine during Communion as a remembrance of what Jesus has done for us and that He will come again. These are reasons for us to be encouraged and strengthened inside. We eat and drink as a sign that we trust God's word in this.

The storm continued, but Paul had found the 'waters of quietness' in his spirit because he had heard the will of God to save them. He was assured and confident of the outcome of the situation. It was also a period of rest following what was, presumably, an intense period of interceding before God for the lives of all those on board. Hearing from God brought about that soundness of mind that we read of in 2 Timothy 1:7. His faith inspired the others to believe that maybe, just maybe, he was right.

Soundness of mind comes from being secure in trust, priorities and outcome; not divided between two masters, not tossed and overwhelmed by the storms. It also comes as we experience the awareness of God's will and greater purpose for our lives. It is easier to withstand when we are assured of His presence with us and His sovereignty over the circumstances we face. We may not get an angelic visitation, but we can remind ourselves and each other of His goodness and faithfulness to those who follow Him.

In another letter, Paul gave us these instructions or practical ways with which to tackle worry and release God's peace and rest into our souls:

> 'Be anxious for nothing, but in everything by prayer and supplication, with thanksgiving, let your requests be made

known to God; and the peace of God, which surpasses all understanding, will guard your hearts and minds through Christ Jesus. Finally, ... whatever things are true ... noble ... just... pure ... lovely ... of good report, if there is anything of virtue and if there is anything praiseworthy – meditate on these things. The things which you learned and received and heard and saw in me [do these things] and the God of peace will be with you.' Phil. 4:6-9

Firstly, through the prayerful process of fixing our minds on who God is, and in His ability to respond to all that we need. The implication is that as we present our requests to God, we entrust those matters to His divine care and action; we trust that He will work in those matters and therefore there is no need for us to worry. We entrust the entire situation *and* its outcome to Almighty God. As we trust Him, we will know the protection of His peace against all attack of fear-filled thoughts and emotions.

Secondly, through choosing to focus on the good things of God's kingdom and make those things our dwelling-place. This does not mean that we ignore the terrible things going on in the world, but that we change our perspective to the power of God's kingdom to overcome every work of the evil one.

Thirdly, through obedience to God's ways. As long as we are within the will of God in our lives, we are on the right path no matter what it holds. Ultimately, it is God's view of us alone that matters. What we are going to is of far greater importance than the things we face now. If we take seriously Paul's invitation to follow his example, to act and speak as he did, then we can look at how he responded in the storm both in prayer, in faith and in eating when God's promise was given.

These things on our part release God's supernatural peace, which goes far beyond anything that we could generate by ourselves. Our focus is critical: focusing on the wind and the waves will cause us to sink in faith but focusing on Jesus despite the storm enables us to keep walking through in confidence.

Reflect and Respond Ideas

Head outside: In stormy weather, pause for a while and pay attention to what is happening and how it makes you feel. Whatever storms you face in life, bring them to God and ask Him to establish His waters of quietness in your soul. Wait on Him and give thanks that He hears you and is with you.

Research something: Investigate the use of fasting as a sign of need and eating as a sign of trust that God has heard.

Ponder further: What are your responses to storms in life? How can these stories enable you to stand and withstand in any future storms?

Get creative: Which storm most captures your focus and imagination? Read the story in full and then respond in creative writing, art, dance or music.

The Sabbath

God knows that He needs to *lead* us beside the waters of quietness; He knows that He needs to lead us to a place of rest where we can recover with Him. Jesus walked the Earth with us and experienced the regular need to go to a quiet place to reconnect with the Father.

Let us begin with the very first Sabbath. All days were and are created by God. Each day is one to give thanks for, to use for God's glory and to praise Him. Yet, from the beginning of creation, God intended His people to have one day of the week set apart from the other six. We read in Genesis that,

> 'God saw everything that He had made, and indeed it was very good.... on the seventh day God ended His work which he had done, and He rested on the seventh day from all His work .... Then God blessed the seventh day and sanctified it....' Gen. 1:31 and 2:2-3

There are three things to note from this passage:

1. He had not exhausted Himself mentally, physically or emotionally. He did not need a lie-in, a roast dinner and a long afternoon nap. It was a model of how we were to live. God did not need a Sabbath: mankind did. It was His gift of grace to His children.

2. The seventh day was blessed and sanctified by God, and He did this *before* the Fall. It was part of the work-life balance that was needed for the health and well-being of mankind even when things were perfect.

3. There is a need to reflect on the labour of the week and to see what has been good.

Ideally, the Sabbath should be a rest from labour and a time set apart to refocus, restore and be refreshed. It should be our opportunity to walk with God and catch up with Him, giving thanks and rejoicing in God's goodness with family and friends. It is not God who needs that time; *we* do. Is it any surprise, then, that it is so contested?

What does God mean by good? For us, it is an adjective that we use for a range of situations, sometimes even sarcastically, and it has become a vague, somewhat meaningless term. God's creation was without fault, joyous, beautiful in every detail. He delighted in what He saw and He called it 'good'. God's goodness is about being pure, perfect and beautiful in holiness so, when He looked at His creation, He saw that it was pure, holy, stunningly beautiful, breath-taking, awe-inspiring, without fault. These are the things we are to think about on the Sabbath: where have we seen God's faithfulness, intervention and protection during the week? Where have we been so thankful to know God's presence with us? What have we heard Him say this week? Where have we seen a glimpse of the breath-taking beauty and glory of our God?

We can also look back and be glad about the things that we have achieved and done well. Naturally, being human, when we look back we will see a mixture of good and bad in our behaviour, right and wrong; but that gives us the opportunity to repent and come back into restored relationship with God if we have not already done so. The Sabbath gives us the time and space to do that.

We look at this now, post-Fall and post-exile from Eden, so our perception of good is different. Part of the consequence of the Fall was the introduction of futility and difficulty in our labour, with the result that it can be difficult to experience satisfaction in our work. Additional stress occurs if you have experienced tension with colleagues or had unjust feedback from a superior; there may be changes to staffing, expectations, funding and any number of variables that can be unsettling. It can be difficult to switch off from work, especially on a Sunday when going back to work the following day is looming. In my first job, there was a strong focus on setting targets for staff which cultivated an atmosphere of criticism and a sense of work never really being good enough. It was difficult to stop and delight in the labour of the week because the pressure was immense, there was always more to do and the goalposts constantly changed so there were always new expectations to meet.

Our souls need rest, just as our bodies and minds do. If our work environment is insecure, challenging or competitive then we need time to refocus on the Kingdom of God; we need time to remember who we really work for and whose opinion matters in the eternal perspective. We need to be able to rest in our identity, worth and purpose in Christ which involves being satisfied and settled in those things, no matter what negative messages we have been sent in our work environment.

We also need to find rest in a job well done and allow ourselves to be satisfied. Do not rush onto the next thing or save it all up for the end of the day when other things will be on your mind but take a 'Sabbath' moment – a moment to 'cease,' a moment set apart for God, a moment of accepting His grace. Give thanks for the achievements of the day so far, no matter how small or insignificant they seem: for getting the laundry out on the line or back in, dinner on the table, children into bed or out to school, assignment done, bills paid, showing kindness to someone we find difficult, keeping our temper when tired ... It is too easy for our sense of worth to be eroded if we are constantly moving onto the next thing to do. We need that Sabbath rest to put our lives back into perspective before Him.

It is also true that we need to find rest in God again after any traumatic time so that we can be restored. In *The Voyage of the Dawn Treader*, the crew went into the Darkness and there found one of the missing lords they had gone to seek. After a lengthy time in the Darkness, on an isle where dreams (or rather nightmares and fears) haunted him, he was described as being in 'an agony of pure fear' and 'a broken man.' The healing he needed came from mental, emotional and physical rest provided by Ramandu.[36] This could easily be a descrip-

---

[36]   Lewis, *The Voyage of the Dawn Treader*, pp. 140 and 160

tion of Elijah and his encounter with God, as we saw in the chapter on Life with God. The restoration process began with Elijah's physical need for food and sleep, giving his brain some time off from the enormity of all he was experiencing.

It is no coincidence, then, that the Sabbath begins and ends with food and sleep because physical, mental and emotional restoration are always linked with each other. Sleep allows the brain and body to process and recover. God does not need that – this is not for His benefit. It is for us. We need that weekly time to rest, to heal and be restored.

Celebrating with Food

Food is a central part of many of the festivals of Israel, either through the thanksgiving offerings after the harvest seasons or through the sharing of meals together where past events were commemorated.

The festivals were instigated by God, as a reminder of the worship and service due to God because of His goodness. They were designated occasions to cease normal activities and routines to focus their hearts and minds on God. This was necessary as Israel tended to forget to prioritise the things of God, failing to keep anything set apart for God and turning to idolatry. Festivals involved bringing offerings to God, such as the Feast of First Fruits, which was to celebrate the barley harvest. The first sheaf of the harvest was to be offered to the LORD, along with a male lamb without blemish. There was to be a grain offering of fine flour mixed with oil and a drink offering of wine. Similarly, the Feast of Weeks, after the wheat harvest, involved the offering of loaves, livestock, grain and drink. There was a sin offering and a peace offering. This was a recognition that all that they had came from the blessing and provision of God. It had to be the first and the finest of the produce of the land to honour God.

The festivals were also used as a means to refresh everyone's memories and to teach the young. It was a method to maintain the stories of the past, to maintain the knowledge of God's faithfulness and goodness.

If we look at the Passover and the feast of Unleavened Bread, we see this clearly. Passover was a commemoration of Israel being commanded to place the blood of a lamb on their doorposts in Egypt, so that the Angel of the LORD would pass over and not bring death to the firstborn son. Passover was celebrated with a meal that had different foods to eat at different points during the retelling of the story, which enforced the message of the story of the Exodus. It was not only an act of remembrance of God's goodness but a multi-sensory teaching tool. This meal was not about passively sitting and hearing the Scriptures. There was the participation element, as well as seeing, touching and tasting different items of food. For example, there were bitter herbs to represent the bitterness of slavery and salt water to represent the tears of the people. Tasting bitter or sweet foods engaged more of the senses so that even if someone 'zoned out' of listening to the story, there was that flavour activating the taste buds and thought processes to help them focus.

When Pharaoh allowed Israel to go they had no time to bake leavened bread, so the feast of Unleavened Bread (celebrated the following day) surrounded the need to remove all leaven from the home and live without it for seven days. This was a physical process to focus the mind and heart on removing sin from one's life, both through changing a regular practice of food preparation but also in tasting something of a different texture.[37] It would become familiar to do this but still something set apart, as the children asked why particular things were done and the adults responded with the story of the Israelites having to pack hurriedly, taking whatever bread they could make quickly so that they could leave Egypt.

The same principle applies to the Sabbath. As Christians, we celebrate the Sabbath on Sundays, but for Jews the Sabbath begins at sunset on Friday evening and continues until sunset on Saturday evening. Therefore, the Sabbath celebrations should begin with a family meal and then sleep. The Shabbat meal is an important family time and an act of worship in the home. The table has the loaves of *challah* bread and wine. Two candles are lit and God is blessed in the prayers spoken. The bread is broken and shared out, with blessings spoken over the family members. A meal is shared and the focus is on having a relaxed

---

[37] See Leviticus 23; Spangler and Tverberg, *Sitting at the Feet of Rabbi Jesus*, p. 247-257 for information about the feasts, the Seder meal and the New Testament fulfilment of all that was waited for.

time together. The following day, there would be an act of worship at the synagogue as a community.

Offering hospitality and sharing meals had a far deeper significance than we give them today. Eating together was a sign of accepting a covenant, that could not be undone. We could look again at the passage in Exodus 24:9-14 where the elders of Israel went up to God, sharing in the meal God had provided. In the making of a marriage contract between two families, there was a point in the ceremony where the prospective bride and groom were invited to sip wine. Doing so indicated acceptance of the marriage; refusal to do so ended the discussions. Meals could be used to bring about reconciliation: once the injured party had eaten, then the matter was dealt with and could not be raised again. It was a sign of accepting the apology and ending the relational separation that the dispute had caused. [38] We saw this with Joseph and his brothers in the chapter on Peace. Joseph did not just verbally accept their remorse and repentance, then turn away. Joseph called his brothers to come physically close once more, thus removing the hidden and the evident barriers of separation.

Communion, or the Lord's Supper, is very much a Jewish festival in the sense that it was originally part of a meal, and it follows the pattern of reading the Scriptures to remember a particular event, with food and drink to reinforce the key aspects. We take bread and drink wine as we retell the story of the Last Supper and meditate on Jesus dying for us at Calvary; remembering that we share in His death and resurrection as we follow Him. It was Jesus's command that we do this as a remembrance of Him. As we take and eat, we confirm the covenant of grace with thanksgiving and humility. Preparing for Communion signals a change in a time of worship: it is time to be still, to allow the Holy Spirit to show us areas where we have sinned and need to repent. It is a solemn moment to put things right with God. Where two people are separated by conflict, the taking of food is a sign of forgiveness: of stating that the conflict has been resolved and that the matter will not be spoken of again. Therefore, we seek forgiveness from God and we eat as a sign of His promise to forgive us as we resolve to turn away from our sins.

---

[38] Spangler and Tverberg, *Sitting at the Feet of Rabbi Jesus*, pp. 143-145

I wonder how Sunday would change for us if we began our Sabbath on Saturday evening? If we began by lighting a candle, blessing God who provided for us and remembering what He has done for us, then having a family meal and a good night's rest?

Celebrating with Praise

Worship in the home and with church family is central. Psalm 92 was written for the Sabbath. It begins,

> 'It is good to give thanks to the LORD, and to sing praises to Your name, O Most High; to declare Your loving kindness in the morning, and Your faithfulness every night ... For You, LORD, have made me glad through Your work; I will triumph in the works of Your hands.' Ps. 92:1-4

Remember, when God is talking about goodness, He is referring to all that is pure, holy and perfect in His character and kingdom. When the Psalmist tells the people that it is 'good' to do something, we are being reminded that these are Kingdom activities that bless our God and us. Therefore, on our day of rest, there is the reminder that it is good to:

- give thanks
- to sing praise
- to declare God's loving kindness and faithfulness
- to triumph in all that God has done.

None of these things are passive. The Psalmist is encouraging the people to engage with the faithfulness and goodness of our God and to respond actively through words of thanksgiving and praise, declarations of His loving kindness, revelling in all that God has done for us. We are to praise and exalt the name of our God: Jehovah, Most High, Alpha and Omega, I AM, LORD of hosts, God who provides...

The Psalm continues by reminding us of the eternal perspective, by contrasting the fate of unbelievers (the senseless man, the fool, the wicked, the workers of iniquity) who will ultimately be scattered and destroyed, no matter how they may prosper now. We need the reminder that, ultimately, God is the one who is Judge and His standards are very different to the world's. This may be a particularly necessary perspective when working in a secular environment. (verses 6-9)

Next, the focus moves to the recognition that God is the one who restores our strength, who rejoices in our endurance for Him, and who anoints us with fresh oil (Ps. 92:10). I believe this is the anointing from Heavenly Father to son, as well as the anointing for our calling. This is not any old oil found in the back of a cupboard – it is fresh and fragrant. The anointing oil for the priests (and we are now a holy priesthood for the LORD) was scented with 'quality spices:' liquid myrrh, cinnamon, cane (with a similar scent to ginger) and cassia (see Ex. 30:22-25). This was a special blend, only to be used in the context of worship. No one else was to make this oil for any other purpose; it was to be set apart.

The Psalm finishes with the promise and confident expectation that righteousness will be blessed with growth and maturity, with fruitfulness and vigour that surpasses natural ability and strength:

> 'The righteous shall flourish like a palm tree... Those who are planted in the house of the LORD shall flourish in the courts of our God. They shall still bear fruit in old age; they shall be fresh and flourishing, to declare that the LORD is upright...' From Ps. 92:12-15

There is a sense of completeness in this Psalm, as could be expected for the Sabbath. It was a break from the normal routine of life and time set apart for the ritual of a holy day. Each part of the Sabbath carried a sense of actively setting things apart: through the preparations, the activities, the act of commemoration, teaching the young and reminding each other of the ways of God Most High. There was a stopping of the work commitments of the other six days of the week and a starting of the setting apart process. God commanded His people to stop and change their routine every seventh day, so that they would regularly rest and act in a way that would restore them spiritually. In so doing, Israel was showing itself to be different to all the nations around. The Sabbath was unique to Israel, and now to those who believe in Christ who are grafted in.

Keeping the Sabbath is a necessary moment in the week to refocus ourselves in thought, emotion and deed. As we focus on God, we regain the eternal perspective and receive the fresh anointing from God for the week to come, which gives us that strength and joy that we need. Being in that right place before God brings such hope: as we are righteous before Him, we flourish and grow, bearing the fruits of righteousness into old age. This should never be about cold, dutiful obedience to avoid punishment, but a joyous relief that God supplies all we need as we are positioned before Him.

Confirming the Covenant

The Ten Commandments were Israel's part of the covenant with God, which was given for their well-being so that they would be spiritually and relationally healthy and whole.[39] They were short, to the point and non-negotiable. The first four commandments dealt with idolatry and maintaining the holiness of God's name and the worship of God. Keeping the Sabbath was part of this group of commands:

> "You shall have no other gods before Me. You shall not make for yourself a carved image; you shall not bow down to them nor serve them. You shall not take the name of the LORD your God in vain. Remember the Sabbath and keep it holy."

Through Ezekiel, God expressed His anger at the breaking of the covenant by His people, including the breaking of the Sabbath which was,

> "... a sign between them and Me, that they might know that I am the LORD who sanctifies them.... That you may know that I am the LORD your God."

They were not keeping the Sabbath holy because Israel's '... heart went after idols.'[40]

We keep the Sabbath as a part of our covenant with God and this

---

[39] See Exodus 20:8-10, Ex. 34:12, 35:1-3
[40] See Ezekiel 20:1-44 for God speaking against Israel's rebellion and His heart for restoration; the verses about the Sabbath are 12-13, 16, 19-20)

turns on who we choose to serve and worship. Our keeping of the covenant necessarily involves our deliberate choice to reject idols – anything that turns us away from keeping our full focus on God. Our part is to remind ourselves of the holiness of God's name and of the need to have hearts that are sanctified by Him and for Him. The Sabbath day is designed to be a regular point in our week to refocus on putting God first in our lives so that, wherever we have lost ground during the busyness of the week, we can reposition ourselves before God and be strengthened once more in Him.

Restoring the Sabbath was part of the rebuilding of Israel after exile. Just as Jerusalem's walls and the temple needed to be physically rebuilt, so Israel needed to be rebuilt spiritually and mentally. Alongside the physical work of clearing rubble and rebuilding, sin needed to be dealt with in repentance and the people restored to the beauty of holiness. It was a process of spiritually returning, repenting and remembering what God had done for them. It was a process of restoring right priorities, the knowledge and understanding of the law within them and restoring that sense of God's holiness and power. (See Neh. 10:28-39)

Having committed willingly to a renewed covenant with God, once Nehemiah left Jerusalem the people went back to their usual practices. Nehemiah's exasperation is clear when he discovered that it was business as usual and the people had broken every single one of their covenant promises. Again.

> 'In those days I saw people in Judah treading wine presses on the Sabbath, and bringing in sheaves, and loading donkeys with wine, grapes, figs, and all kinds of burdens, which they brought into Jerusalem on the Sabbath day...
>
> Then I contended with the nobles of Judah, and said to them, "What evil thing is this that you do, by which you profane the Sabbath day? Did not your fathers do thus, and did not our God bring all this disaster on us and on this city? Yet you bring added wrath on Israel by profaning the Sabbath."' Neh. 13:15 and 17-18

Nehemiah's words may seem overly strong, but his perspective was based on having seen the ruined city of God and the effects of exile on the people. Exile was the means used to bring about attitudes of repentance, which was a profoundly hard experience. Yet, they were committing all the same offences as if nothing had happened. Had they learned nothing? The people were labouring on the Sabbath and were trading with other nations, which Nehemiah described as profaning the Sabbath - something evil.

It is important to recognise that Nehemiah was not angry because an individual or family had found themselves unable to keep the Sabbath for a while because of a crisis or out of dire financial need. He was angry because the whole people had deliberately and collectively rejected all Sabbath rest; consciously ignoring a clear command from God. No one had prevented them from keeping the Sabbath and no one was compelling them to work on the Sabbath – it was rebellion. It seems ludicrous that the people of God rebelled against His command to rest! Ludicrous and tragic. Their hearts were turned away from God; they simply did not desire to honour Him. They preferred to keep labouring and to keep every day the same. They preferred to keep the gates open seven days a week.

Nehemiah's response was to speak clearly to the people, but also to take charge over the city gates. The gates were the access points to the city: the point at which a city could control who came and went, and when:

> '... as it began to be dark before the Sabbath, ... I commanded the gates to be shut, and charged that they must not be opened till after the Sabbath. Then I posted some of my servants at the gates, so that no burdens would be brought in on the Sabbath day.... And I commanded the Levites that they should cleanse themselves, and that they should go and guard the gates, to sanctify the Sabbath day.'
> Neh. 13:19 and 22

There was a physical and spiritual role in keeping the gates, as we see by Nehemiah's choice of the Levites, the priestly tribe, as gatekeepers. They were to cleanse themselves first, as they would for their temple duties, then to close and guard the gates during the Sabbath. The Levites had long combined practical duties for maintaining and guarding the holy places, objects and practices of God, alongside the call to praise and bring thanksgiving morning and evening. When Israel had been brought out of Egypt, the Levites were appointed as the guards and carriers of the tabernacle, and guardians of the camp of the LORD. Later, they had charge over the temple.[41] Now, they were given the responsibility and authority to monitor the access to the city of Jerusalem for the sole purpose of keeping the Sabbath holy – set apart, sanctified to the LORD.

The command to keep the Sabbath, given by God in Genesis and Exodus and again by Nehemiah during the rebuilding process, was very deeply opposed. God's blessings came as Israel kept the covenant, so Satan did whatever he could to stop them from keeping the covenant. God wanted His people to be set apart in worship of Him alone, the one true God. Satan wanted them to be like everyone else, engaging in worship to anything other than God or focused on work ... anything to stop them from honouring God. Whatever God wanted to be set apart, Satan drew the people away into the desire to be like everyone else. The covenant was pivotal in the relationship between God and His people, so that was what was so consistently undermined. The people could have kept the covenant and did keep it for seasons, but there was a strong pull towards the things of the world that they did not resist.

We are under the covenant of grace, so the blood of Christ is now the pivotal element to our relationship with the Father. However, we should not ignore the Mosaic covenant because that is the guide to righteous living. We are still to love the LORD our God with all our heart, mind and strength; and out of our love for Him, we desire to serve and obey Him; we have a desire to live rightly before Him. Having a day set apart is still God's intention for us, even during busy times of the year. To an agricultural society, the instruction was that '...even during the ploughing season and harvest you must rest.' (Ex. 34:20-21, NIV) Some things cannot be avoided: family crises oc-

---

[41] See 1 Chronicles 9:17-27, I Chron 23:25-30 and 1 Chron 26 where certain Levites were appointed gatekeepers of the temple; others were appointed musicians (with a system of accountability, as we see in 1 Chron 25:6)

cur, parenting never stops, pipes burst, cars break down and so on, irrespective of what day it is. We do not live in a perfect world and we cannot control everything that happens around us. In all this, it is important to remember that God knows your circumstances and the essential commitments you need to juggle. If your heart desire is to keep the Sabbath and to honour God but your circumstances are blocking that, then bring it to Him and ask Him for His enabling. Remember that your heart position is critical here: God sees your heart and will respond to your desire to meet with Him.

Just as the Levites were appointed as gatekeepers, we need to have that same attitude of responsibility and authority when it comes to our lives. What do we allow to access our minds and hearts? What are we listening to, buying into, absorbing into our attitudes and perceptions? We have a priestly responsibility in guarding the gates of our own lives and of our churches; we have an authority and a responsibility to guard against compromise and becoming blended with the things of the world. In the Bible translation used, the Scripture refers to the 'wine, grapes, figs, *and all kinds of burdens ...*' being brought into Jerusalem (my emphasis). Bringing in wine, grapes and figs sounds wonderful, but burdens do not. We read in chapter one about the order and boundaries of creation. We are to have boundaries between work and rest, but we need to decide and establish those boundaries for ourselves as the Holy Spirit guides us. We are to 'close the gates' to the things that oppose our Sabbath rest.

How can we put that into practice? We know that keeping the Sabbath will be opposed because it is God's will for us, because it benefits and strengthens us. Keeping the Sabbath was designed to restore and deepen our relationship with God, clearing any blockages that have got in the way, and restoring our strength and joy. This is supremely important for us: it opens the way to access the treasures of the Kingdom of God and it is why it is so strongly contested. Therefore, begin by putting your spiritual armour on so that you can stand and withstand to keep the Sabbath. We are gatekeepers to our thoughts and emotions, so bring them under authority in Christ and resolve to keep the Sabbath. Position yourself before God, with heart, mind and strength focused on honouring Him.

Sabbath Response

REJOICE: praise, sing, give thanks, declare God's goodness, we claim and proclaim God's victory.

Close the gates to complaining, bitterness, discontent, envy, ways where you dishonour others in your speaking or thinking, defeatist or hopeless thoughts.

REMEMBER the eternal perspective: that righteousness before God is more valuable than anything the world can give us.

Close the gates on any way in which you feel that righteous living is not worth it, that keeping set apart for God is a waste of time.

REPENT of anything that has left the gates open to things that do not please God but that also leave you burdened with things that should not have been allowed access.

Close the gates to sin, to rebellion, to any way in which your heart is pulled towards the ways of the world. Close the gates to compromise and half-heartedness towards God.

RECOMMIT yourself to Him and to the covenant of grace.

Close the gate to legalism and any striving to find your own righteousness and salvation (for example, through work and achieving in a particular way).

RECEIVE that anointing of joy and strength from God, to continue to minister His grace to the world around us.

Close the gate to any cold-hearted, dutiful obedience of God that excludes exuberant love for Him; close the gate to the spirit of heaviness, cynicism, jadedness and apathy. Let the tiredness wash away as you sit at His feet and enjoy His presence.

REST in His presence, in the relief that He has control over all things; knowing that as we sit at His feet with love and adoration, we flourish, grow and bear fruit.

Close the gate to all of your striving and efforts to make your own way to righteousness and salvation; close the gate to all endeavours to come up with great plans and solutions to whatever you face; close the gate to all your attempts to control and hold everything together.

CONCLUSION

Jars of Treasure

Throughout each chapter, we have looked at the treasures of the Kingdom of God which we can discover as we go through the darkness. We have used the metaphor of building strong foundations and walls of faith and truth, relationship with God, hope, peace, joy and rest. We have also used the military metaphor of being armed with the living and powerful things of God's Kingdom that equip and enable us so that we can stand and withstand in the darkness. There is a metaphor we have not yet used, though.

One of the fundamental truths of the darkness is that this is where we find out that we are jars of clay.

We are made of earth. Shaped by the hands of God, special and unique in His sight, but still, made of earth.

We are fragile. In the darkness, we cannot ignore our vulnerability and our inability to save ourselves.

A jar is designed to be filled with something. We so often feel empty and search for the missing thing that will help us feel all that we want to be: confident, capable, successful, secure, happy. It is God who fills that emptiness. It is God who holds all things together and it is our loving, powerful, victorious God who gently holds us, His fragile jars of clay who try so hard but often get battered and bewildered by life. Wherever we come to the end of our own resources, emotionally, mentally, physically, spiritually, He wants to fill that gap with Himself.

We need to be filled with the knowledge of salvation and all that means for us: to take hold of it, to be anchored and protected by it. God wants to fill us with His treasures of truth, relationship, faith, wisdom, hope, peace, joy and rest. He wants us to be jars of clay, full of the indescribable, priceless gifts of His heart.

A jar is not designed to work miracles. But wonderfully, God's miracles involve jars.

He filled an empty jar with oil for a destitute widow who was willing to give Elijah her final meal. That jar of oil did not run dry again.[42] For the one who was out of the food needed for living, God provided abundantly. When we are empty and come to Him to be filled, confessing that we cannot meet our own need, He pours out the oils of His kingdom: joy, anointing, healing, blessing, light, sustenance, fragrance.

He transformed empty jars at a wedding, too. At Jesus's instruction, the people filled the empty jars with water and God turned that into the finest of wines.[43] This was not a life or death situation, but God provided abundantly and joyously. Victoriously, perhaps, as a hint of what would one day be experienced by His people at the wedding feast of the Lamb and His Bride. When we come to God, needing that which is in us to be transformed, He exchanges the ordinary for something extraordinary.

To the church at Corinth, Paul wrote these powerful words:

> 'But we have this treasure in jars of clay to show that this all-surpassing power is from God and not from us. We are hard pressed on every side, but not crushed; perplexed, but not in despair; persecuted, but not abandoned; struck down, but not destroyed...
>
> ...we know that the one who raised the Lord Jesus from the dead will also raise us with Jesus and present us with you in His presence. All this is for your benefit, so that the grace that is reaching more and more people may cause

---

[42] 1 Kings 17:8-16. See also 2 Kings 4:1-6 where Elisha performed a similar miracle, filling many jars with oil
[43] John 2:1-11

thanksgiving to overflow to the glory of God.

Therefore, we do not lose heart.

Though outwardly we are wasting away, yet inwardly we are being renewed day by day. For through our light and momentary troubles, an eternal glory for us is being achieved that far outweighs them all. So we fix our eyes not on what is seen, but on what is unseen. For what is seen is temporary, but what is unseen is eternal. 2 Cor. 4:7-9,14-18, NIV

Our God works through jars, lovingly moulded by His hands out of the earth He called into being. We are His workmanship, His design, the one act of creation that was to be in His likeness.

We can experience seasons in life when it feels exactly like being crushed and abandoned; where there seems to be no point to the difficulty and we cannot see that it glorifies God or benefits us. It can seem futile and worthless, certainly neither fleeting or momentary. But we should not lose heart. Why?

Because one day, we will be raised with Jesus and stand before our Father. Until then, the more we need and accept His grace, the more that will be available through us to others. Until then, the more we lean into God for all our strength, hope and joy, the more we will be shaped into His likeness. We will be increasingly filled with His resources, rather than our own limited supply. We will increasingly recognise that what is being achieved is only through the work and power of God, not man.

Because whatever happens in our physical lives, spiritually there is daily renewal and a weight of eternal glory that will far outweigh whatever we go through now. That is so hard to grasp as we have experienced suffering in some form, but we have not experienced the weight of glory. This is why we are called to focus on the things of faith: the unseen things that will not be marred or depreciated in value depending on current markets; the unseen things of eternal and perfect worth.

Because God knows that we are made of clay; He knows that we are fragile, that we experience brokenness all too easily. It is through that state that He shines all the more clearly to the world around us, because the strength and joy that we know is coming from a source other than us.

Because we are jars of clay, called to contain treasures that are desperately needed by us personally and the world around us. What we cannot do of our own strength and ability, we do in God's strength and enabling. We are not called to solve anyone's problems but to point to Christ: to come alongside them, weeping when they weep, sharing in their griefs and praying for them to be strengthened in their hearts with the strength of God, and to abound in hope by the power of the Holy Spirit.

Yes, we are fragile, easily broken jars of clay. But we have access to the treasures of God and every time we fix our eyes on Christ and trust Him to fulfil His word, the more we are filled with that treasure. We have access to the tools of the Kingdom which can drive back any enemy of hell. We can be jars of clay that are forces to be reckoned with – believers who stand and withstand, with shields locked together and strong in Christ. We are jars of clay with an eternal glory to come that Satan can never steal or destroy.

The darkness has an end but the glorious treasures of God's presence will be ours forever and ever and ever... Amen!

BIBLIOGRAPHY

Bible translations and concordance

Unless otherwise stated, Biblical text and word definitions are taken from:
'The Spirit-Filled Life Bible, New King James Version.' (Thomas Nelson, 1991)
Used by permission of HarperCollins Christian Publishing. www.harpercollinschristian.com

Additional translations used:
'Holy Bible', New International Version (International Bible Society, Hodder and Stoughton, 1991)

Additional definitions:
Strong, James. 'The New Strong's Exhaustive Concordance of the Bible' (Thomas Nelson, 1990)
Used by permission of HarperCollins Christian Publishing. www.harpercollinschristian.com

Books

Cornwall, Dr. Judson and Dr. Stelman Smith, 'The Complete Dictionary of Bible Names,' (Bridge-Logos, 1998) Used with permission of Bridge Logos, Inc.

Eldredge, John and Stasi, 'Captivating,' (Thomas Nelson, 2005)

Lewis, C.S., *The Silver Chair,' (Lions, 1992)*

Lewis, C.S., *'The Voyage of the Dawn Treader,' (HarperCollins, 1992).* Extracts used with permission.

Spangler, Ann and Lois Tverberg, 'Sitting at the Feet of Rabbi Jesus,' (Zondervan, 2018)

Used by permission of HarperCollins Christian Publishing. www.harpercollinschristian.com

Websites used

www.britannica.com

University of Nottingham videos, accessed 26 May 2020

https://www.youtube.com/watch?v=5aD6HwUE2c0

https://www.youtube.com/watch?v=b2YrZNahqiw

www.ingramcontent.com/pod-product-compliance
Lightning Source LLC
Chambersburg PA
CBHW041136110526
44590CB00027B/4030